CONVERSATIONAL NARRATIVES

A HYBRID DISCOURSE GENRE

A Study in the Field of Linguistic Pragmatics

by LOREDANA IORDACHE

To the memory of my grandparents.

Loredana Iordache

LOREDANA IORDACHE

CONVERSATIONAL NARRATIVES

A HYBRID DISCOURSE GENRE

A Study in the Field of Linguistic Pragmatics

Scientific advisors: Prof. Dr. **ALEXANDRA CORNILESCU**
Prof. Dr. **DANIELA IONESCU**
Prof. Dr. **ILINCA CRĂINICEANU**
Associate Prof. Dr. **DIANA HORNOIU**

Cover design: Leo Orman

Front cover illustration: *Conversation* (1981), a picture by Berthe Morisot (1841–1895).

© 2014 ePublishers. ISBN 978-606-8499-91-8

All rights reserved.

This book can also be acquired in Kindle format. Kindle format ISBN: 978-606-8499-92-5.

For more information about this book please write to ePublishers, info@ePublishers.info.

EXPERTS' OPINIONS ON THIS BOOK

A Study in the Field of Linguistic Pragmatics

The present book is a study in the field of linguistic pragmatics, by using *conversation analysis* and microsociolinguistics as an extension of speech act theory, as well as in the field of applied linguistics by offering an analysis of a genuine Romanian conversational corpus.

The study is first of all important for its theme - that of conversational narratives, since it is the first comprehensive research of this issue in Romanian research.

Chapter 1 deals with the theoretical framework of the research which is based on the integration of two theoretical perspectives, *conversation analysis* and *narrative analysis*. Narrative analysis offers the instruments necessary for the micro analysis of narratives as fragments per se, whereas conversation analysis offers the basis for the integration of narratives in the context of conversational interaction. Chapter 2 views conversational narratives as texts *having certain linguistic features* and content traits. Chapters 3 and 4 focus on the narrative as process. Chapter 3 investigates the content of the story proper, analysing its communicative functions, in other words it analyzes the functions of narratives as message. Chapter 4 examines the interaction between narrative and conversation from the perspective of *the interactional role* of cooperation between the two discourse genres, the perspective adopted being again that of conversation analysis.

Chapter 3, **The functions of conversational narratives,** is the most extended of all chapters and considers conversational narrative as a complex multifunctional message. It is the author's merit to have completed and systemized the discussion on the functions of conversational narrative starting from complete theories on the functions of language. In the present case, the author opts for Halliday, discriminating mainly between the ideational, interpersonal and textual functions. These three functions are detailed by using the theory of the communicative code on the functions of language proposed by Jakobson. The two theories (Halliday's and Jakobson's) are convergent, both viewing language from the perspective of communication. The advantage of this combination is obvious in the discussion on the *interpersonal* function, which can be detailed in an *emotive* (expressive, according to Bűhler) function (which constructs the speaker), a *persuasive* function, which focuses on the interlocutor, a *phatic* function, which maintains the channel of communication and expresses the concern for the mutual saving of the interlocutors' faces. The right assumption adopted by the author is that in each and every case there is a *dominant function*, which relates to the purpose of communication, that is to the very illocutionary or perlocutionary dimension of the story, whereas the other functions are present but subordinate (it is the case of the *referential* and *textual* functions) or simply absent (the *poetic* function). The chapter offers a coherent and integrative perspective on the complexity of the functions of conversation analysis, on the complexity of the literature in the field. The analysis is entirely original, the only stories discussed being the ones taken from the corpus collected by the author. From a methodological point of view, the chapter makes extensive use of the Speech Act Theory and the Politeness Theory, with many sociolinguistic elements.

All in all, through its structure, the present study outlines an original theory of conversational narratives, proposing a reading grid of these narratives. The endeavour is synthetic and integrating, the author reevaluating the reviewed literature and systemizing it according to her own ideas.

The thesis demonstrates the reading of a very vast literature (about 250 titles), the text relying at all times on arguments, authoritative arguments included. The study integrates and continues the Romanian research on conversation.

The corpus is highly relevant and excellently analysed. The stories have been given titles, which permits us to identify them easily in the different moments of the analysis.

The linguistic sections provide the interested readers with lists of formulas, clichés, etc., the present study enriching the picture of Romanian oral discourse.

The thesis is very nicely and correctly written; it is a pleasant read.

Professor Dr. Alexandra Cornilescu
University of Bucharest

A Book Based on a Corpus of Spoken Romanian

A book that finds its due place in the rich international and national literature generated by the interest in theories which avoid the fracture between the linguistic world and the extralinguistic one, such as discourse analysis, the theory of verbal interactions – namely conversation analysis, narrative analysis – is constructed with intelligence, patience, humour, but also with scientific accuracy around a frontier, original and well-delimited theme: the structure, the characteristic features and the functions of brief stories or narrative sequences occurring in everyday conversation.

A book which is based on a corpus of spoken Romanian – narratives embedded in conversations recorded by the author with the participants' permission, transcribed according to the international conventions in the field and then translated into English –, a corpus which adds to the materials collected, published and commented upon by reputable researchers, with considerable achievements in the field of sociolinguistics, such as Laura Dascălu-Jinga, Liliana Ionescu Ruxăndoiu, Marina Ciolac, Liana Pop.

A book which proves that such narratives – influenced by the constraints of dialogue, – in the broad sense of the word – have a length which anyone can recognize due to the specific opening and closing formulas used by the storyteller, a structure which is easy to identify and to describe, as well as a series of syntactic features (relatively simple noun phrases with a small number of constituents, temporal alternations marking the separation of narrative episodes or reaching the climax of the story, discourse markers, and only rarely subordinate connectors, phatic elements sometimes associated with address terms, fragments of reported speech) and lexical features (words derived by diminutival or augmentative suffixes, idioms, slang, taboo terms) which distinguish them from other discursive productions. A book which proves that narratives embedded in conversation have precise communicative purposes, in other words, functions which can only be revealed as a result of a careful, fine, scrupulous analysis. We are talking about – a plurality of functions – which narratives serve simultaneously in communication, but among which one is the major, dominant one – and it depends mostly on the speaker/narrator's intention(s) –, and the other two or three are secondary. These functions which the recipients of the discursive production are always quite soon aware of, being urged to or only authorized to take part in the construction of the respective narrative(s) form the basis of a genuine typology of narratives embedded in conversation.

A book which, besides proposing such a typology, has the merit of highlighting the social and contextual factors which are decisive in granting the right to speak to one of the speakers in order to engage in storytelling, since that discursive production must be relevant for the interactional context in which it is introduced and all the conversationalists have to be actively involved in the act of narration.

A book full of interesting information, stimulating ideas for those who will read it, a book which introduces us with great ability to the secrets of pragmatic, sociolinguistic and linguistic research, but also a book which offers reliable study material to the potential young researcher either eager or just curious to engage in similar analyses.

Moreover, a book which, in spite of what one might think after having gone over the table of contents more or less carefully, is easy and enjoyable to read.

Professor Dr. Alexandra Cuniță
University of Bucharest

Theoretical Concepts Excellently Used

Loredana Iordache proposes a very ambitious and complete approach to the way in which a narrative is embedded in a conversational act. This is the reason why the analysis proposed in the present thesis is that of the story *per se* and of the conversational framework, which occasions or justifies the teller's story.

Dialogical or conversational narratives occur in real conversational or interactional situations with participants engaged in a conversational act. The common strategy of such types of interactions is negotiation and the specific forms of narrative are strongly collaborative narratives, in which two or more speakers engage in narrating a familiar experience.

Loredana Iordache's research work is structured in five chapters which form a systematic apparatus of empirical analysis, based on the speech act theory and the latest communication theories in functional linguistics.

The theoretical concepts are excellently used and prove to be effective and challenging in the proposed analysis. The aim of the thesis is to propose a detailed radiography of all the ways of pragmatic interpretations of a special kind of narrative, i.e. the dialogue-framed narrative. The present work stands proof of a consistently working model of application of communication theories, which may ultimately lead to the identification of certain types of conversational narratives, in other words, to a set of socio-linguistic *universalia* relevant for verbal interaction.

Professor Dr. Daniela Ionescu
University of Bucharest

A Reliable, Comprehensive and Complex Study

Loredana Iordache's book is a reliable, comprehensive and complex study, situated at the interface of the linguistic and pragmatic description of different types of narratives framed by dialogue from the perspective of conversation analysis, discourse analysis, speech act theory and politeness theory.

Narrative embedded in dialogue represents a specific form of discourse genre which combines conversation, interpreted as a mode of socio-cultural behaviour with narrative, which represents the archetypal mode of organizing human experience.

The theoretical framework in which the author places the analysis of the functions of narrative in conversation is one which brings together the perspective of conversation analysis and the perspective of discourse analysis, as well as the pragmatic theories of Speech Acts (Searle (1969)), The Cooperative Principle (Grice (1975)), Politeness Theory (Brown & Levinson (1987)) and Impoliteness Theory (Culpeper (1996)).

With convincing arguments, very well illustrated by the examples in the corpus, the author shows that the narrative embedded in conversation is a mixed discourse genre which preserves the formal features of classical narrative but also borrows a lot from the linguistic features characteristic of spoken language at the level of vocabulary and of the less elaborate syntactic structure of the sentences.

This type of narrative is far less structured syntactically than the written one, it is fragmented or based mostly on the simple coordination or juxtaposition, on the ellipsis of certain verbal phrases. The structure of noun phrases is simple, usually lacking in epithets, the use of interjections, vocatives and familiar or diminutival address terms confers dynamism to the story, mixed with digressions and subjective-affective involvement, which prevails over the syntactically well-structured communication of the message.

The vocabulary used in narratives framed by dialogue is colloquial and comprises mostly idioms, slang, clichés, taboo terms and words derived by diminutival or augmentative suffixes.

The pragmatic functions of narratives in conversation are analysed from the perspective of their double status (i.e., stories embedded in conversation) in the theoretical framework provided by the analysis of the language functions proposed by Halliday and Hassan (1989) and Jakobson (1960). On the basis of the corpus she analysed the author proposes a very interesting and original hierarchy of the functions identified in this type of narratives, from the dominant ones to the peripheral ones on the basis of the intention criterion formulated by the theory of conversation (Grice (1975)) and by the theory of speech acts (Searle (1979)).

In analysing the narratives embedded in conversation from this perspective, the author observes the multifunctionality principle of language proposed by Jakobson, emphasizing not only the dominant function but also the secondary functions accompanying it, describing them, as well as the linguistic means through which they are rendered.

In the last chapter of the study the author analyses the interactional features of this hybrid discourse genre, showing that they are the result of the integration of narratives in dialogue according to sociological variables, such as the interlocutors' age, sex and level of education.

The innovative contribution of the present work is the creation of a typology of narratives embedded in conversation on the basis of several criteria, such as the internal structure of this hybrid discourse genre, the degree of fictionality, the novelty in point of information, the factors triggering the narratives or the topics of this type of fragmentary narratives.

The author proves to be a genuine, fully-fledged and talented researcher who bases her analysis on an impressive amount of original data collected from spoken Romanian. Her study is extremely clear and coherently written, and it uses an extended and an up-to-date bibliography.

Professor Dr. Ilinca Crăiniceanu
Spiru Haret University, Bucharest

The First Romanian Comprehensive Study of Narratives in Conversational Discourse

Loredana Iordache's book brings an element of novelty to Romanian linguistics, being the first comprehensive study of narratives in conversational discourse. Basing her analytical endeavour on an original corpus of naturally occurring conversations, the author offers an extensive and fine-grained analysis of narratives in spoken Romanian. The study is also remarkable for the typology of conversational narratives established on the basis of linguistic and interactional features'.

Associate Professor Dr. Diana Hornoiu
Ovidius University, Constanța

TABLE OF CONTENTS

EXPERTS' OPINIONS ON THIS BOOK 5
   A Study in the Field of Linguistic Pragmatics 5
   A Book Based on a Corpus of Spoken Romanian 6
   Theoretical Concepts Excellently Used 7
   A Reliable, Comprehensive and Complex Study 8
   The First Romanian Comprehensive Study of Narratives in Conversational Discourse 9
ACKNOWLEDGEMENTS 14
INTRODUCTION 15
CHAPTER 1. THEORETICAL FRAMEWORK. SETTING UP THE CORPUS 21
   1.0 Introduction 21
   1.1 Conversation Analysis – an overview 21
      1.1.1 Conversational Structure: key concepts 22
         The turn-taking system 23
         Overlapping talk 24
         Adjacency pairs 26
         Repair mechanisms 27
      1.1.2 Conversation Analysis and its relevance to conversational narrative research 29
   1.2 Narrative Analysis and its relevance for the study of conversational narratives 31
      1.2.1 Key concepts and terms in Narrative Analysis 34
      1.2.2 The Internal Structure of Conversational Narratives 40
     Why does the structure of conversational narratives differ from that of monologic narratives? 48
         Levels of conversational narratives 48
         Types of clauses in conversational narrative discourse 49
      1.2 Pragmatic Theories as Auxiliary Analysis Tools for the examination of conversational narratives 50

1.4 Research Methodology 56

    1.4.1 Data collection 56

    1.4.2 Transcription of the data 57

        I. Temporal and sequential relationship 57

        II. Aspects of speech delivery, including aspects of intonation...58

        III. Other markings 59

    1.4.3 Locating narratives in transcripts 59

    1.4.4 Translation of the data 60

1.5 Conclusions 60

CHAPTER 2. LINGUISTIC FEATURES OF CONVERSATIONAL NARRATIVES 62

2.0 Introduction. Overview of chapters 3 and 4. 62

2.1 The embeddedness of stories in dialogue 64

2.2 Linguistic markers indicating the transition from conversation to narrative.....................67

    2.2.1 Formulaic story openers/closings 68

    2.2.2 Tense switching...73

        The narrative past 73

        The narrative present 75

        a). Conversational historical present/The retrospective present...75

        Tense Alternation (the narrative past/the CHP) 77

        b). The prospective present..80

        The narrative future...82

2.3 The oral style of conversational narratives 83

    2.3.1 Spoken vs. written language..83

    2.3.2 The orality of narratives in talk-in-interaction...85

    A. The syntax of conversational narratives 85

        interjections 87

        exclamatives...87

        Reported speech..93

    B. The vocabulary of conversational narratives...97

2.4 Conclusions 103

CHAPTER 3. THE FUNCTIONS OF CONVERSATIONAL NARRATIVE......................106

3.0 Introduction 106

3.2 The Functions of narratives in conversational interactions 110

3.3 The ideational (or referential) function.. 111

    Transmitting knowledge to the audience 112

3.4 The interpersonal function... 116

    3.4.1 The emotive function... 116

        Constructing a particular social, cultural or professional identity..................................... 118

        a). The narrators' socio-cultural identity... 131

        c). The context/cotext of occurrence of a narrative 131

    3.4.2 The persuasive function.. 146

        Illustrating a point one is advocating in the conversation 148

        Justifying, explaining or accounting for one's actions (or those of others).................... 150

    3.4.3 The phatic function 152

        Entertaining the audience.. 154

        Gossip... 158

        Small talk: Establishing, maintaining or transforming social relationship. Ratifying group/family membership and reinforcing group norms and values... 165

3.5 The textual function 170

    3.5.1 The metalingual function... 177

        Clarifying a linguistic term.. 178

    3.5.2 The poetic function 180

        Achieving dramatic effect.. 180

3.6 Conclusions 182

CHAPTER 4. INTERACTIONAL FEATURES OF CONVERSATIONAL NARRATIVES 185

4.0 Introduction 185

4.1 Interactional Features of Conversational Narratives.. 186

    4.1.1 Story Relevance 186

        A) Story relevance in point of the novelty of the content... 187

        B) Story relevance in point of the interlocutors' involvement in the ongoing narrative 194

    4.1.2 Tellability rights or speakers' right of telling stories 199

    4.1.3 The interactive, often polyphonic nature of conversational narratives 201

    4.1.4 The unfolding of stories across several turns of talks 203

4.1.5 The fragmentary nature of stories across extended and interrupted discourse..........205
4.2 Conclusions 209
CHAPTER 5. FINAL CONCLUSIONS 212
BIBLIOGRAPHY 218

ACKNOWLEDGEMENTS

I am grateful to many people for helping me with this thesis, but above all, I wish to thank God, who has shown me that nothing is impossible when you trust in Him. This is how I managed to write the present thesis and raise two energetic small children.

In the actual process of writing the dissertation, first and foremost, I would like to thank Professor Alexandra Cornilescu (University of Bucharest), my PhD supervisor, for her expert knowledge, advice and bibliographic support. I cannot thank her enough for her patience and encouragement, particularly at times when things did not seem to go in the right direction.

I am also grateful to Professor Alexandra Cuniță (University of Bucharest) for her moral support and help with the administrative issues while she was head of the Doctoral School.

My gratitude is also extended to my friends and colleagues: Valentina Barbu, Garofița Dincă, Simona Mazilu and Raluca Burcea for bibliographic support, advice and encouragement. A special thanks goes to my husband, Petrișor Iordache, who guided me to find a series of books which were fundamental for my research.

I also wish to thank Veronica Vasile, my colleague and fellow sufferer, for her support and advice in matters where our theses intersect.

The work with the corpus has proved to be extremely time-consuming. I would like to thank my friends, relatives and acquaintances for having accepted to be recorded. I could not have succeeded in transcribing such vast material without the help of my sister and my friends, whom I am forever indebted. For having helped me choose the most appropriate versions in matters of translation of the Romanian corpus into English I wish to thank my friend, Fabiola Popa and Fr. John Downie.

Last, but by no means least, I am very grateful to my family. It would not have been possible for me to write and actually finish this doctoral thesis without their help. I cannot thank them enough, especially my mother, husband and mother-in-law who helped me take care of my two children, Pavel and Nectaria.

I thank my children for their smiles and laughter, which gave me the strength of going one step further with the dissertation. I thank my son, Pavel, who, barely four years old, took the initiative of helping me finish the thesis by actually taking a pen and scribbling lines on each and every page of one of my drafts. I also wish to thank my little daughter, Nectaria, for having calculated the angle correctly before dropping my laptop to the ground at about ten months of age. This way, the damage was minimal and, fortunately, my data and materials have not been ruined.

Finally, I would like to thank my godparents, Felix and Maria Trușcă, my confessor, father Vasile Gavrilă, as well as my friends, Fabiola Popa, Mădălina Balaș, Alina Cosma, Gina Răducan, Cristina Mailat, Raluca Băloiu, Ana Maria Panainte, Garofița Dincă, Carmen Dochia, Raluca Burcea, Paula Halitzchi, Brigitte Sighete, Ruxandra Lambru, Mariana Badea, Angela Mătrescu and Florica Danciu, for their moral support and encouragement throughout these difficult years.

Bucharest, September 7th, 2013.

INTRODUCTION

The aim of the present paper is to examine and analyse various aspects concerning the phenomenon of storytelling in conversational interactions. We started our research from the investigation of this theme in the English domain and we propose to discuss this problem on a Romanian corpus of conversational narratives that we have set up. The dimensions of this study are, on the one hand, *linguistics and pragmatics*, and, on the other hand, *microsociolinguistics*, in the sense defined by Brown and Levinson (1987) [1978]. The socio-cultural variables which we took into consideration are age, gender and level of education. Our assumption is that there is a set of anthropological features, conversation analysis universalia, identical for both English and Romanian, which can be correlated with the socio-linguistic particularities of the researched subjects. The bridge between the strictly linguistic elements and the micro socio-cultural ones is represented by the discourse strategy of positive and negative politeness (Brown and Levinson, 1987), conjoined with the rules governing turn-taking in conversational interactions (Sacks, Schegloff and Jefferson, 1974).

The conversational narratives which will be examined in this paper will illustrate relevant points and supply linguistic evidence for the hypotheses made in this study. These narratives are excerpts extracted from our own Romanian corpus, which consists of about thirty hours of audio-taped recordings of naturally-occurring, face-to-face, formal and informal conversational interactions.

The present paper is an *empirical study*, which focuses on the interweaving of two basic forms of communication: *the narrative* and *the dialogue*. The reason why we chose to investigate this mixture of two different types of discourse – conversation and narrative – is given by the naturalness and high frequency with which stories occur in conversational interactions, as 'conversation is the natural home of narrative, and the most familiar context of storytelling for most of us. Storytelling is a common part of conversation between friends and family members' (Norrick, 2007:127).

As far as we know, few studies have been conducted in Romanian on the subject of conversational narratives, among which none is extensive. We are going to briefly discuss these works below, highlighting their contribution to stories in talk-in-interaction.

Ştefănescu (2011) examines the use of *discourse markers* in an interactional story, emphasizing their multifunctionalism in both conversational and narrative discourses. The study starts from the idea of narration as a conversational event, pointing out the three levels of conversational narratives: the story proper, the act of narration and the conversational frame.

Hornoiu (2008) investigates gender-related conversational discourse. One important aspect revealed by her research paper with respect to conversational narratives is the fact that the latter represent a locus which favours *the construction of social identities*. A remarkable empirical finding in this sense is the fluctuating nature of storytellers' identities. Unlike some variation sociolinguists, who claim that speakers' identities remain constant in spite of contextual changes (as they are assumed to be permanent properties of speakers), Hornoiu argues that telling one's experience(s) in the form of stories is a way of emphasizing certain aspects of one's identity.

Chiricu (2007) examines *reported speech* in conversational interactions, conversational narratives included, whereas Bălășoiu (2004) discusses the same issue in a corpus of oral dialectal, mostly narrative, texts collected in linguistic interviews.

Șerbănescu (2007) discusses intercultural communication, by bringing together two perspectives: the anthropological and the communicative - linguistic ones. The work highlights the similarities and differences between the different communicative styles of people representing different cultures. The last chapter of the study examines the characteristics of the Romanian people's communicative style, however, failing to illustrate them with concrete examples from a spoken corpus of Romanian. This task will be completed in a subsequent book of the author's, Vasilescu (2007a).

Vasilescu (2007a) resumes the topic regarding the specific communicative style of the Romanian people, began in her prior work, Șerbănescu (2007), this time illustrating it with a series of examples taken from three corpora of spoken Romanian which have been consulted and analysed beforehand. In her research paper the author discusses various issues with respect to our national culture (argumentation, speech acts, Grice's cooperative principle and its four related maxims, the politeness system, etc.) and also brings to the fore various *patterns concerning the Romanians' particular style of telling stories*. In this sense, the following features are worth mentioning: preference for a chronological organization of the events in a story, abundance of details, tendency towards subjectivity, dramatization, etc.

Buja (2008) focuses on oral narrative discourse in non-conversational settings with the purpose of examining the first language acquisition of narratives. Her cross-sectional study[1] is based on

---

[1] A cross-sectional study examines a set of variables in a group of subjects of different ages.

naturalistic sampling[2] and traces the development of *tense* and aspect forms, as well as of *discourse connectors* in subjects that range from preschoolers to university students.

Gafu (2009) deals with oral narratives collected both during social interviews and during conversational interactions among family members and friends, with the purpose of capturing the manner in which the individuals in the Romanian urban society relate to their current dwelling setting, the city. The second aim of her research paper is to inventory the *narrative types* which are characteristic of urban family life. Among these, the author lists family stories, personal experience stories, contemporary legends, jokes (Rom. 'bancuri' and 'farse') and oral historical accounts.

In the context of the previous research in the field, our thesis is meant to be a comprehensive study of Romanian conversational narratives. It also proposes to contribute to the enrichment of the data of spoken Romanian[3] with material comprising narratives in talk-in-interaction.

Having therefore based our present research on the information conveyed by earlier studies in English and Romanian concerning narratives in talk-in-interaction and on the data gathered in our own corpus of Romanian conversations comprising conversational narratives, we have proposed to find an answer to the following ***theoretical questions***:

1. What are the formal properties of conversational narratives?
    a). What are the language features of conversational narratives?
    b). What are the interactional features of conversational narratives?
2. What is the purpose of introducing a narrative in the ongoing conversation?
3. Which sociolinguistic variables influence the telling of a story?
4. Is there a typology of stories in talk-in-interaction?

We will now present the ***outline of the present study***. Our thesis comprises an introduction, one theoretical chapter, three applicative chapters and one chapter summarizing the conclusions of our research.

---

[2] Naturalistic sampling deals with the recording of samples of a subject's spontaneous usle of language in familiar and comfortable settings and the analysis of the obtained information.

[3] The corpora of *spoken Romanian* published so far are *ROVA* (2011) (edited by Dacălu Jinga); *CORV* (2002) (Dacălu Jinga); *IVLRA* (2002) (edited by Ionescu-Ruxăndoiu); *IV* II (2007) (edited by Ionescu-Ruxăndoiu). Some of these corpora were published in volumes dedicated to corpus collection alone, whereas others were included in volumes comprising applicative studies, which combine corpus collection with its description. The latter are (*ROVA* (2011) (edited by Dacălu Jinga); *IV* II (2007) (edited by Ionescu-Ruxăndoiu) and (Hornoiu, 2008).

The Introduction presents our theme of investigation – the hybrid discourse genre of conversational narratives –, the dimensions of our study, a review of the previous Romanian research in the field, as well as the research questions and the outline of the present dissertation.

Chapter 1 deals with the theoretical framework related to narratives in the ongoing interaction. The conceptual apparatus proposed in this chapter is taken from *an eclectic approach* to analyzing conversational narratives, which is crucial for the examination of the complexities of conversational interactions. This approach is based on two approaches to discourse, namely *conversation analysis* and *narrative analysis*, as well as on the pragmatic *theory of speech acts* (Searle, 1969), Grice's *Cooperational Principle (CP) and its four related maxims* and *politeness theory* (Brown and Levinson, 1987 [1978]) and its parallel counterpart, *impoliteness theory* (Culpeper, 1996); (Culpeper et al., 2003). The conversation analysis approach relies on the model of organization and structuring of conversation elaborated by Sacks, Schegloff and Jefferson (1974), whereas narrative analysis has its starting point in a method of analyzing the internal structure of stories devised by Labov and Walevtzki (1967). The speech act theory refers to language being used with the purpose of performing actions, such as producing a certain effect in the recipient, whereas the politeness theory starts from the concept of *face* coined by Goffman (1955) and continues with the elaboration of *positive* and *negative politeness strategies*, used by speakers as means to achieve their conversational goals.

The data base and methodology used in collecting and transcribing the Romanian material, as well as in translating it into English, are also put forward in this chapter.

Chapter 2 examines the *linguistic features* of conversational narratives found in the literature, illustrating them with relevant excerpts taken from the Romanian corpus. We focus upon the linguistic traits marking the passage between the discourse genres of dialogue and narrative: *opening/closing formulas* and *the switch in tense* (from the present tense of the conversation to the past tense[4] of the narrative). We look at the various ways in which a story is triggered in conversation: by means of a conversational detail (an *entailed* narrative), by means of a question (an *elicited* narrative), or by means of the presence of an object or person in the local environment (an *environmentally cued* narrative). We insist on a specific linguistic property of conversational narratives bestowed on them by their being embedded in the larger framework of dialogue: the *orality*[5] of stories in talk-in-interaction, both in point of *syntactic structure* and *vocabulary*.

---

[4] We will see that the narrative present and the future are also an option.
[5] This feature is characteristic of spoken language.

Chapter 3 examines the functions of storytelling in conversation, based on the language functions developed by Halliday & Hasan (1989), detailed by reference to the functions of language proposed by Roman Jakobson (1960). According to the principle of the *multifunctionality of language* proposed by Jakobson and the Prague School linguists, and supported by Halliday & Hasan (1989), conversational narratives will be pointed out to serve several functions simultaneously. However, since we have found that not all functions are prominent, we range them hierarchically, from the dominant function to the minor ones. We identify the main function of a given conversational story, by relying on *the intention-based criterion* (Arcand and Bourbeau (1995) apud Hébert (2007)), which is synonymous with Grice's (1975) and Searle's (1979) idea of the purpose of a speech act. As most narratives in talk-in-interaction have been found to have overlapping functions, the present analysis is not limited to the main function, but also tackles the other, secondary function(s).

A few additional aspects are dealt with when discussing certain functions of narratives in conversation. In connection with the interpersonal function, we consider the use of *topics* as revealing for the storyteller's socio-cultural identity, for his/her relationship with the interlocutors and for the context/cotext of occurrence of a particular narrative. The sociolinguistic variables of *age, gender, and level of education* are shown to be determinant factors for topic selection in narratives embedded in conversation.

The *internal structure* of conversational narratives is discussed in relation to the textual function. From this point of view, we discriminate between *canonical* and *non-canonical narratives*.

Chapter 4 deals with *the interactional features* of conversational narratives, among which the *speakers' right of telling stories*, which is secured by the *relevance* of stories in the conversational framework which engenders them. Other characteristic properties of narratives resulting from their intersection with conversation are the interactive, often *polyphonic nature* of conversational narratives, their *unfolding across several turns of talk*, and, last but not least, the *fragmentary nature* of stories across extended and interrupted discourse. This chapter also presents two narrative forms which are characteristic of stories embedded in conversation: *rounds of narratives (story sequences)* and *collaborative stories*, which promote a sense of solidarity and harmony among speakers.

Chapter 5 Final Conclusions emphasizes the relevance of our study for the present-day research of narratives in talk-in-interaction and proposes a typology of conversational narratives based on criteria which proved pertinent for the present research. Thus, with respect to the internal structure of conversational narratives, we distinguish between *canonical* and *non-canonical stories* (Georgakopoulou, 2006b; Ervin-Tripp and Küntay, 1997; Ochs and Capps, 2001; Labov and Waletzky, 1967). The examination of the ongoing narratives from the point of view of their source leads to the binary opposition: *firsthand* versus *secondhand* narratives (Schank (1990) apud Özyildirim (2009:1210)), whereas with a view to the degree of fictionality of the events presented in the conversational narratives, we distinguish between *fictional* and *non-fictional* narratives (Preece, 1992). According to the contribution of one or several narrators to the enfolding narrative, we discriminate between *narratives told by a single narrator* and *collaborative accomplishments* (Goodwin, C. & Goodwin, M., 1990; Jefferson, 1978; Ochs et al., 1992; Norrick, 2000; Sacks, 1992; Sacks, 1978), whereas according to the frequency of the succession of nearly identical narratives in conversation, we identify *single narratives* and *rounds of narratives* or *story sequences* (Sacks, 1992; Kŭntay and Şenay, 2003; Coates, 2003; Arminen, 2004). Finally, in point of the context/cotext of occurrence of conversational narratives, we encounter the following categories of narratives: *entailed narratives, elicited narratives* and *environmentally cued narratives* (Kŭntay and Şenay, 2003). Several types of narratives are added to the already existing typology, by grouping them according to the following criteria of classification: the novelty of the narrative's informational content for the recipient and the topic selection in the conversational narratives. In point of the former criterion, we distinguish between *narratives presenting new information* and *narratives based on old information*, whereas in point of the topic tackled by the narrators in their stories, we draw a larger list.

CHAPTER 1.
THEORETICAL FRAMEWORK. SETTING UP THE CORPUS

1.0 Introduction

The aim of the present chapter is to provide a theoretical framework suitable for the analysis of conversational narratives. For this purpose, we have resorted to an integrated framework which combines two approaches to discourse, both relevant for the analysis of conversational narratives that represent the object of our investigation in the subsequent chapters: *conversation analysis* and *narrative analysis*. The tools provided by narrative analysis will enable us to engage in a micro-analysis of the act of narration, whereas the concepts advanced by conversation analysts will serve as basis for the integration of narratives into the overall context of conversational interactions, that is, into turn-by-turn talk. The analysis of conversational turns will be based on *pragmatic theories*: Speech Act Theory (Searle, 1969), including Grice's Cooperative Principle (CP) (1975), and its four related maxims, as well as Politeness Theory (Brown and Levinson, 1987 [1978]) and Impoliteness Theory (Culpeper, 1996); (Culpeper et al., 2003).

1.1 Conversation Analysis – an overview

Conversation Analysis (CA) is a branch of ethnomethodology[6] which started out with the seminal works of Sacks (1964; 1972); Sacks, Schegloff, and Jefferson (1974); Schegloff (1968); Schegloff and Sacks (1973) and Pomerantz (1985) on conversational interactions. The model of conversation analysis that they proposed concerns the way conversationalists produce and interpret conversation, as *a form of social interaction* (Ionescu-Ruxăndoiu, 1999:43). The merit of CA researchers is to have focused on

---

[6] An approach to discourse developed by sociologist Garfinkel, H. (1967), which is concerned with the fact that social action does not only display knowledge, but also creates it (Schiffrin, 1994:233).

data collection – recordings of spontaneous conversational interactions, which they transcribed in minute detail, so as to reproduce the actual sounds of conversation – both linguistic and non-linguistic details – (verbal and non-verbal sounds, stutters, laughs, false starts, repetitions, hesitations, precise pronunciation, silences, interruptions, etc.) (Hilbert, 1990:798); (Schiffrin, 1994:235) and to measure time to fractions of a second (see Jefferson, 1984, 1989). The advantage of preserving the data in recorded and transcribed forms is that it permits their examination and reexamination. Conversation analysts regard the phenomena in the recorded data as *conversational constancies* rising from the specificity of conversational interactions (Hilbert, 1990:800). In fact, the conversation analytic data have been found to transcend both culture and personal volition, approaching 'the status of *species-specific social behavior*' (Boden (1983) apud Hilbert (1990:798)).

Utterances are viewed as being contextually relevant for one another: each utterance is shaped by a prior utterance and shapes the next one. Therefore, CA is concerned with the problem of social order and how language creates and is created by social context (Schiffrin, 1994:232). CA transcripts do not focus on the social context of talk (social identities of speakers, settings, personal attributes, etc.), since analysts believe that these features may be interpreted locally (Schiffrin, ibid.:235).

It is the merit of conversation analysis to have found that conversational activities underlie the other, more specialized types of social activities[7] (Bogen, 1992:276); (Sacks, Schegloff and Jefferson, 1974:730).

In what follows we will present the key-concepts bearing on the organization and structuring of conversation, as proposed by the model of conversational structure outlined by Sacks, Schegloff and Jefferson (1974), Sacks (1992), Schegloff (2000), and Duncan (1974) and then consider the relevance of these concepts to conversational narrative research. We have, by no means, included all the concepts put forward by conversational analysts, but only those we will resort to in our analysis of conversational narratives in the chapters to come.

1.1.1 Conversational Structure: key concepts

Conversation, or talk-in-interaction is the conversational analysts' field of research. It was defined as 'a vehicle for interaction between parties with any potential identities, and with any potential

---

[7] Sacks, Schegloff and Jefferson (1974:730) state that "[it] appears likely that conversation should be considered the basic form of speech-exchange system, with other systems on the array representing a variety of transformations of conversation's turn-taking system, to achieve other types of turn-taking systems."

familiarity' (Sacks, Schegloff and Jefferson, 1974:700), or, in the case of dyadic conversation, between a speaker and an auditor[8] (Duncan, 1974:164-165). The *methodological novelty* of CA consists in studying *recordings of unplanned, naturally occurring conversations* (Duranti, 1997:247). As a result of his investigations of conversational exchanges, Sacks concluded that communication is organized *sequentially*. This entails another characteristic feature, namely *the succession of speakers*, which proved to be systematic, orderly and rule governed (Duranti, ibid.:247); Norrick (2000:107).

The turn-taking system

One of the fundamental ideas put forth by conversational analysts is that conversation is organized and structured by *turn-taking*. According to this principle, everyone has the chance to talk in a conversational interaction, in spite of the absence of a pre-allocated order of the speakers' contributions and of the turns being unequally distributed in terms of length[9] among the participants to the interaction. These matters (order at talk and talk length) are negotiated during the conversational interaction[10] (Sacks, 1992, vol.1:710); (Duranti, 1997:248); (Trudgill, 1995:110). The finding that speakers alternate with no gaps and no overlaps (or brief ones) determined CA researchers to devise a set of rules accounting for such smooth transitions (Ionescu-Ruxăndoiu, 1999:41), (Rovenţa-Frumuşani, 2004:41), (Hornoiu, 2008:90). These rules have two components: *the turn constructional component and (ii) the turn-allocational component* (Duranti, ibid.).

We will now focus on *the structure of a turn*, which can vary from a linguistic point of view. Thus, a turn can be constructed out of a word (or a single lexical item), a phrase, a clause or a sentence. These units have been referred to by conversational analysts as *turn-constructional units (TCUs)*. The end of such a unit has been called a *transition-relevance place (TRP)*, since it represents the point at which another party could start talking and therefore, speaker-change might (but need not) occur (Sacks, Schegloff and Jefferson, ibid.:700-702); (Fox, 1987: 10); (Duranti, ibid.:249); (Hornoiu, ibid.).

Another important issue of the turn-taking system is, besides the *turn-constructional component* discussed above, the way parties organize their talk-in-interaction by selecting speakers, i.e. the *turn-allocational component*. According to the two rules governing the transition of speakers so as to minimize gap and overlap, the three ordered options are: current speaker selects next speaker, next speaker self-

---

[8] According to Duncan (1974) a *speaker* is defined as 'a participant who claims the speaking turn at any given moment', whereas an *auditor* is 'a participant who does not claim the speaking turn at any given moment'.
[9] Some speakers tend to dominate the conversation, whereas others produce only a few utterances.
[10] See also Ionescu-Ruxăndoiu (1991:29); Hornoiu (2008:90); Rovenţa-Frumuşani (2004:48).

selects as next, or current speaker continues (Sacks, Schegloff and Jefferson, 1974:702); (Ionescu-Ruxăndoiu, 1999:45); (Hornoiu, ibid.:91).

Now a few considerations need to be made on the contextual constraints governing a turn exchange. These contextual factors, which are *sociological variables*, such as age, gender and socio-hierarchical relations (rank, status, power) holding among conversationalists determine not only the length of a turn, but also who may (even may not) or must speak first or last in a conversation. For instance, in many western cultures, older people or those holding a higher rank speak first and are not supposed to be interrupted until they select the next speaker. Similar constraints apply to women in traditionally male-dominated western cultures. Thus, men have been shown to take the floor more often than women, hold it for a longer period of time and interrupt women more often than the other way round (Van Dijk, 2008:205).

Next we will discuss one important phenomenon which might occur at *transition-relevance places (TRPs)*, when speaker change is effected: *overlapping talk*.

Overlapping talk

The turn-taking organization represents a system in which the parties get to speak in an orderly manner (Schegloff, 2000:1), the basic feature of conversation being that one party talks at a time (Sacks, Schegloff and Jefferson, 1974). However, it may happen that participants should talk simultaneously in conversation (Ionescu-Ruxăndoiu, 1999:46). However chaotic this may seem, not all instances of overlapping talk mean that all overlaps are interruptions (Tannen (1983) apud Hayden (1987:252)), or that people do not listen to each other (Jefferson, 1984:43) (however, not the same can be said for overlaps in legal settings[11]); on the contrary, overlap may be 'a matter of fine-grained attention' (Jefferson, 1986:153).

Overlapping talk has been classified into *competitive* (problematic, in need of overlap resolution system) and *non-competitive* (e.g., an ignored blip, or a collaborative co-construction) (Schegloff, 2000:32-33); (Fox, 1987:10-11); (Hornoiu, 2008:94). The following four types of *overlapping talk* are treated as *non-problematic*:

a). *"terminal overlaps"* in which the second speaker starts talking by virtue of the first speaker's incipient finishing. The overlap is very brief, as the first speaker completes his/her preceding turn.

---

[11] In legal settings, overlapping speech is often thought to hinder the understanding of participants and to obstruct the court proceedings (Hayden, 1987). For an extensive account, also see Atkinson, J. M., and Drew, P. (1979); Walker, A. (1980).

These instances of overlap may also be the result of the second speaker's misinterpretation of the first speaker's utterance as complete, while the first party keeps going, within his/her rights (Jefferson, 1986:154). Building on Sacks et al.'s (1974) assertion that the potential completion, rather than the actual completion of a TCU is transition relevant, Liddicoat (2004:451) demonstrates that terminal overlaps may be accounted for by the recipients' tendency of predicting, while listening to the on-going talk, the current speaker's possible completion point (rather than waiting to see if it is actually complete) and attempting to self-select as the next speaker, while the previous party goes on speaking beyond the potential completion.

(1) N: Also he said that (0.3) 't what you ea:t, (0.2) end how you[12]
     wash yer face has nothing tih do with it,
          (0.8)
     H:Yer kiddin//g.
     N: nNo:,

b). "*continuers*" (such as *uh huh, mm hm*, context-fitted assessment terms, etc.), which show that the recipient understands that the current speaker is taking an extended turn at talk (Hornoiu, 2008:94).

c). various types of "*conditional access to the turn*", which include *word search, anticipatory completion and collaboratively built sentences,* in which the ongoing speaker allows or even invites the recipient to intervene during the former's speaking turn, as long as the latter helps complete the turn-in-progress (Hornoiu, ibid.).

d). various "*choral/chordal*" *phenomena,* which are produced simultaneously, and not serially (that is, one after the other). This category includes *laughter, collective greetings, leave-takings, or congratulations,* which are either mandated (e.g., choral congratulations), or allowed to be produced simultaneously, and not serially (e.g., overlapping continuers) (Hornoiu, ibid.).

In *competitive overlap* turn-taking rules are violated, as the next speaker starts talking before the projected TRP of the current speaker's turn constructional unit (Fox, 1987:11):

(2) H: En I nearly wen'chhrazy cz I//: l:lo:ve that mo:vie[13].
    N: y: Yeah I know you lo:ve tha::t.

Although most overlaps come to an end very quickly, some of them may be considerable in length and many overlaps turn out to be the locus of hitches and perturbations in the production of the

---

[12] The transcription of the excerpt is the one adopted by Fox (1987).

[13] For transcription conventions see Fox (1987).

talk. With regard to the participants' attitude towards overlapping talk, it should be noticed that there are cases in which the speakers may attend to whether the production or the understanding of talk has been impaired or not and also may attend to the overlapping talk's consequences upon the subsequent direction of talk (Schegloff, 2000:10). For instance, the overlap of an address term might be regarded as having potential serious consequences, if the term is unheard, given its 'relation-formulating properties' (in the literature, address terms have the role of formulating and maintaining the status of a relationship[14]) (Jefferson, 1973:48).

With respect to the role simultaneous talk plays on people's conversational styles, Tannen (1984, 1989) has showed that it is a linguistic feature which occurs frequently in the high involvement style, being used by the speakers for precise purposes, such as *building rapport* and *signaling involvement*. On the other hand, the lack of overlapping talk (in the case in which the first speaker stops talking when a second party self-selects before completion), or silence on the part of the first speaker, is indicative of a high *considerateness style*, in which speakers avoid talking at the same time in order to consider the principle not to impose.

Adjacency pairs

As an approach designed to investigate the structure and process of social interaction, CA distinguishes three *levels of conversational organization*: a). *the local level,* which consists of two turns: the current one and the next one; b). *the level of recurrent sequences,* which consists of three-four turns or even more; c). *the global level,* which comprises all the turns in a conversation (Ionescu-Ruxăndoiu, 1991:29); (Ionescu-Ruxăndoiu, 1999:52).

The *adjacency pair* is another crucial concept for our analysis. It represents the basic unit of conversational structure and plays an important role at the local level of conversational organization (Ionescu-Ruxăndoiu, ibid.:30); (Ionescu-Ruxăndoiu, 1999:50). An adjacency pair is a sequence made up of two utterances, which are produced by two different speakers and which are in close proximity to one another (Duranti, 1997:250). The first part of the adjacency pair makes relevant a particular type of action from another participant. Common examples of such pairs are: 'question-answer', 'greeting-greeting,' 'invitation-acceptance/decline', 'offer-acceptance/rejection', 'complaint-denial', 'compliment-acceptance/rejection', 'challenge-rejection', request-grant/refusal', 'instruction-receipt' (Fox, 1987:12); (Ionescu-Ruxăndoiu, 1999:50); (Ionescu-Ruxăndoiu, 1991:30).

The adjacency pair below is an example in which A's complaint makes relevant B's denial:

---

[14] See Brown, R. and Ford, M. (1961) on address terms.

(3) A: Hey yuh took my chair by the way an' I don't think that was very nice.
B: I didn' take yer chair, it's my chair.

It may also happen that the second part of the adjacency pair does not follow right after the first part, but is separated from it over a sequence of turns. The example below in which an insert expansion intervenes between the first and the second part of the adjacency pair is a case in point (Sacks, Schegloff and Jefferson, 1974:716); (Fox, 1987: 12); (Ionescu-Ruxăndoiu, 1999:50-51):

(4) A: May I speak to President Regan?
B: May I ask who's calling?
A: Nancy.
B: Ok.

Since in all situations there are preferred courses of action, the first part of an adjacency pair has a *preferred*/unmarked second and a *dispreferred*/marked second. The preferred second is indicative of what is considered to be normally expected, whereas the dispreferred second entails a larger structural complexity[15] and signals an indirect discursive strategy in accordance with the requirements of linguistic politeness (Duranti, 1997:260); (Ionescu-Ruxăndoiu, 1991:30); (Ionescu-Ruxăndoiu, 1999:51).

The adjacency pair below displays a preferred (grant- B_1) and a dispreferred second (refusal- B_2) in response to a request.

(5)A: Can you help me tomorrow morning?
B_1: Yes, sure.
B_2: Mmm, I'm sorry, I'm afraid I can't. I have classes then.

Repair mechanisms

Repair mechanisms are another aspect worth taking into consideration when analysing talk-in-interaction. Their role is to deal with turn-taking errors and violations (Sacks, Schegloff and Jefferson, 1974:700), as well as with problems in speaking, hearing and understanding (Schegloff, Jefferson and Sacks, 1977:361). The 'repairable' or 'the trouble source' is a term used for that which the repair addresses.

A distinction between the terms 'repair' and 'correction' becomes pertinent at this point. 'Repair' is not limited to 'correction', having a wider scope. *Correction* refers to the replacement of an error by its correct counterpart, whereas *repair* is a more general term, as it is neither dependent upon, nor limited to replacement. For instance, a 'word search' (which occurs when a speaker cannot access a word in due

---

[15] The structural complexity of dispreferred seconds may manifest itself in components whose role is to preface the utterance.

time) is not a correction or a replacement (Schegloff, Jefferson and Sacks, 1977:362-363); (Duranti, 1997:261); (Dascălu Jinga, 2002b:31).

There are various *types of repair* mentioned in the conversation analysis literature[16]. *Self-repair* (i.e. repair done by the party who initiated the repairable item) is distinguished from *other-repair* (i.e. repair done by one of the speaker's interlocutors) (Schegloff, Jefferson and Sacks, ibid.:361-362); (Dascălu Jinga, ibid.:34). Self-repairs may be either *self-initiated* (i.e. repair done by the speaker without prompting) or *other-initiated* (i.e. repair done by the speaker after the repairable item has been prompted to him by another party) (Schegloff, Jefferson and Sacks, ibid.:364); (Ionescu-Ruxăndoiu, 1999:52-53). With respect to other-correction, as a particular type of other-repair, Jefferson (1987:88-89) notes that it may be accepted (and then the new term is adopted) or refused (the new linguistic item is ignored and the first term is used again) by the first speaker. A special case is that of *'abdicated other-correction'*, in which a recipient can and should correct a non-self-correcting speaker, but he/she does not, treating the error and its correction as inconsequential, and by so doing, minimising the importance of the mistake (Jefferson, 2007:447).

Repairs may be used for *manipulative* purposes: to gain time to think or to hold the floor, by preventing another party to intervene at the next TRP, thus producing 'singly-developed floors' (as opposed to 'collaborative floors'), which represent a characteristic feature of competitive conversational styles in which the interlocutors tend to dominate the floor. The non-deployment of repair in contexts where it would be relevant may be interpreted as being indicative of agreement and intersubjectivity (Hornoiu, 2008:93).

Repair mechanisms, in particular error-correction devices may *convey interactionally the speaker's identity* as well as the degree of familiarity of the speaker to the context in which he/she speaks and to his/her interlocutors. Even if a speaker may have access to a range of terms, he/she assigns one set in his/her 'home' environment, and another set to unfamiliar environments and people. For instance, an individual may self-correct by switching an informal term for a more formal variant of the same concept when in a non-familiar environment or/and speaking with unfamiliar recipients in order to confer a degree of finesse to his/her utterance. Or, it may happen that one of the other parties involved in the conversation may correct the speaker in case he/she uses a word that may be deemed inappropriate for the respective context, by providing a more appropriate variant of the previous term/repairable item

---

[15] Works on repair devices include Schegloff, Jefferson and Sacks (1977) and Jefferson (1974, 1984, 1986, 1987, 2007).

(other-correction). This discrimination does not apply exclusively to the words a party selects when speaking, but also to the pronunciation, tone of voice, etc. (Jefferson, 1974:191-192).

1.1.2 Conversation Analysis and its relevance to conversational narrative research

Narratives acquire a series of properties[17] due to their being embedded within the larger framework of conversation. These formal features may be understood by means of the concepts proposed by conversation analysts. In what follows, we will consider the relevance of these concepts for conversational narrative research.

Sequentiality, that is, determining whose turn it is to speak, is obviously the main issue. Everyday narratives are seen as sequentially organised activities, whose 'structure emerges on-line and is negotiated by the participants' (Georgakopoulou, 2007:4). The problem with conversational narratives is that they usually take more than one turn to complete and that a longer turn may contain not just one sentence, but a large number of sentence-like units. This is why it is not always easy for recipients to identify which is the end of the narrator's turn. In this case, it is the storyteller's duty to signal to the listeners that he/she is engaging upon a longer turn so that the audience might be able to adapt their conversational behaviour accordingly, and allow the narrator to finish his/her story (Mandelbaum, 1987:145); (Drew, 2005:82); (Sacks, 1992); (Norrick, 2000:107). This is done by means of a *story preface*, whose role is twofold: to announce that the speaker is going to need to hold the floor long enough to finish his/her story and to indicate what sort of response is expected on the part of the listener upon the end of the story. The tellers often provide the recipients with an abstract containing a brief summary of the tale that is about to be told as well as an evaluation of it, which reflects the narrator's standpoint with respect to the recounted events (Sacks, ibid.); (Norrick, ibid.). Just as in an adjacency pair, where a question is expected to be followed by an answer or an offer by an acceptance/a refusal, etc., so do stories require a response on the part of the recipients, either in the form of a *comment* (Fludernik, 2009:48) or even in the form of another, subsequent, *parallel story*. Such a story[18] usually mirrors the first in point of characters, topic, action and even phrases used by the speaker in recounting it (Sacks, ibid.); (Norrick, ibid.).

---

[17] These properties will make the object of chapter 4 of our thesis.
[18] This type of story is called a 'second story'. For further information, see chapter 4.

Another aspect of sequentiality is *recipient design* (cf. Sacks et al., 1974:272). This concept refers to the fact that the teller conceives his/her story by taking into account the identity of the recipient and the situational context in which the narrative emerges. This property of the ongoing story influences issues such as 'topic selection, word selection, ordering of sequences as well as options and obligations for starting and terminating conversations' (Niemelä & Rauniomaa, 2010:229). We may therefore postulate that in asymmetric relations determined by power and distance variables, narratives are constrained in point of length of turns at talk and in point of speakers' priority to get and hold the floor. Thus, the elderly and the hierarchical superior are privileged against younger people and those in an inferior position to go first and hold the floor for a longer time interval, as well as to interrupt their interlocutors during the process of storytelling.

In examining the occurrence of spontaneous narratives in conversational interactions, conversational analysts have emphasised the influence of active listeners who make comments or even turn into full-fledged co-narrators: 'in spontaneous conversation all stories are diffuse and negotiated to a greater or lesser degree' (Norrick, ibid.:136). Thus, the involvement of recipients into the story performance may somewhat alter the course of the story, so that the outcome of the process of narrating may be different from what the teller initially had in mind. The story may even be suspended if it fails to meet the audience's expectations.

The mechanism of *repair* is used by both tellers and listeners in the process of (co-)narration. Storytellers may use self-repair devices as a means of manipulating the audience (Hornoiu, 2008:93) in their attempt to hold the floor (to get on with the story and eventually finish it) and prevent another party to intervene at the next TRP, as for instance, when the tellers cut themselves off and restart by rephrasing at story beginnings and transition relevance places. The auditors may also intervene into the structure of the conversational story by making remarks that act as repairs (other-repair devices), as for instance, in cases where the teller cannot recall a linguistic item and the latter is provided by the listener (Schegloff, Jefferson and Sacks, 1977:362-363) or when a term used by the narrator is deemed inappropriate by the recipient who subsequently supplies a better variant. This variant is not restricted to words alone, it may well be the case of a more appropriate tone of voice, or manner of pronunciation (Jefferson, 1974:191-192), as for example, when one of the parties intervenes to mimic the speech of one character in the story, which renders the story more vivid and even funnier (should the story take the form of an anecdote). The auditors' refrainment from using repair devices in contexts where such devices would be relevant is thought to be a sign of agreement and intersubjectivity (Hornoiu, 2008:93).

Another relevant aspect for conversational narrative research is *overlapping talk*. In traditional narratives one expects a single teller to weave his/her story starting from topic talk, while his/her interlocutors listen carefully to what is being told. In other words, one party talks at a time and, upon completion, another conversationalist is either selected by the current speaker or self-selects (Sacks, Schegloff and Jefferson, 1974). In such cases overlapping talk is unlikely to occur. However, recent studies have pointed to the frequency of narratives that are told by co-narration, especially in informal contexts, among friends and family members (cf. Tannen (1984, 1989); Blum-Kulka (1993); Ochs and Taylor (1992a, 1992b, 1993, 1995); Ochs, Smith and Taylor (1989); Norrick (2000)). This is the locus where non-competitive overlaps are most likely to occur. Such overlapping talk is not to be misjudged as interruption but rather as a means of showing involvement in the storyline and establishing a relationship between co-narrators that is based on emotional affinity (Tannen, 1984, 1989).

We will use the concepts presented above in the subsequent chapters of our study.

Now, we will put forward another approach which is crucial to our research – *narrative analysis*.

1.2 Narrative Analysis and its relevance for the study of conversational narratives

Narratives have been studied by researchers in various fields: anthropology, sociology, linguistics, literature, psychology.

The *anthropologic perspective* acknowledges the crucial role played by narratives in human culture and civilization. Whereas Barthes & Duisit's (1975:237) diachronic perspective points out the fact that the roots of narrative are thrusted in the history of human civilization: 'Narrative starts with the very history of mankind', Schiffrin (1996:167) draws on the central place narratives hold in all human activity and communication (cf. Threadgold, 2005:268):

'The stories that we tell about our own and others' lives are a pervasive form of text through which we construct, interpret and share experience: we dream in narrative, daydream in narrative, remember, anticipate, hope, despair, believe, doubt, plan, revise, criticise, gossip, learn, hate and love by narrative.'

From a social and psychological viewpoint, narratives are seen as the 'primary way through which humans organize their experiences into temporally meaningful episodes' ((Richardson (1990) apud Ozyildirim (2009:1210)):

'People organize their personal biographies and understand them through the stories they create to explain and justify their life experiences. When people are asked why they do what they do, they provide narrative explanations. It is the way individuals understand their own lives and best understand the lives of others.'

Also, narratives are '*selections* rather than *reflections* of reality' (Burke, 1962), since in the process of narration we do not limit ourselves to accurately reporting a certain experience, but we take a step forward and distance ourselves from the event, thoughts and emotions we experienced at some point in the past and reexamine them from a social and psychological viewpoint. Moreover, recipients are enabled to do the same thing (Ochs, 2004:276); (Ochs, 1997); (Richardson (1990:118) apud Ozyildirim (2009:1210)). As Goffman (1974:504) points out,

'A tale or anecdote, that is, a replaying, is not merely any reporting of a past event. […] A replaying, in brief, recounts a personal experience, not merely reports on an event. A replaying will therefore incidentally be something that listeners can empathetically insert themselves into, vicariously reexperiencing what took place.'

From a linguistic perspective, a narrative has been defined as *a sequence of temporally ordered events* (Smith, 1999:489); (Zafiu, 2000:42). In the same line, a narrative was shown to consist of 'a sequence of narrative clauses (clauses containing a verb in the simple past tense or sometimes the historic present tense) whose order matches the real time order of the events described in those clauses' (Thornborrow and Coates, 2005:3); (Pridham, 2001:10). Other similar definitions view the narrative as a story which tells about facts that have happened or are happening and which are organized as a sequence of events (Berger (1997:4) apud Ozyildirim (2009:1210)) and as 'a perceived sequence of nonrandomly connected events' ((Toolan (1988:7) apud Franzosi (1998:519)). Likewise, Labov (1972:360) regards the narrative as 'one method of recapitulating past experience by matching a verbal sequence of clauses to the sequence of events which (it is inferred) actually occurred' (cf. Franzosi, 1998:519); (cf. Ozyildirim, 2009:1210) and *a minimal narrative* as 'a sequence of two clauses which are temporally ordered'. If the order of the narrative clauses is reversed, the semantic interpretation of the original temporal sequence is altered ("I punched this boy/and he punched me" vs. "This boy punched me/and I punched him") (Ozyildirim (2009:1210)), (Labov (1972:360) apud Franzosi (1998:522)). However, not any sequence of two temporally ordered events can make up a story (Rimmon-Kenan (1983:19) apud Franzosi (1998:520)), the respective events must be *logically coherent*: for instance, the following two sentences 'Joan took her plane at 5 pm' and 'Peter drove to the airport at 8 pm' would make up a story only if later sentences established a logical connection between those two sentences, e.g., 'They had both been looking forward to spending the weekend together'. Also, they must disrupt an initial state of equilibrium. This entails a reversal of situation. Reversals may reccur in a story along the sequence: initial state → disruption→new state→disruption→new state→...→final state (equilibrium) (Franzosi, 1998:520-521).

From a *literary, narratological viewpoint* the narrative, as a text type, has been defined in terms of the well-formedness criterion as having a *fixed structure, made up of a beginning, a middle and an end* (Aristotle, English translation, 2000:12). The formalist and structuralist narratologists pointed out the two facets of the term *narrative: story* and *discourse*[19]. The first notion designates the content of the narrative, namely the sequence of events, whereas the second one refers to the process through which the events are presented (Chatman, 1975:295); (Chatman, 1978:19-20); (Toolan, 2008:39-40).

Another crucial distinction in literary theory, which actually preceded the binary opposition *story* and *discourse,* was launched by Forster (1923), between the concepts of *story* and *plot*. The difference was shown to lie in the distinct way of organizing the events or 'incidents'. Thus, in a story, events are organized in sequence, whereas in a plot they are liked by cause and effect. The two sentences below illustrate the distinction in question:

"The king died, **and** the queen died." (story)

"The king died, **and** the queen died **of** grief." (plot)

We can notice that the events in the first sentence succeed one another and are connected by the coordinative copulative conjunction 'and', whereas in the second example, the events are also linked by the subordinate conjunction of cause '(because) of', which institutes the cause-effect relation underlying the events. Our conclusion is that the cohesion between the causally linked events in the plot is stronger than that standing between the temporally linked events in the story.

Considering the perspectives presented above, we will base our present research on the hypothesis postulating that narratives represent a property of the human species. Previous studies conducted on spontaneous narratives in interaction seem to support our tenet: 'Telling stories is a

---

[19] These concepts will be discussed in details further on, when referring to the notion of narrative.

human universal of discourse' (Jaworski and Coupland, 2006:25) and 'we are all narrators in our daily lives, in our conversations with others' (Fludernik, 2009:1). Therefore, it is no wonder that narratives may be found in any age, place and society, under multiple forms, in fields like: literature, theatre, cinema, painting, comics, news items, conversations (Barthes & Duisit, 1975:237); (Barthes (1977:79) apud Franzosi (1998:517)); (Cohan & Shires, 1988:1). Narrative is therefore international, transhistorical and transcultural (Barthes & Duisit, ibid.); (Barthes apud Franzosi, ibid.).

Our dissertation focuses on *conversational stories*. According to most narrative analysts, they represent the prototype of narratives (Ochs and Capps (2001) apud Herman (2009:35)); (Fludernik (1996) apud Herman (2009:35)). In the same line, Norrick (2007:127) acknowledges that 'conversation is the natural home of narrative, and the most familiar context of storytelling for most of us' and that 'narrative grows from and thrives in the concrete conversational context' (2000:19).

For the purpose of our research we will be using, as pointed out in the introduction of the present chapter, *narrative analysis* as an essential tool in the study of storytelling in conversation when analysing the storytelling performance of conversationalists, that is, their engagement in telling stories at some point during a conversational interaction. Narrative analysis refers to a set of 'analytic methods for interpreting texts that have in common a storied form' (Riessman, 2008). It focuses on how elements are ordered in a story, why some components are rated differently from others, and how perceptions of the past, present and future are shaped. Narrative analysis also counts as a social science methodology, as it has been found that conversational narratives vary according to the social context within which they are gathered (home, school, work, etc.) and as it gives the recipients the chance to display their points of view and make evaluations (Garson, 2008).

1.2.1 Key concepts and terms in Narrative Analysis

In what follows, we will introduce several *key concepts and terms* employed by narrative analysts[20]. These notions will guide us in the subsequent chapters into building our own analysis of the data in the corpus we have collected. But first and foremost, a few words need to be said on the meaning of several, apparently common terms which we will be making use of in this paper.

---

[20] among whom the most prominent are Chatman (1975), Polanyi (1982), Blum-Kulka (1993), Garson (2008), Norrick (2000), (2007), Bamberg (2004a), Georgakopolou (2006a), (2006b), (2008), Toolan (2008), Fludernik (2009) and Herman (2009).

A distinction between *narrative* and *non-narrative* discourse should be set up from the very beginning. The criterion underlying this dichotomy resides in the presence/absence of event clauses in these two types of discourse. Thus, a narrative has been defined as a sequence of events progressing in time (Smith, 1999:489). Or, in other words, the narrative mode of discourse presupposes the presence of both event and state clauses, whereas the non-narrative mode of discourse does not contain more than one single event clause (Polanyi, 1982:511). Toolan (2008:36-37) proposes three main criteria underlying a narrative: sequential and interrelational events, forgrounded individualities and an evolution from a state of crisis to one of resolution. It ensues that a text that lacks these qualities does not qualify as a narrative.

Within narrative discourse, we discriminate between *written and oral narratives,* and, within the latter category, between *monologic and dialogic narratives*. *Monologic* narratives, on the one hand, are told in non-conversational contexts, as is the case of stories elicited in interviews (cf. Labov and Waletzky (1967)), stories told as retellings of films (cf. Tannen (1993)), picture stories, or even previously read stories. On the other hand, *dialogic or conversational* narratives are told at some point during a genuine, naturally-occurring everyday conversation[21], characterized by turn-taking[22], and are strongly dependent on the interaction between the conversational participants (Fludernik, 2009:47). Therefore, their characteristic feature is the negotiation between interactants: they are 'always interactive, *negotiated*, and not simply designed for a particular audience by a single teller' (Norrick, 2007:127). We refer here especially to the case of *collaborative narratives*, in which two or more speakers engage in telling a jointly experienced or familiar story but also to narratives told by a single speaker, whose narrative performance and final product (the story) is very much shaped by the recipients' contributions – comments, questions, etc. In other words, the conversational story may take up various (sometimes unexpected) turns, so that no one (not even the teller) may know what the conversational narrative will actually look like in the end. And all this is due to the recipients' new status: the audience is no longer passive, but is actively involved in the storytelling process (Norrick, ibid.:137).

Some conversational narrative analysts distinguish between the notions of *narrative* and *story*. At this point, we believe it is imperative to discriminate between these two terms, but beforehand we will turn our attention to the notion of *narrative*. According to Bamberg (1997:335), the concept of *narrative* has a double reading. Approached traditionally or structurally, it refers to the representation of certain events that took place in the past, whereas from a pragmatic, performance-based viewpoint, it is

---

[21] We will henceforth refer to narratives told in conversation as being *embedded* in conversation. According to Fludernik (2009:47), conversational narratives represent an essential constituent of conversational interactions holding between interlocutors.
[22] This term was explained in the section dedicated to conversation analysis.

synonymous with the act of telling. This distinction put forward by Bamberg (1997) is not a new discovery in the field of linguistics. It goes back to the earlier studies of narratologists, who firstly discriminated between the two dimensions of a narrative, basically between *story* and *discourse*. These concepts have received different denominations throughout the years: from Russian formalists' (Propp, 1928) *fabula* and *sjuzhet*, to French structuralists' (Benveniste, 1966); (Barthes, 1966) *histoire* and *discours* and Chatman's (1978) *story* and *discourse*. The first part of the above dichotomies refers to the *content*- the chain of events, the protagonists involved in these events, as well as the settings-, whereas the second part designates the *means* by which the content is rendered, or, in other words, the *process* through which the story is shaped (Chatman, 1975:295); (Chatman, 1978:19-20)[23]. Briefly speaking, the story represents the 'what', whereas the discourse is the 'how' of what is communicated (Chatman, ibid.). In the same line, narrative analysts speak of *the event structure* (the chronological sequence of events, as they happened in the real world) and *discourse structure* (the sequence of events, as presented by the narrator in the narrative) (Brewer & Lichtenstein, 1982:473), of *narrated events* (the events recounted in the story) and *narrative events* (the situations in which the stories are told) (Bauman, 1986:112).

In this paper, we will be using the term *narrative* in a narrower sense, meaning only genre, and not discourse. For the second reading of the term, namely the act of telling a story, we will be using the term *narrative discourse* or *storytelling performance,* which we will discuss later on, in the forthcoming pages of this section. With respect to distinguishing between the terms narrative and story, we define *narrative* as a sequence of at least two[24] coherent (past, present, or future tense) clauses describing an action or a change of state (Norrick, 2000:28); (Polanyi, 1982:509); (Labov and Waletzky, 1967); (Ochs, 1997:189) and a *story* as a narrative in the past, having contextual relevance and containing the teller's evaluation (Norrick, 2007:128); (Polanyi, 1982:511). In this line, story is acknowledged as a subclass of narratives having an affective component, i.e. the quality of entertaining the recipients (Brewer & Lichtenstein, 1982:473). Therefore, the term *story* is a subordinate of the superordinate term *narrative*, qualifying as one of the various narrative genres, along with plans, simultaneous reporting of what is currently going on (e.g., sportscasting), generic descriptions of what used to be the case in the past, or what is normally the case in the present as well as descriptions of wished-for, yet unrealized events. Other researchers, as for instance, Georgakopoulou (2006a, 2006b, 2008); Bamberg (2004a); Bamberg and Georgakopoulou (2008); Ervin-Tripp and Küntay (1997); Ochs and Capps (1996) advance the narrower term, *story*, as a rough equivalent of the broader term, *narrative*. Georgakopoulou (2006a) points out that in conversation,

---

[23] See also Toolan (2008:39-40); Blum-Kulka (1993:364); Franzosi (1998:519-520); Bottez (2007); Buja (2008:9-10); Herman (2005:25); Schmid (2010:186); Scholes et al. (2006:288).
[24] A narrative consisting of only two coherent clauses describing an action or a change of state counts as *a minimal narrative*.

unlike the sociological narrative interview (such as the one conducted by Labov and Waletzky (1967)), there is a high frequency of variations from the narrative prototype of non-shared, personal experience past events. Such are 'stories' of shared events, 'stories' of future or hypothetical events (which focus on events that might have happened but actually did not), and narratives that lack culminating events (as it is the case of habitual narratives), to name but a few[25] (Georgakopoulou, 2006a, 2006b); (Ervin-Tripp and Küntay, 1997); (Riessman, 1993). At the same time, Georgakopoulou (2006a) acknowledges the necessity of building up a new analytic vocabulary, which should refer to the 'neglected' stories or stories which are still 'in the fringes of narrative research'. In this sense, she proposes the coinage of affirmative definitions instead of negative ones (i.e., a-typical, non-canonical, non-conventional stories, marginal cases). The terms Georgakopoulou (2006a, 2006b), Bamberg (2004b) and Bamberg and Georgakopoulou (2008) suggest are *small stories, small stories-in-interaction, story-lines, ongoing narratives* and *narratives-in-interaction* (cf. Herman, 2009:5). These terms draw attention on the qualities of conversational narratives. For instance, the denomination *small stories* points to the fragmentary character of such narratives and is also meant as a counterpart of the modernist 'grand narratives'. The terms *story-lines* and *ongoing narratives* reflect the fluidity, plasticity, open-endedness, and dynamic nature of conversational narratives, whereas the more neutral term, *narratives-in-interaction,* refers to the context of occurrence of such stories, that is, social interaction, which implies another quality of these narratives: their dialogical nature. In the present dissertation, we will be using the terms *conversational narrative, conversational story, ongoing narrative and narrative-in-interaction* interchangeably, referring to the different narrative genres we might encounter in our data.

When we speak of a *performed story*, we will envisage it as being similar to a theatrical performance, i.e., being dramatized by the speaker, or theatrically staged. Such a story will display at least some of the following series of performance features: alternation between conversational historical present (CHP) and the past tense, direct speech, asides, repetition, expressive sounds, sound effects, motions and gestures (Wolfson, 1978:216-217).

The pair of terms *stories* and *reports,* as designating two basic genres of narratives, definitely deserves our attention. These concepts are both co-hyponymic genres of the superordinate term narrative and 'concern specific events which occurred at specific times in the past relative to the time of narration' (Polanyi, 1982:511). They differ in terms of the function they have at the level of conversation: thus, a narrator who presents a *report*[26] limits himself/herself to revealing a picture of what

---

[25] *Non-canonical narratives* will be examined at length in chapter 3 of the present paper.
[26] Reports usually lack a story's climax and resolution.

went on during a particular time period. In contrast, the tellability of a *story* (i.e. its value or its worthiness to be told) resides in the entertainment value given by the exceptional nature of the events narrated and in the story's moral point (of view) or message the narrator wishes to convey (Polanyi, 1982:515); (Fludernik, 2009:48); (Wolfson, 1978:216). The performance features[27] used by the storyteller in staging his/her story play a crucial role in distinguishing a performed story from a mere reporting of past events (Wolfson, ibid.:223).

Among the various types of narratives we have encountered during our research, for the immediate purpose of conversational narratives, we are interested in the following recurrent types[28] : *collaborative narratives, second stories* or *response stories* and *elicited stories*. Thus, we will speak of a *collaborative narrative* (or a *co-told story*) whenever at least two participants to the talk-in-interaction engage in joint storytelling of a familiar event. We will define a *response story* or *a second story* as a tale told by one conversationalist right after a preceding story, preserving either the same topic or the same type of story (Sack, 1992); (Norrick, 2000:28), whereas when we refer to an *elicited story*, we will have in mind a narrative told in response to a request made by one of the interactants (Ervin-Tripp & Küntay, 1997); (Norrick, 2000:28).

As to the participants in a conversation who are involved in the process of telling or listening to a conversational story, we will distinguish between the following participant categories: the terms *teller, storyteller and narrator* will be used interchangeably to designate a conversationalist who engages into the act of telling a story. Those participants to a conversation who come to listen to a story shall be named *listeners, recipients, auditors, or audience* – these terms will also be used interchangeably, with the specification that none of them refers to passive conversationalists, but, on the contrary, to active partners who interrupt the tellers for repair or correction and even contributions of their own to the ongoing story. Those participants in the conversation whose contribution to the development of the ongoing story is substantial (as for instance, in point of detail, dialogue, evaluation of the story) are to be acknowledged as *co-tellers* or *co-narrators* (Norrick, 2000:27-28).

In the interpretation of stories, participants employ *frame concepts* (or *scripts* in Garson's terms (2008)). These terms refer to expectations we have about story patterns and about the relations holding between the elements of a story by encoding 'prototypes for objects, sequences of events, and causal relationships, which facilitate recognition, categorization and memory of stories'. Frame concepts also guide tellers into selecting appropriate stories for a given context and into indicating to the audience

---

[27] i.e., alternation between conversational historical present (CHP) and the past tense, constructed dialogue, asides, repetition, expressive sounds, sound effects, motions and gestures.
[28] These types of stories, as well as others, will be dealt with in chapters 2, 3 and 4 of our paper.

what to expect and the way they should respond (emotionally) to these stories (Tannen, 1978, 1979); (cf. Tannen, ed. 1993 apud Norrick (2000:8)). As frame concepts point to conventional, canonical narratives, they are used as basis for the comprehension of new, unexpected components which lead to the recognition of a diversity of conversational narratives, such as personal anecdotes, dream tellings, fight stories, etc. (Garson, 2008); (Norrick, 2000:44). In other words, *stories* expand on frame concepts, or scripts, by encompassing non-canonical events and adding evaluations which denote the narrator's viewpoint. Stories told in a competitive and interactive conversational interaction are usually fragmented, but one can also find instances of monologic narratives in spontaneous conversation (Labov (1997) apud Garson (2008)).

In the present paper we use the term *storytelling performance*[29] meaning *narrative discourse* or *narrative act* and define it as a speaker's engagement into the telling of a story at some point in the conversation (Fludernik, 2009:157). Storytelling performance is determined by the local conversational context, in that it departs from and returns to it and, therefore, is both designed for and co-determined by the conversationalists that act as recipients of the ongoing tale (Norrick, 2000:12). More often than not, conversational narrative performances are *diffuse*, due to common features of spoken language, such as repetition, formulaicity and disfluencies (pp.3-4), and *polyphonic* – meaning that the current story is being told by more than one conversationalist who also compete to formulate its point-, its most stable elements appearing to be background information, evaluative comments and dialogue (p.16), (Norrick, 2007:128).

In point of *modes of performance* or telling, we will discriminate between three main modes of performance: *monologic, dialogic* and *polyphonic*. In *monologic* narratives, only one teller is in control of the floor, the recipients responding indirectly and supporting the telling, however, without being involved in the tale. Such narratives may be either initiated by the teller or told in response to a question from another party. *Dialogic* narratives usually display a question/answer format, regardless of the tale being self- or other-initiated, whereas *polyphonic* or multivoiced narratives are constructed in close collaboration between several conversationalists (Blum-Kulka, 1993:385-386).

Another important contribution to the field of narrative analysis is the model devised by Ochs and Capps (2001:1-58), as discussed by Herman (2009:34-35) and Georgakopoulou (2006a:237-238)). According to this paradigm, conversational narratives can be described along the following five dimensions: *tellership, tellability, embeddedness, linearity/temporality* and *moral stance*. *Tellership* refers to the

---

[29] The term *performance* is originally theatrical but has later on been adopted by anthropology and sociology to describe the spectacle of genuine, everyday life (Threadgold, 2005:265).

producer of the story, showing if the story is told by a single narrator or is co-narrated. *Tellability* points out whether the story is rendered in an effective rhetorical way or whether it is only a teller's poor attempt to render an event with low tellability. In point of the *embeddedness* dimension, a narrator might either take a longer turn to tell his/her story, which becomes detached from the conversational context in which it is told, or, on the contrary, he/she might narrate, by taking a turn of talk that is no longer than the previous or subsequent turns of the conversational interaction he/she is engaged in, and thus, the story is said to be embedded in the discourse flow surrounding it. *Linearity* is indicative of the way events are recounted in the story. This can be done on a single, linear causal-temporal axis or on multiple axes. *Moral stance* refers to the speaker's passing judgment on him/herself and/or other characters in the events he is reporting.

In what follows we will turn our attention to conversational narratives, endeavouring to distinguish them from the more general term of oral narratives and to define them in terms of their impact on two different fields of research: linguistics, social anthropology and socio-psychology.

Having these broad definitions in mind, we will now turn to the internal structure of a conversational narrative.

1.2.2 The Internal Structure of Conversational Narratives

Regarding the structure of a conversational story, we will discuss it in terms of the most significant model elaborated by the American sociolinguist William Labov (Labov and Waletzky (1967) and Labov (1972)), who provided a method of analyzing the internal structure of stories. The framework devised by Labov has been heavily drawn upon by most researchers of conversational narratives (Franzosi (1998); Berman (1998); Norrick (2000); Pridham (2001); Lambrou (2003); Holmes (2005); Fludernik (2009) and Ozyildirim (2009) – to name but a few), although, originally, it was designed to apply solely to narratives of personal experience elicited in sociolinguistic interviews. In what follows we will present the concepts elaborated by Labov and Waletzky (1967) and Labov (1972) and discuss the limits of their applicability to conversational stories.

A monologic story presenting a personal experience, told by a single narrator in an elicited interview, was shown to have the following structure: *abstract, orientation, complicating action, resolution* or *result, evaluation and coda*[30].

Abstract: represents one or two initial clause(s) in a narrative which summarize(s) the entire story. Sacks (1992:18) proposed the term 'story preface' as an alternative to Labov and Waletzky's (1967) notion of 'abstract' of a narrative. A story preface has the role of announcing that a story is going to be told by one of the interactants (and therefore that the storyteller intends to be talking in alternate positions until the story is over) and of signaling the sort of evaluative response the narrator expects from the recipients at the end of the story.

Orientation: gives background information on the time, place, the characters in the story and their initial behaviour. Its function is to inform the recipients about the coordinates of the story. Listeners are usually provided with orientation components at the beginning of a narrative, however, this is not necessary the case, as we may find orientation clauses at any point in the narrative, whenever the teller feels the audience needs more clarification on the spatial-temporal framework of the story (Buja, 2008). In the same vein, Schiffrin (1981:48) points out that the narrator sometimes needs to introduce orientation clauses into the complicating action so as to 'add information which the hearer needs in order to understand or interpret the significance of 'adjacently reported events'. Also, embedded orientation clauses may be evaluative if the provided information is indicative of the value of the recounted events relative to the point of the story. Orientation clauses are not temporally ordered, which means that, were they to be rearranged, the recipients' understanding of the background and of the narrative events would not change. Orientation usually refers to 'existing states (e.g., we were C.I.T.'s) and extended processes (e.g., we were all going out for lunch) which may begin before the narrative action itself and continue during that action' (p. 49).

Complicating action: consists of narrative clauses that inform the recipients about what happened. It contains the *climax* or *high point* of the story.

Resolution or *result*: informs the hearer about how the complicating action was resolved. At the same time it is indicative of the ending of the events by releasing the tension created by the succession of events in the complicating action.

---

[30] *Coding schemas* are usually used by researchers, after transcription, to label the elements that make up the narrative structure. For instance, one may use a set of structural/functional categories to label the segments of a narrative, as follows: AB= abstract, OR= orientation, CA= complicating action, EV= evaluation, RE= resolution, or CO= coda (Garson, 2008).

Evaluation: consists of comments made by the speaker about the event that he/she experiences. It represents the emotional aspect of the story, accounting for the tellability of the story (why it is worth telling). It often interrupts the main action, for thoughts and feelings, expressing the storyteller's involvement and highlighting what is interesting to the narrator or to the recipients. Among the linguistic structures functioning as evaluation devices one can mention emphasis, parallel structures and comparatives, with modals, negatives and future ranging among the most important. Schiffrin (1981:59) distinguishes between two types of evaluative clauses, namely *internal* and *external evaluation*. External evaluation clauses 'comment on and interpret events for the audience from a perspective outside the narrative action' (p. 48), whereas internal evaluation consists of clauses in which 'narrative events convey their own importance, and make obvious contributions to the point of the story' (p. 59). The *evaluative* element does not hold a fixed place in the narrative structure: that is why one may notice evaluative utterances at any point during the narrative performance (Pridham (2001:15) and Ozyildirim (2009:1218)). The role of the evaluation is of utmost importance, as it indicates the way the teller intends the story to be perceived by the listeners (Pridham (2001:20).

Coda: signals the end of the story, representing the narrator's ultimate comment, the later or present perspective, sometimes providing a short summary of the story or even a moral, worth presenting to the story recipients. It may be evaluative, pointing out the effects of the event on the narrator. The coda also has the function of returning the recipients to the present moment by pinpointing the relevance of the narrated events to the present situation (Schiffrin, 1981:48). In this sense, it acts like a bridge that connects the realm of the story to the teller-recipient present (Toolan, 1997 apud Buja, 2008:15).

Now a few things need to be said about *the internal structure of stories*, as highlighted by the Labovian model. First of all, it is an *anthropological concept*, as it exists independently of a particular language (Buja, 2008:15). Therefore, we may assume that it may be recovered in oral narratives in any language. Secondly, it may be extended to all types of narratives- as we shall see later on, in another chapter of the present paper-, and not restricted only to the oral personal experience narratives, which represented Labov's collection of data. As pointed out by Jaworski and Coupland (2006:25) 'all verbal narratives share a basic structure', irrespective of their variation in form and function. Thirdly, not all the elements in the Labovian framework are equally important. Thus, a conversational story might not contain all the elements evinced by the Labovian model - however, if it does, the elements, excepting the evaluation, usually observe the above-given order – (Pridham (2001:15); Ozyildirim (2009:1218); Buja (2008:16)). Similar evidence comes from Ervin-Tripp & Küntay's (1997:6) and Georgakopoulou's

(2006a, 2006b) database of conversational narratives which, unlike Labov and Waletzky's elicited stories, were un-elicited and whose narrators did not engage in a long performance that should hold the floor for a considerable amount of time. Consequently, we may assert that the extension and application of Labov's model of the internal structure of narratives to spontaneous stories in talk-in-interaction trigger the distinction between *compulsory* and *optional components* (Ionescu-Ruxăndoiu, 1991:40). *Complicating action* is deemed as obligatory for the formation of a narrative, containing the climax or high point of the story (Ozyildirim, 2009:1211); (Labov (1972:370) apud Franzosi (1998:522)). *Resolution* is also most likely to be present in any conversational narrative though not all narratives have a clear resolution – some may report a problem but fail to present a solution (Buja, 2008:15-16). *Orientation*, like the other two elements, *complicating action* and *resolution* is believed to be *compulsory* for the internal structure of narratives embedded in dialogue (Ionescu-Ruxăndoiu, ibid.). At the other end of the continuum lie the *optional* elements: *preface/abstract* and *the coda*. Empirical evidence supporting this claim comes from Chafe (2001:677) and Ozyildirim (2009:1218). The latter's study on Turkish oral and written personal experience narratives (PEN) revealed that, while all of the written narratives exhibited a fully-fledged narrative structure, some of the oral, conversational narratives lacked the *preface/abstract and the coda*. Also, in many conversational narratives in English, the climax of the story is displaced towards the beginning of the story in order to enhance suspense (Fludernik, 2009:47). Thus, a story may start with a key utterance of the story's protagonist and only afterwards provide the necessary background details, followed by the main action, which culminates with a fully detailed account of the climax (Polanyi (1978) apud Fludernik (2009:47)). Regardless of the total or partial display of the elements in the internal structure of a conversational story, the teller has at his/her disposal various conventional ways of pinpointing where they are in the ongoing story. Thus, in indicating climactic moments, tellers often shift from past to conversational historical present (CHP)[31] or use connectives followed by adverbs or interjections. The same use of CHP marks the evaluative remarks on the story addressed by the teller to the recipients (Buja, 2008:16); (Wolfson, 1978:225).

Therefore, we may postulate that the internal structure of a prototypical narrative will display all the components *(preface/abstract anticipating the topic, orientation, complicating action, resolution, evaluation, and coda)*, whereas a marginal case will only contain the obligatory elements, lacking therefore precisely those elements whose role is to delimit the narrative passage from the surrounding ongoing talk: *the preface/abstract and the coda* (Ionescu-Ruxăndoiu, 1991:40); (Ervin-Tripp and Küntay, 1997); (Ştefănescu,

---

[31] Conversational historical present (CHP) designates the present tense which is employed to refer to past events.

2011:280). However, recent research has shown that we can find narrative passages in spontaneous conversation which partially lack even those elements believed to be essential for the narrative structure: 'the presence of a climactic complicating action, or closure of the storyline with a resolution'(Georgakopoulou, 2006b).

Norrick (2000) extended and refined the framework elaborated by Labov and Waletzky (1967), by adding the following elements:

Narrow frame: represents the transition from orientation into main action.

Main action: is represented only by active verbs in past tense and no continuing actions.

Result: indicates the direct effects of main action.

Using the concepts developed by Labov and Waletzky (1967) and Labov (1997), as well as those he himself added, Norrick (2000:29) proposed a method meant to ease the recipient's task of comprehending the narrative produced by the teller. Such a task may sometimes be difficult to complete in the ongoing course of talk due to the polyphonic nature of conversational narratives, as, confronted with 'disfluencies, syntactically incomplete utterances, tense shifts, speaker shifts, interruptions and digressions', the listener may find him/herself in the position of piecing together the elements of a narrative, just like in a jigsaw puzzle. This method presupposes eliminating adventitious talk, disfluencies, corrections and interruptions, consolidating narrative clauses by filling in the understood elements (as for instance, in the case of syntactically incomplete sentences) and combining teller and audience contributions, if need be, to get the gist of the story – a complete and coherent basic narrative.

In what follows, we will endeavour to indicate the internal structure of a prototypical conversational narrative with the purpose of showing that it evinces all the components identified by Labov and Waletzky (1967) in their theoretical framework. The excerpt below is taken from Norrick's (2000) corpus of conversational narratives:

(1) First Job
1 *Ellen*: *what was your first job?*
2 *April*: *first job, um oh*
3   *that was at the Halsted Burger King*
4   *in Halsted Minnesota.*
5 *Ellen*: *that near your house?*
6 *April*: *about six miles away.*
7 *Ellen*: *m-hm.*
8 *April*: *and they- they built it brand new,*
9   *and I was one of the first employees.*
10   *and because of that*
11   *we ah- um we had a head honcho woman*

12   *from International Burger King*
13   *come and train everybody in.*
14   *because there was like thirty of us?*
15 *Ellen: wow. Yeah?*
16 *April: and uh we had about a week of training*
17   *and I remember*
18   *the most embarrassing moment of my life*
19   *happened then. {laughs}*
20 *Ellen: {laughing} what does that mean? {laughing}.*
21 *April: {laughing} um no this is just-*
22   *I can't believe I did this*
23   *but- um I was really nerv-*
24   *well it was my first job,*
25   *and I was nervous*
26   *and there's so much to learn.*
27   *I mean y'know there's so many things at Burger King*
28   *you have to [make and uh-]*
29 *Ellen: [how old were you?]*
30 *April: I was like a sophomore in high school.*
31 *Ellen: okay.*
32 *April: yeah, [the summer after my sophomore year.]*
33 *Ellen: [you were young,] okay.*
34 *April: and um we were learning the drive-through*
35   *and just the thought of speaking on-*
36   *into that microphone*
37   *and y'know into outside-*
38 *Ellen: yes.*
39 *April: and you have to pretend to take orders*
40   *and, and I was so embarrassed.*
41   *and the first time I had to do it*
42   *I said "welcome to McDonald's*
43   *[may I take your order?"]*
44 *Ellen: [oh no {laughing}.]*
45 *April: and everybody just laughed at me {laughing}.*
46 *Ellen: {laughing} did you try and pull it off like a joke*
47   *like you meant to say that?*
48 *April: no. {laughing}*
49 *Ellen: no.*
50   *{laughing} good job.*
51 *April: yeah, that was my very first job.*

If we examine the fragment above following Norrick's guideline, we can easily identify the internal structure of the present conversational story as being made up of an *abstract, orientation, complicating action, resolution, evaluation,* and *coda*.

ABSTRACT
I remember the most embarrassing moment of my life happened then

ORIENTATION
(It was my) first job
that was at the Halsted Burger King
in Halsted Minnesota
I was one of the first employees

I was like a sophomore in high school
yeah, [the summer after my sophomore year.]

COMPLICATING ACTION
we ah- um we had a head honcho woman
from International Burger King
come and train everybody in
and uh we had about a week of training
and um we were learning the drive-through
and the first time I had to do it
I said "welcome to McDonald's
may I take your order?"

RESOLUTION
and everybody just laughed at me {laughing}

EVALUATION
and just the thought of speaking oninto
that microphone
and y'know into outside-
I can't believe I did this
but- um I was really nervous
and I was so embarrassed
the most embarrassing moment of my life

CODA
yeah, that was my very first job.

In our story, the abstract provides the audience with a general view about what kind of story to expect, namely one about a most embarrassing situation. The orientation supplies information regarding the characters in the story – in our case, the storyteller herself and other employees, like her – and the spatio-temporal framework against which the events took place: the storyteller's first job at Burger King in Halsted Minnesota, in the summer after her sophomore year in high school. The complicating action of the present story refers to the sequence of events that actually took place: the storyteller and the other employees were trained and then were made practice taking orders. The climax of the story is represented by the main character's blunder the first time she had to take orders: instead of welcoming customers to Burger King, she uttered the name of the competing company, McDonald's. The resolution element indicates the way the events reached a closure: there was general laughter following the teller's utter mistake. The evaluative component of the story resides in the comments made by the speaker on the events recounted, which reflect the emotional aspect of the experience: the narrator's nervousness and embarrassment. In the present story, the narrator's evaluation is external, as she uses specific evaluative devices, such as a negative modal ('can't') and emphasis ('so', 'really') to comment on the events for the recipient from outside the story action. Finally, the coda renders a brief summary of the story by concluding that the story was about the teller's first job.

Unlike the conversational story above, the following excerpt is illustrative of an ongoing narrative whose internal structure evinces only part of the components present in Labov and Waletzky's (1967) theoretical framework. The fragment below is taken from Leung's (2009) corpus of conversational narratives:

(2) Rottweiler
1 Nadia: Yvonne has # I mean #
2   Ashley has # a Rottweiler ((muffled, barely audible because of food in her mouth))
3 Yvonne: what?
4 Nadia: Yvonne has # I mean # WHOA
5   Ashley has a Rottweiler =
6 Yvonne: = I know # so does Courtney
7 Nadia: it ate their cat
8 Lisa: it ate their cat =
9 Yvonne: = no # I thought it smuushed it
10 Lisa: yeah
11 Nadia: it smuushed it
12 Yvonne: and it was still playing with it # and um
*   ((nonverbal demonstration of actions))*
13   r::ah::p ((lifts both arms into air))
14   w::am::p ((moves arms to indicate struggling))
*   ((mouth moves to indicate eating))*
*   ((hands on lap))*
*   ((munching sound))*
15 Lisa: squush
16   what was that ((high squeaky voice))
17 Yvonne: heh heh heh

The above dynamic collaborative narrative is told by three adolescent friends. It starts and ends abruptly, lacking an abstract and a coda as well as the evaluation element. The orientation gives minimum information on the protagonist of the story – Ashley's dog, a rottweiler –, without specifying the actual time and location of the event that is to be recounted. The complicating action component, which represents the events taking place in the narrative, namely, Ashley's dog attacking her cat, is rendered mostly by the use of onomatopoeia and body language, than words and phrases, as one would have normally expected. The same holds for the resolution of the story, which consists of body movement and a high squeaky voice.

ABSTRACT

ORIENTATION
Ashley has # a Rottweiler

COMPLICATING ACTION
it ate their cat

> *it smuushed it*
> *and it was still playing with it # and um*
> *r::ah::p ((lifts both arms into air))*
> *w::am::p ((moves arms to indicate struggling))*
> *((mouth moves to indicate eating))*
> *((hands on lap))*
> *((munching sound))*

RESOLUTION
> *squush*
> *what was that ((high squeaky voice))*

EVALUATION
> -

CODA

Why does the structure of conversational narratives differ from that of monologic narratives?

Now let us consider why the structure of a conversational story told in a face-to-face interaction is different from the structure of a monologic narrative elicited in an interview. A conversation presupposes the presence of at least two participants who might compete to take the floor. It is precisely this competition to gain the floor that influences and alters the form of the story the speakers try to tell, as, in their attempt to hold the floor, they may omit information and focus on the point of the story, doing their best to persuade the audience that the story they tell is worth hearing, so as to prevent another participant from self-selecting at a transition relevance place[32] and running the risk of being interrupted or, what is worse, of never getting the chance to finish his/her story, should the story seem boring or pointless to the audience (Herman, 2009:34); (ibid.:38-39).

Levels of conversational narratives

Another fruitful contribution to the conversational narrative research comes from Fludernik (2009:48). She points out that spontaneous, naturally-occurring conversational narratives have two basic levels[33]: 1). *the level of communication between speaker and listener(s)* and 2). *the level of the story proper.* The *communicative level* consists of frame elements (they are represented by the *abstract, orientation* and *coda* in Labov and Waletzky's (1967) theoretical framework), which make it possible for the speaker to switch from the communicative situation to the story proper and back again. The level of communication between teller and recipient is also active throughout the storytelling, whenever the storyteller addresses the auditors by making comments (e.g., 'Of course, that's quite typical of Karl. He was never backward

---

[32] This term was already discussed in the section dedicated to conversation analysis.
[33] See also Ștefănescu (2011:283-287).

at making rude jokes.') and explanatory remarks (*delayed orientation*) (e.g., 'The house stands as you know, at the edge of the forest'). It is also functional whenever the recipients are actively involved in the storytelling process, by nodding, inserting appreciative phrases (*Aha, right, I see*) and making comments (*Scandalous! Typical! That's terrible!*). *The story level* has an episodic structure, meaning that there are several successive episodes which make up a story. Each episode has three stages: the *opening*, the *climax* and the *resolution*, whereas the beginning and ending of the tale are explicitly marked by an abstract and a coda, respectively.

Types of clauses in conversational narrative discourse

For Labov, a monologic personal experience narrative contains two types of clauses: *narrative* and *evaluative*. As a result of our investigation of our own collected corpus, we may assert that this constituency is not restricted to personal experience narratives elicited in interviews but is also evinced by most types of conversational narratives. Narrative clauses have a referential function, as they transmit data concerning the events, characters and settings in the story. Evaluative clauses have the role of evaluating the story and thus suspend the sequence of events of narrative clauses (Ozyildirim, 2009: 1211-1212). Evaluation reflects the point of the narrative: why it was told and what the narrator wishes to convey. It relates the events presented in the narrative to the narrator's value system (Labov (1972:366) apud (Ozyildirim (2009: 1212)). Evaluation may appear in various clauses: free clauses that 'comment on the story from outside': e.g., "And it was the strangest feeling"; or in clauses that evaluate characters in the story: e.g., "I just closed my eyes". It can also be embedded in the narrative, 'in the form of extra detail about characters': e.g., "I was shaking like a leaf", of 'suspension of the action via paraphrase or repetition; 'intensifiers', such as gesture or quantifiers: e.g., "I knocked him all out in the street"; elements that compare what happened with what did not or could have happened or might happen; 'correlatives' that tell what was occurring simultaneously; and 'explicatives' that are appended to narrative or evaluative clauses' (Johnstone (2001:638) apud Ozyildirim (2009: 1212)).

In what follows, we will illustrate, on the basis of fragment (1), the two types of clauses – narrative and evaluative – contained by a conversational narrative. In our excerpt, the narrative clauses, which assure the temporal progression of the story, are not compact or grouped together, as one may think, but, on the contrary, scattered throughout the conversational narrative – lines 11-13 (*'we ah- um we had a head honcho woman/ from International Burger King/ come and train everybody in.*'), 16 (*'and uh we had about a week of training'*), 34 (*'and um we were learning the drive-through'*), 41-43 (*'and the first time I had to do it/ I said "welcome to McDonald's/ [may I take your order?"]*),45 (*'and everybody just laughed at me {laughing}'*). In the case of the present conversational narrative, the evaluative clauses interpose between the narrative clauses – lines 18 (*'the most embarrassing moment of my life'*), 22-23 (*'I can't believe I did this/ but- um I was really nervous'*), 25 (*'and I was nervous'*), 35-37 (*'and just the thought of speaking on-/ into that microphone/ and y'know into outside'*), 40 *('and I was so embarrassed')* –, suspending the unfolding of events in favour of their evaluation and interpretation for the recipients. The storyteller evaluates the story both internally (from the inside – lines 25, 35-37 –) and externally (from the outside – lines 18, 22-23, 40 –).

Next, we will now turn our attention to additional linguistic tools, which are useful for our analysis of narratives-in-interaction.

1.2 Pragmatic Theories as Auxiliary Analysis Tools for the examination of conversational narratives

Besides the two approaches presented above – *conversational analysis* and *narrative analysis* (a branch of discourse analysis) –, our discussion of the narrative fragments in the corpus will heavily rely on two well-known pragmatic theories: the theory of social roles - *Politeness theory* (Brown and Levinson, 1987 [1978]), paralleled by *Impoliteness theory* (Culpeper, 1996); (Culpeper et al., 2003) and the theory of meaning – *Speech Acts theory* (Searle, 1969). References to Grice's *Cooperative Principle (CP)* (1975) and its four related maxims will also be made. In what follows, we will endeavour to demonstrate the relevance of these theories to our analysis.

The role of narratives in conversational interactions can be interpreted by using the concepts of speech acts and of politeness strategies. Thus, at the *level of the utterance* or at the microanalysis level, *speech acts* help us understand indirect speech acts, irony and figures of speech, whereas at the macro *level of analysis*, of *the conversational interaction*, we can use speech acts to analyse the relations between turns, the transactional function shaping reciprocal relationships between interlocutors. At the *micro level* of analysis, politeness may be expressed by speakers within a turn by means of speech acts, whereas at the *macro level* of the conversation or turn-by-turn talk, *politeness strategies* are used to achieve various conversational goals, such as, for instance, constructing or maintaining harmonious relations between conversationalists (Thomas, 1996:155-158). For instance, the entertainment function of narratives in conversation is an instance of a positive politeness strategy, as the storyteller is concerned with catering for his/her interlocutors' positive face needs. Choosing the appropriate interactional strategy on a particular occasion depends on the *intermediate variables* proposed by Brown & Levinson (1987) [1978]: *the social distance, the relative power of the hearer over the speaker* and *the absolute ranking assigned to an imposition* in a particular culture (Hornoiu, 2008:13). Thus, in the case of equal power relationships between interactants and in the absence of the social distance between them, the speaker will adopt a positive politeness strategy, characterized by collaboration and a high degree of interruptions, promoting a sense of solidarity between the conversationalists. At the other end of the continuum, in the case of unequal power relationships and in the presence of social distance between interlocutors, the speaker will adopt a negative politeness strategy, characterized by no interruptions and minimal back-channeling, with the conversational aim of displaying respect for his/her interlocutor.

Research on speech act theory postulates the possible extension of this theory to discourse analysis, the main argument being that 'speech acts are not isolated moves in communication: they appear in more global units of communication, defined as conversations or discourses' (Moeschler, 2002). One essential aspect of speech act theory is to account for how we can understand figures of speech, such as metaphor, irony, hyperbole, and indirect speech acts in the course of conversation. Apparently, the hearers' ability to make sense of these matters, i.e. to understand the meaning in context of the speaker's utterance, relies both on linguistic competence and knowledge of the conversational background. These are the two elements enabling the listeners to make inferences from the speaker's utterance and from the assumption that the speaker observes Grice's conversational maxims[34] (Vanderveken, 2002:12); (Mey, 1993:83).

Starting from the assumption that the cooperation between the teller and the recipient resides in the participants' ability of drawing inferences, we may explain why

in the process of narrating the speaker does not have to state everything explicitly, as he/she may rely on his/her interlocutors' capacity of understanding the implied meanings of the linguistic items he/she uses (Mey, ibid.). This entails that in order to qualify for a good conversationalist, the speaker must adapt his speech according to his/her interlocutor's social profile: age, gender and social status, to the contextual/cotextual circumstances in which the conversation takes place as well as to the hearer's cognitive abilities. In considering the latter aspect, the speaker may choose what 'to make explicit', or, on the contrary, what 'to leave implicit'. Unless he/she does that, the speaker risks that the implicit meaning of his/her utterance might not be recovered by the audience (Grundy, 1995:142). In point of

---

[34] The conversational maxims proposed by Grice are not, in fact, norms that the interlocutors must observe, but actually expectations that they have of the speakers (Reboul & Moeschler, 2001:49).

the availability of the cotext to the recipient, if a narrator is telling a story, he/she has to take into account, among others, the recipient's knowledge of the recounted event. Supposing the recipient is not familiar with certain details in the story, the teller will have to supply extra information regarding those facts. If, on the contrary, the audience is acquainted with certain aspects of the narrated event, the speaker may omit them.

In some cases, *flouting Grice's maxims* does not necessarily mean that one does not collaborate with one's interlocutors. The pragmatic effect speakers want to get through their use of language is a case in point (Mey, 1993:75-77). For instance, in telling a story a narrator may make use of irony or banter, metaphor or litotes, thus violating the maxim of quality, in saying something he/she believes to be untrue (Cornilescu & Chițoran, 1994:224); (Reboul & Moeschler, 2001:49). Or, the teller may not observe Grice's maxim of quantity ('be as informative as possible') (Reboul & Moeschler, 2001:49) in telling a joke: for entertainment reasons the speaker will not reveal the punchline of the joke to his audience from the very beginning. For these reasons, the speaker will make use of certain narrative tricks: deliberately leaving out information, misleading, uninforming, or disinforming his/her interlocutors (Mey, 1993:76), gambits which are clearly intended to refrain the recipient from understanding the genuine intended meaning of the spoken utterances.

The Speech Act theory has proved relevant for our analysis of conversational narratives as stories have been found to be told by the speaker to an audience with the purpose of influencing the recipients' actions and social practices (Abma, 2004). This is precisely the domain of speech acts, of language being used with the purpose of performing actions, as for instance, creating and discharging obligations, influencing the thoughts and actions of others, and creating new states of affairs and new social relationships (Sperber and Wilson, 1986:243). Thus, a story that functions as an apology may be told by the speaker with the purpose of determining the recipient to forgive him/her for having erred, or a narrative that takes the form of a complaint may be told to make the audience sympathize with the speaker (this may also imply getting the recipient to change his/her mind). In this sense, we may propose that *stories* are, functionally speaking, *macro speech acts* as they form a body of utterances via which speakers perform actions.

As indicated above, people use stories to perform actions, to change something in/about the speaker, or to produce a certain effect in his /her interlocutor. The success of the speaker's intention, however, depends on the hearer's recognition of the speaker's respective intention (Reboul & Moeschler, 2001:45). In case there is more than one interpretation of an utterance as two different speech acts, most of the times, it is the speech event -the circumstances (the context and cotext included) surrounding the utterance, or, in our case, the body of utterances which make up the story, the background information which refers to the interlocutors' mutual knowledge- that facilitates the hearer the understanding of the speaker's communicative intention (Yule, 1996:47-48); (Reboul & Moeschler, 2001:51).

In what concerns the relevance of *Politeness theory* to our analysis, it emerges from the fact that the meaning of a story is socially constructed (in the sense that a speaker tells a certain story to a certain audience/recipient with a certain purpose at a particular moment in the conversation) (Abma, 2004). The use of each of the three main politeness strategies advanced by Brown & Levinson (*positive politeness, negative politeness,* and *off record*) is bound to social determinants, such as the relationship between speaker and recipient and the potential insulting character of the message conveyed by the speaker (Brown & Levinson, 1987:2). Surprisingly, underpoliteness is often used for establishing or maintaining familiarity and solidarity with the interlocutor, whereas overpoliteness can convey superiority or ironic distance (Leech, 1991:144). Consequently, the less the imposition of the act, the less powerful and distant the conversational partner is, the less polite the speaker will need to be (Culpeper, 1996:355); (Sorea, 2007a:139).

The obvious gap between the said and the implied can be put down to *politeness* (Brown & Levinson, 1987:2) as 'a strategy for cooperation with least cost and maximum benefits to all interlocutors' (Mey, 1993:74):

"In general, people cooperate (and assume each other's cooperation) in maintaining face in interaction, such cooperation being based on the mutual vulnerability of face. That is, normally everyone's face depends on everyone else's being maintained, and since people can be expected to defend their faces if threatened, and in defending their own to threaten others" faces, it is in general in every participant's best interest to maintain each others' face" (Brown and Levinson, 1987:61)

In collaborative talk the speakers' aim is to build up their interlocutors' positive face, avoiding at the same time to say something that might constitute a threat to the recipients' negative face. This aim may not be achieved easily, as participants to conversation are liable to 'lose face' with every turn at talk they take. For instance, a speaker may say something he/she did not really mean to say as a result of being provoked by his/her interlocutor, or he/she may say something he/she did not want to share with the audience. The speaker might also be bullied by an interlocutor who does not like him/her or who wants to exploit him/her for his own benefits (Mey, 1993:72). Thus, *stories* may function as *face-threats* in a competitive conversational style or as *face-saving strategies* in a collaborative conversational style. For example, a story might represent a threat to the positive face of one of the recipients if it refers to a situation in which that specific person is presented as doing something that is not socially acceptable. A story that would constitute a threat to one of the recipients' negative face is a story in which the speaker would relate an event that would present the recipient as being dependent on something/someone or as being imposed on by others. Conversely, narratives may also be designed by their tellers with the purpose of saving one's own/or one of the addressees' positive or negative face. A story functioning as a positive face-saving strategy would recount a situation in which the person who has suffered the face threat is shown to be accepted and liked by others, whereas a narrative related with the purpose of saving one's own or someone else's negative face would present that person as acting independently from what the others said or did.

Politeness Theory has been shown to have a bearing on the structure of daily basis conversation. Hand in hand with conversation analysis, politeness helps to 'communicate the essentials of social relationships' (Brown & Levinson, 1987:38). It seems that face considerations are extremely influential in a certain area of study of conversation analysis, called *preference organization*, in that they determine which types of answers are preferred and which ones are dispreferred in a conversational interaction. For instance, agreement is preferred because disagreement is a face threatening act (FTA), self-repair is favoured against other-correction, as the latter may implicate that self is either misguided or incompetent, acceptances of offers or requests are preferred to refusals, as the latter would mean lack of consideration as well as would non-answers (instead of their answers counterparts) to questions. An offer-acceptance sequence is favoured against a request-acceptance sequence as A's determining B to make an offer is less face risky than A request something of B, as B might refuse the request, but not withdraw the offer (ibid.:38-39).

Face considerations also account for *'conflicting requirements'*, such as the preference for either compliments or self-denigrations. In response to a compliment, the recipient has to choose between agreeing with the compliment or denigrating himself/herself. Both of these choices pose some problems with respect to either the speaker's or to the addressee's face. Agreeing with the compliment means disregarding the constraint against self-praise. The proper way to deal with this dilemma would be to produce intermediate utterances, like for example, 'agreements with praised downgrade, agreements about praise worthiness but with praise shifted to third party, return compliments'. Self-denigrations, on the other hand, are problematic in that the hearer's agreement with the speaker's previous turn in which a compliment is produced, runs counter to the constraint against criticisms of others. Again, intermediate stands seem to be the appropriate solutions in dealing with this problem: 'agreement with self-inclusion, implicit agreement by silence or minimal acknowledgement'. Therefore, the preference for agreement and the constraint against criticism of others are dictated by positive face considerations, whereas the constraint against self-praise is grounded on the rationale that a raising of the self equals a lowering of the other, in the same way as with the honorifics, raising the other implicates lowering of the self (Pomerantz, 1978); (Pomerantz (1984a) apud Brown & Levinson (1987:39)).

A feature of preference organization is the activation of face-preserving strategies and techniques. For instance, a delay (instead of a preferred turn) following a first turn signals the hearer's intention not to produce the preferred action, as expected by the speaker. This gives the speaker of the next turn the opportunity to reformulate his/her utterance so as to make the initial claim more acceptable, or even withdraw it, thus avoiding an actual rejection on the part of the hearer (Brown & Levinson, 1987:38).

It has also been pointed out that FTAs also occur at the level of conversational structure. Thus, turn-taking violations, such as interruptions, not minding other-selection, not bothering to respond to the previous turn, as well as opening and closing procedures, are all FTAs (Brown and Levinson (1987:233) apud Culpeper (1996:358)).

The concept of face is also observed in the process of the narrator's construction of identity through storytelling. Thus, in his/her attempt to build a certain portrait of himself/herself for the audience, the speaker strives to achieve the balance necessary for social acceptance between 'self-aggrandizement' and 'self-effacement' (Dyer and Keller-Cohen, 2000:297).

These pragmatic theories are also meant to counterbalance the shortcomings of narrative analysis. Within the framework of the latter theoretical approach, the focus is on the content of the narrative, whereas the meanings embedded in the language used in telling the story are completely ignored. Moreover, narrative analysis often disregards 'the larger interactive and discursive context' (Abma, 2004). Speech Act theory and Politeness theory make helpful tools in determining what is going on socially in a conversational interaction containing narratives.

We will now turn to the research methodology on which we base our empirical study.

1.4 Research Methodology

In presenting the research methodology employed in our dissertation paper, we will focus on the following matters: the collection of the data, the transcription of the recordings and the methods used in detecting and locating narrative segments in talk-in-interaction.

1.4.1 Data collection

This section will provide information on the methodology used for the collection of the data in this work.

Our data consists of audio-taped recordings of naturally-occurring face-to-face conversational interactions. The recordings were made in Bucharest (between September 2007 and June 2011), Arad (between July and August 2008) and in various mountain locations (in 2010) in both familiar settings (the participants' homes, fast-food restaurants, parks, mountain chalets), during casual chats among friends and/or family members, and formal encounters, during professional meetings. The database was collected using a Sansa audio recorder.

The participants were males and females between 17-75 years of age, twenty-four males and twenty-four females, living and working in Bucharest and Arad. The informants were grouped into four age groups: teenagers (17-19), young people (20-35), adults (36-50) and old people (51-75).

The interactions took place in familiar and formal settings, both in pairs and in groups of three or four people within the same age group and in two different age groups, among same-sex and both sexes informants. The topic of discussion was up to the participants.

The samples included in this paper total around thirty hours of audio-taped talk containing spontaneous extended discourse. In some of the sessions the participants to the conversation were aware they were being recorded, in others they were not, but were told about it afterwards. In both cases, all informants granted permission that the recorded material should be used for linguistic analysis.

1.4.2 Transcription of the data

The recordings were transcribed by adopting the transcription conventions employed in conversation analysis, including thus sufficient detail for a fine-grained analysis (Ochs, Schegloff and Thompson (1996) apud Hornoiu (2008:231-232)). A word of caution is in order here: our use of capital letters serves two purposes only: to indicate proper nouns and to mark the speakers' emphasis of certain linguistic items.

The conversations have been transcribed phonetically. However, in the transcription of foreign (usually English) words used by our Romanian informants, we chose, for accuracy reasons, to observe their common, original spelling. In the transcription, pseudonyms have been assigned to the participants to protect their identity.

Here is the 'key' to the transcription of the conversational narratives in the corpus we gathered:

I. Temporal and sequential relationship

[Separate left brackets, one above the other on two successive lines with utterances
[by different speakers, indicate the point of overlap onset.

] Separate right square brackets, one above the other on two successive lines with
] utterances by different speakers, indicates a point at which two overlapping utterances both end.

= Equal signs come in pairs: one at the end of a line and another at the start of the next line or one line shortly thereafter. They are used to indicate the following:

1. If the two lines connected by equal signs are by the same speaker, then there was a single continuous utterance, with no break or pause, which was broken up in order to accommodate the placement of overlapping talk.
2. If the lines connected by two equal signs are by different speakers, then the second followed the first with no discernable silence between them or was latched to it.

(0.5) Numbers in parentheses indicate silence, approximately represented in tenths of a second. Silences may be marked within an utterance or between utterances.

(.) A dot in parentheses indicates a "micropause", hearable but not readily measurable, usually less than 2 tenths a second.

II. *Aspects of speech delivery, including aspects of intonation*

The punctuation marks are not used grammatically, but to indicate intonation.

. The period indicates a falling, or final, intonation contour, not necessarily the end of a sentence.

? Similarly, a question mark indicates rising intonation, not necessarily an interrogative sentence.

, A comma indicates continuing intonation, not necessarily a clause boundary.

:: Colons are used to indicate the prolongation or stretching of the sound just preceding them. The more colons, the longer the stretching. On the other hand, graphically stretching a word on the page by inserting blank spaces between the letters does not indicate how it was pronounced; it is used to allow alignment with overlapping talk.

becau- A hyphen after a word or part of a word indicates a cut-off or self-interruption, often done with a glottal or dental stop.

word Underlining is used to indicate some form of stress or emphasis either by increase loudness or higher pitch. The more underlining, the greater the emphasis.

Word Upper case indicates especially loud talk; the louder, the more letters in upper case.

WOrd In extreme cases, upper case may be underlined.

° The degree sign indicates that the talk following is marked as being quiet or soft.

°word° When there are two degree signs, the talk between them is marked as being softer than the talk around it.

Combinations of **underlining** and **colons** are used to indicate *intonation contours* as follows:

w**o**:rd If the letter(s) preceding a colon is/are underlined, then there is an inflected *falling* intonation contour on the vowel (you can hear the pitch turn downward).

wo:rd If a colon is itself underlined, the there is an inflected *rising* intonation contour on the vowel (i.e., you can hear the pitch turn upward).

↑↓ The up and down arrows mark sharper rises or falls in pitch than would be indicated by combinations of colons and underlining, or they may mark a whole shift or resetting of pitch register at which the talk is being produced.

> < The combinations "more than" and "less than" symbols indicates that the talk between
< > them is compressed or rushed. Used in the reverse order, they can indicate that a stretch of talk is markedly slowed or drawn out.

< The "less than" symbol by itself indicates that the immediately following talk is "jump-started" i.e. sounds like it starts with a rush.

III. *Other markings*

((cough)) Double are used to mark the transcriber's description of events, rather than representations of them.

(word) When all or part of an utterance is in parentheses, or the speaker identification is, this indicates uncertainty on the part of the trascriber, but represents a likely possibility.

( ) Empty parentheses indicate that something is being said, but no hearing, or in some cases speaker identification, can be achieved.

(bu::t)/ (goo:d) Two parentheses separated by a slash represent alternative hearings of the same spate of talk

We will now present the method we have used in finding the narrative segments in our conversational data.

1.4.3 Locating narratives in transcripts

In order to identify candidate instances of narrative segments, the following methods were adopted (Kuntay and Ervin-Tripp, 1997:114): reading over the datasets for large-level indicators of narrative such as reference to past events or irrealis events, prefaces by narrators, prompting by audiences, or audience evaluations. Also, the narrative passages we have spotted intuitively were verified by automatic search, i.e. computerized search for specific linguistic markers such as temporal connectives. Once we identified the narratives, the next step was to proceed to the investigation of their linguistic and interactional features, their internal structure, functions and typology.

1.4.4 Translation of the data

Last but not least, we translated the interactional narratives in our Romanian corpus into English. In the process of translating, we weighed the cultural elements carefully and then decided to adopt either a *documentary* or an *instrumental translation*[35], depending on what we thought to be the focus of the various conversational narratives in our data. Thus, we basically tried to preserve the original type of expression from the source language into the target language. However, at times, we decided to adapt the source frame and style to target audience, as for instance, when translating proverbs, address terms, general extenders[36], idioms, or slang. Finally, for accuracy reasons, we verified our translation with a native speaker, Fr. John Downie.

The following chapter will discuss the formal linguistic properties of conversational narratives, features acquired as a consequence of the narratives' being embedded in talk-in-interaction.

1.5 Conclusions

The aim of the present chapter has been to set up a theoretical framework, which would provide several key-concepts to be used later on, in the subsequent chapters of this paper, in the analysis of the conversational data, analysis which focuses on the conversational narratives performed by storytellers in their interventions.

The chapter proposed an integrated approach which combines two approaches to discourse which have been found relevant for the analysis of conversational narratives: **conversation analysis and narrative analysis**. We have argued that the tools provided by narrative analysts are helpful in our microanalysis of the storytelling performance and that the concepts forwarded by conversation analysis will be used in order to fit the stories into the conversational context of turn-by-turn talk. Also, we have

---

[35] For more information on these types of translation, see Sorea (2007b:72-73).
[36] For further details on the matter, see chapter 2.

shown that, additionally, the *speech act theory* (Searle, 1969), along with *the cooperative principle* (Grice, 1975), as well as the *politeness* (Brown and Levinson, 1987 [1978]) and *impoliteness theories* (Culpeper, 1996); (Culpeper et al., 2003) make helpful tools for the present analysis, in that they provide both a linguistic and a sociolinguistic perspective of conversational narratives.

Finally, we presented the research methodology we employed in our present research: the collection of the data, the transcription of the recordings, the methods used in detecting and locating narrative segments in talk-in-interaction, and the translation into English of the conversational narratives in our corpus.

CHAPTER 2.
LINGUISTIC FEATURES OF CONVERSATIONAL NARRATIVES

2.0 Introduction. Overview of chapters 3 and 4.

The aim of the present chapter is to discuss the relation between narratives and the linguistic context in which they are embedded, that is, the ongoing talk. In this sense, we will endeavour to identify a set of linguistic features which characterize Romanian conversational narratives. For this purpose, we will rely on relevant works in the literature devoted to *narrative analysis (narratology)* included). As shown in the first chapter, conversational narratives have been approached from various perspectives*: linguistic, anthropological, social, and psychological. From an **anthropological perspective** (Barthes & Duisit, 1975), narration has been described as *an essential property of the human species*[37]:

'Moreover, in this infinite variety of forms, it [narrative] is present at all times, in all places, in all societies; indeed narrative starts with the very history of mankind; there is not, there has never been anywhere, any people without narrative; all classes, all human groups, have their stories' (p. 237).

From a literary, **narratological viewpoint**, it has been pointed out that a narrative, as a text type, has a *fixed structure, consisting of a beginning, a middle and an end* (Aristotle, English translation, 2000:12). Finally, from a **linguistic perspective**, a narrative, as a mode of discourse, has been defined as *a sequence of temporally ordered events* (Smith, 1999:489).

We will show that, even if they are brief, narratives embedded in conversation have the same structure as the classical narrative. Also, the aim of our work being the study of narrative within the larger framework of dialogue[38], we are concerned with a specific feature bestowed on narratives by

---

[37] In the same line, Fisher (1987:xi) proposes 'a reconceptualisation of humankind as Homo narrans' and that 'all forms of human communication need to be seen fundamentally as stories'.
[38] We have used the terms *dialogue* and *conversation* interchangeably, since the slight difference between them is not significant for the purpose of our paper. For futher information on this matter, see *DICȚIONAR GENERAL DE ȘTIINȚE. ȘTIINȚE ALE LIMBII* (1997).

their being engendered by dialogue: their *orality*, given by both their syntactic structure and by the vocabulary characteristic of spoken language. We will also focus upon a special problem: marking the passage from one type of discourse to another – from conversation to narrative and back again – by means of specific linguistic markers: *opening/closing formulas* and *the switch in tense* (from the present tense of the conversation to the past tense of the narrative). We will also examine the various ways in which stories are engendered by conversation: by means of a conversational detail (*entailed* narratives), by means of a question (*elicited* narratives), or by means of the presence of an object or person in the local environment (*environmentally cued* narratives).

The linguistic features of conversational stories will be illustrated with relevant excerpts extracted from our corpus of conversational interactions comprising ongoing narratives. This corpus amounts to about 30 hours of naturally-occurring, face-to-face conversational interactions, containing genuine conversational narratives, which were recorded in familiar settings, during casual chats among friends and/or family members as well as in more formal settings, during professional meetings[39].

Chapter 3 focuses on the *functions* of narratives within the conversational framework in which they are embedded. We start from the paradigm of the functions of language proposed by Halliday & Hasan (1989) and detail it by reference to the functions of language proposed by Jakobson (1960). Conversational narratives will be shown to serve several functions simultaneously, in accordance with the principle of the *multifunctionality of language* proposed by Jakobson and also supported by Halliday & Hasan (1989). For systematicity reasons, we will range the functions in a *hierarchy* and identify the main function by relying on *the intention-based criterion*, which is synonymous with Grice's (1975) and Searle's (1979) idea of the purpose of a speech act.

While chapter 2 mostly discusses the formal linguistic properties of conversational narratives, chapter 4 deals with the *interactional properties* of narratives, discussing various issues, among which the relevance of stories and the speakers' right of telling them. These aspects are examined in terms of the framework of conversation analysis and its related concept of turn-taking in conversation (Sacks, Schegloff and Jefferson, 1974). We have also investigated the manifestation of the sociological variables of age, gender and level of education in discourse as well as the pragmatic discursive strategies of positive and negative politeness used by the speakers in our corpus (Brown and Levinson, 1987 [1978]).

---

[39] For more details about the corpus, see chapter 1 of the present paper.

The first linguistic matter we discuss is the occurrence of narratives within the larger frame of the ongoing talk, a phenomenon which confers specific properties to these narratives. We will show how stories depart from and return to another discourse genre, the dialogue.

2.1 The embeddedness of stories in dialogue

A crucial trait of conversational stories[40] is that they are framed by dialogue. A dialogue may engender a narrative when a word or phrase in the ongoing talk reminds one of the parties of a certain event, thus triggering a narration. This type of narratives

having as a starting point a certain *detail* in the conversation has been called an **entailed narrative**. Alternatively, a story may be triggered by *a question* asked by one of the interactants – it is the case of **elicited narratives** – and by a process of association with the presence of *an object or person in the local environment* – as is the case of **environmentally cued narratives** – (Iordache, 2009a). The respective narrative may be 'topically coherent'[41] (cf. Sacks, 1968) or not with the previous talk, that is, the teller may elaborate his/her story starting (or not) from the same topic that has been tackled in the foregoing talk (Jefferson, 1978:220). Conversely, a completed story may bring about a discussion on the same topic (or on a similar one) as the one tackled in the narrative. The conversation is often reengaged having as a starting point a certain detail in the story that reminds one of the recipients of a particular event which will make the subject of a new discussion (Jefferson, ibid.). All in all, narratives are always relevant, even though they are not always topically coherent.

Fragment (1) below is illustrative of the case of *entailed* conversational narratives which start from a detail in the ongoing talk and are built on the same topic as the one set by the preceding conversation. Upon coming to an end, participants re-engage the conversation on a topic tangential with the one tackled in the story.

*(1) Meci de fotbal/*Football match

---

[40] Our discussion will not be restricted to *stories* in interaction: we will also take into account *narrative passages*, since we are more interested in the linguistic perspective of conversational narratives, rather than in the narratological viewpoint. For economic reasons related to their production within the framework of turn-by-turn talk, such narrative passages usually have a minimal complicating action and may even lack climax and resolution.
[41] *Topical coherence* is roughly defined as 'a current utterance standing in an appropriate, continuous relationship to ongoing talk' (cf. Sacks, 1968).

1B: **Pleșan** *când l-a luat Dinamo de la Craiova era jucătoru' lu' Craiova*
   when Dinamo took Pleșan from Craiova he was Craiova's player
2 *ținea echipa-n spate*
   he was the leader of the team
3P: *ții minte când a plecat (0.2) de la U Craio:va?=*
   do you recall when he left U Craio:va
→4B: = *țin minte și-acuma c-am fost la meciu' cu Cluju'*
   I still recall that I went to the match against Cluj
5 *de conducea Cluju' cu doi-zero la pauză*
   Cluj led two-nil at the break
6 *și i-a bătut cu trei-doi*
   and they beat them three-two
7 *ce-a făcut?*
   what did he do
8 *a dat două goluri*
   he scored two goals
9 *unu' cu capu' unu' din lovitură liberă și-o pasă de gol (0.2) (   )*
   one by head from a free kick and a goal pass
10R: *băi Bog[dane*
   say what Bogdan
11B: [*și-am înjurat de mi-a venit dracii*
       and I swore like a sailor
12R: (   )
13B: *da (0.1) da' traba e că dup-aia a ajuns la Dinamo și s-a lăsat*
   yeah but the thing is that after that he went to Dinamo and he grew lazy

The narrative in excerpt (1) – lines 4-9 and 11 – relates a personal experience of the narrator's, B, who happened to watch a football match between the Universitatea Craiova and Universitatea Cluj football teams. The story is elaborated on the same topic (a football match) as the previous talk – rendered here in lines 1-3 –, which refers to the performance of one of the footballers in the Romanian football championship. The present story is introduced in the conversation with the role of elaborating on the speaker's argument in line 2 ('*ținea echipa-n spate*') ('he was the leader of the team'). The ending of the story re-engages the conversation – lines 12-13 – on a topic tangential with the one tackled by the teller in his story: the speaker goes on by expressing his dissatisfaction regarding the lack of professionalism of the respective football player.

The fragment below exemplifies an *elicited narrative*, which is prompted by the interlocutor's question.

(2) După gărzi/ After shifts
1D: *și cum reușești să te refaci (0.2) după gărzi*
   so how do you manage to recover after your shifts
2C: *nu prea reușesc să mă refac după gărzi ( ) partea cea mai rea [este că*
   I can't really recover after shifts the worst part is that
3D: [*dormi câteva ore când vii*
   acasă?=

                                                                  do you sleep for a few hours
            when you get home
4C: =nu prea (0.1) de oboseală (0.3)
         not really because of the fatigue
5   mă gândesc la diverși pacienți la ce puteam să fac și n-am făcu::t =
         I think of the various patients of what I could have done but I didn't
6D: îhî (0.4) și din ce <u>cauză</u> (0.5)
         yeah and why
7C: mă rog (0.1) cauzele sunt evidente nu-i vorba de [asta
         well the causes are obvious it's not that
8D: [sunt destul de clare=
                                                         they are pretty obvious
9C: = și ajungi acasă la 2:30-3:00 mănânci ceva mai vorbești cu familia îți faci o baie=
         and you arrive home at half past two or three o'clock you eat something you talk to your
         family you have a bath
10D: =da
         yeah
11C: (0.4) mai stai (0.2) te mai gândești (0.1) și deja s-a făcut seară de te culci
         you take some time you think it over and before you know it it's already evening and you
         go to bed

The story in the excerpt above is elicited in line 1 ('*și cum reușești să te refaci (0.2) după gărzi*') ('so how do you manage to recover after your shifts') by C' interlocutor, D, who manifests interest in C's resting programme after the night shift. D's concern for C's needs is a positive politeness strategy, which is used by D to grant C the floor so that she could give a recount of a particular aspect of her professional life.

Excerpt (3) below is an instance of *environmentally cued narratives*, which are triggered by the presence of an object or person in the local environment.

<u>(3)Undița/ Fishing line</u>
26L: *fii atent fii atent*
         watch this watch this
27C:*a:::: și io am rămas cu undița agățată într-un copac odată*
         oh I myself got my fishing line stuck in a tree once
28   *asta când mergeam cu ea pe umăr fără să mă uit la nimic în jur*
         this was while I was walking with it on my shoulder without looking around
29   *((L și A râd))*=
         ((L and A laugh))
30C:=*și eram cam așa:în mijlocul sălbăticiei (0.1)*
         and I was almost in the middle of the wilderness
31   *adică n-avea cine să m-ajute pe-acolo*
         I mean there wasn't anybody to help me there
32L: *și ce [(   )?]*
         and what
33C: *[făcusem rost] de un scăunel de pescuit parcă cum să zic*=
         I managed to get a fishing chair or something

34A: =((râde))
      ((laughs))
35C: bine am tăiat firu' până la urmă [((râde))]
      well I eventually cut the thread ((laughs))
36A: [((râde))]
                                         ((laughs))

The story above is recounted as a result of the speaker's having noticed, in the
immediate surroundings, a little boy holding a fishing line, which got tangled in the branches of a tree. Thus, the respective person and object remind the teller, C, of a similar situation, which is immediately brought to C's interlocutors' attention. Due to its hilarious nature, the story seems as if it were cut out of a Charlie Chaplin film: the recipients may visualize C as a boy, strutting in the middle of nowhere, his fishing rod on his shoulder, when, unexpectedly, the object he is holding gets stuck in a tree. Then, when he finally manages to get a fishing chair and get on it, what he actually does is cut off the thread. The hearers' reaction to such a situation can be just one: bursting into laughter – lines 29, 34 and 36.

We will now focus on the passage from one discourse genre to another – dialogue to narrative – and back again.

2.2 Linguistic markers indicating the transition from conversation to narrative

Next, we will deal with the linguistic elements delimiting talk-in-interaction from narrative passages. We will emphasize the role played by opening/closing formulas and tense in indicating the boundary between the discourse genres of dialogue and narrative. Firstly, we will examine formulaic story openers/closings.

2.2.1 Formulaic story openers/closings

The emergence of stories into the ongoing interaction and their re-engaging the ongoing talk is announced by the use of conventional formulas, marking the beginning and the end of a story, respectively. In what follows we will turn our attention to this very matter.

The literature on conversational narratives has pointed out that in order to mark a story's beginning and grasp their interlocutors' attention as well as their availability of listening to the story, narrators often utilize specific formulas (Sacks, 1992; Norrick, 2000; Vasilescu, 2007a:81; Iordache, 2010c:227). The investigation of our corpus has confirmed these findings: after having examined the stories which make up our Romanian corpus we encountered the following inventory of **formulaic story openers**: *'odată'* ('once'), *'îmi aduc aminte că'* ('I recall that'), *'ţin minte şi-acuma'* ('I still recall'), *'ţi-aduci aminte când?'* ('do you recall when?'), ('ce ne-a mai speriat pe noi atuncea') ('how scared we got then'), *'mai ştii'* ('do you recall'), *'prima experienţă'* ('the first time'), *'a doua oară'* ('the second time'), *'a treia oară'* ('the third time'), *'ţi-am povestit despre ...?'* ('have I told you about ...?'), *'revenind la treburile astea'* ('getting back to our business'), *'apropo de asta'* ('by the way'), *'hai să-ţi spunem'* ('let us tell you'), *'păi hai să-ţi spun de la început'* ('well let me tell you from the beginning'), *'să-ţi povestesc'* ('let me tell you'), *'hai să-ţi mai povestesc ceva'* ('let me tell you another story'), *'da' ia spune-i mă cum a fost cu ...'* ('come on tell her about'), *'de unde să-ţi încep să-ţi spun mai întâi?'* ('where shall I start?'), *'v-am zis?'* ('have I told you about?'), *'haideţi să vă zic'* ('let me tell you'), *'vreau să-ţi spun că'* ('I mean that'), *'asta e una de i-am speriat pe toţi'* ('this is one which frightened everybody'). These formulas may be grouped according to the following criteria:

a). *neutre formulas*, which introduce a story whose topic is unknown, 'a puzzle' for the audience (e.g., *'hai să-ţi mai povestesc ceva'*) ('let me tell you another story') ;

b). *more engaging formulas*, which anticipate the topic of the events in the narrative, thus preparing the listeners with respect to the sort of story they should expect and the kind of response they should provide at its end (Sacks, 1992; Norrick, 2000) (e.g., *'asta e una de i-am speriat pe toţi'* ('this is one which frightened everybody'), *,ce (ne-a mai speriat pe noi atuncea) mai ştii'*) ('how scared we got then').

A particular strategy used by tellers to introduce their story to the audience is the use of questions which constrain the hearers to answer 'what' (Sacks, 1972 apud Norrick, 2000) : *(e.g. 'ştii ce mi-a zis mie o şefă de-a mea'?)* ('what do you think a boss of mine told me?'), thus selecting the interlocutor as the next speaker.

The following fragments point out that the storyteller introduces her story through a story opener.

(4) Carismă/ Charisma
1A: **ți-am povestit despre** *studentul meu ca:re (0.3) ((râde)) cu carisma ?*
    have I told you about my student who ((laughs)) with charisma
2G: *nu =*
    no you haven't
3A: *= a (0.1)* **nu ți-am pove[stit?**
    oh haven' t I
4G: [*nu (0.1) ce carisma ?*
                                    no what charisma
5A: *ă: (0.5) vorbeam despre success (0.3) și: despre carismă*
    well we were talking about success and charisma

The introduction by speaker A of the story opener *('ți-am povestit despre')* ('have I told you about') in line 1 and its reiteration, this time in the negative form, in line 3 *('nu ți-am pove[stit?')* ('haven' t I') have the role of announcing the story and inserting it in the ongoing conversational interaction as well as arousing the recipient's interest in the narrative that is about to be told. Moreover, this opening formula accounts for the speaker's cautiousness with respect to the relevance or newsworthiness of the upcoming story. By checking the novelty of the story for the listener, the speaker makes sure she will not disqualify herself as a narrator.

(5) Râde ciob de oală spartă[42]/ The pot calls the kettle black
1C: *ua::i* **mai ții mai ții minte** *faza cu profa de is- de geografia Angliei? ((râde))*
    oh do you recall the incident with the teacher of Engish geography ((laughs))
2   *și (0.1) ((râde)) Cristina Pop (0.1)* **nu mai știi** *[((râde))*
    and ((laughs)) Cristina Pop don't you recall it ((laughs))
3T: [*da*
                                                            yeah
4C: *ua:i ((râde)) deci aveam o profă de geografia Angliei (0.2)*
    oh ((laughs)) well we had a teacher of Engish geography

In order to introduce a story which is familiar to one of the hearers and to prompt her into co-narrating, speaker C uses a formula which is specific for the introduction of familiar stories in conversation 'do you recall when?' – line 1 *('ua::i mai ții mai ții minte')* ('oh do you recall'), and then reformulates it in the negative, 'don't you recall' – line 2 *('nu mai știi')* ('don't you recall').

---

[42] We have given titles to our excerpts since they are part of narratives which are stored and which we intend to list in an Appendix.

Among formulaic story openers, which announce the suspension of the conversation and the beginning of a narrative, we distinguish the category of **temporal connectors.** Their role is also to ensure the cohesion of a text on the syntactic level and its coherence on the semantic level (Halliday and Hasan, 1983:10); (Halliday and Hasan, 1989:73); (Buja, 2008:61). This is why speakers use temporal connectors to link clauses, sentences and ideas, respectively. In our corpus we have found that the Romanian narrators used the following repertoire of temporal connectors: *"când* (when), *într-o zi* (one day), *a doua zi* (the second day), *odată* (once), *într-o seară* (one evening), *ieri* (yesterday), *ieri dimineață* (yesterday morning), *azi dimineață* (this morning), *azi* (today), *astăzi* (today), *acuma* (now), *vineri/sâmbătă* (on Friday/on Saturday), *în weekend* (at the weekend)".

The fragment below points out that a *temporal connector* indicates the beginning of a narrative passage.

*(6) La slujbă/*At the mass
1M: *nu ți-ai dat seama nu?*
    you haven't thought of this have you?
2A: *păi cred că de două ori la Sfânta Ecaterina și o dată la Gorgani*
    well I think I go twice to St. Catherine's and once to Gorgani's
3   *dar **acuma** am împăcat ambele părți*
    but this time I've reconciled both sides
4   *am fost la Sfânta Ecaterina* (0.3) *am stat cam până la sfârșitul slujbei*
    I went to St. Catherine's I stayed almost to the end of the service
5   *și pe urmă am fost și la Gorgani și m-am întâlnit și cu prie°tenii°*
    and then I went to Gorgani's as well and met my friends too
6L: *cu cine?*=
    who?
7A:= *cu prietenii așa*
    well my friends

In the fragment above speaker A presents a short report[43] of what she did that day (attending the mass and meeting her friends). The passage from casual conversation to the narrative embedded within it is marked by a temporal connector, the adverbial ‚*acuma*' ('now') – line 3, along with the switch of tense, from the present of the conversation to the narrative past.

The combination of *a formulaic story opener* and of *a temporal connector* is also a common means of introducing a story in conversation.

*(7) La munte/*In the mountains

---

[43] For more information on *reports*, see chapter 1.

1 R: **hai să-ți spunem** (0.2)
    let us tell you
2 **când** am coborât noi din tren (0.3) "cum mergem"
    when we got off the train how shall we go
3 "păi a : (0.2) luăm taxiurile
    well let's take the taxi
4 luăm taxiurile (0.2) ca să nu mai mergem pe jos și ajungem pân' la Crăcănel"
    we take the taxi so as not to go on foot and we reach Crăcănel

In the excerpt above, R recounts what happened on her latest trip to the mountains. After the story proper has been announced by a story preface in line 1 *('hai să-ți spunem')* ('let us tell you'), the speaker further introduces her story through the temporal connector 'when', followed by a verb in the past tense in line 2 *('când am coborât noi din tren')* ('when we got off the train how shall we go'). These linguistic markers have the role of signalling to the listener that the story is unfolding right before their eyes. That a story is being told is very important for a listener to realize as social conventions, such as politeness, require his/her attention and active participation in the story recounted by the speaker.

The use of the temporal connector 'când' ('when') in the fragment above has the role of introducing the narrative into the conversational interaction, of ensuring the smooth passage from one type of discourse to another, as it links the two clauses both syntactically and semantically, thus contributing to the cohesion and coherence of the text.

Just as there are formulaic story openers indicating the beginning of a narrative passage, there are also **formulaic story closings,** marking the end of narratives and the return to turn-by-turn talk. However, while there are many story openers, there are fewer story closings, which are more difficult to spot than the former, presumably because stories have natural endpoints provided by the climax and the resolution. The role of these formulaic phrases is to bring the teller into the present, as the end of the narrated event coincides with the end of the narrative event (Norrick, 2000); (Iordache, 2010c:229-230).

Our own corpus confirms that the frequency of occurrence of formulaic story closings is extremely reduced. Instead of the closing formulas, the Romanian speakers seem to prefer to end their stories by what we shall call *summary utterances*, which are similar to a curtain that is drawn at the end of a theatre play. Their role is to summarize the narrated event *('da și-asta-i povestea cu copiii')* ('yes and this is the story with the children') or/and to evaluate the story *('mă rog asta-i așa (0.1) for fun')* ('well this is just for fun'). Sometimes, they may take the form of *proverbs*, transmitting the morale or lesson of the story (*'râde ciob de oală spartă'*) ('the pot calls the kettle black').

We will present a list of the repertoire of evaluative phrases used by the subjects in our corpus in ending their stories: *'mare-amenințare știi?'* ('great threat you know'), „mă da' cum a putut copilul ăla' ('how on earth could that child'), '*Doa::mne ce clasă mă/ acolo într-adevăr nu puteai rezista*' ('oh God what a class/you simply couldn't make it there'), '*în orice caz nu am văzut niciun arici*' ('anyway we haven't seen any sea urchins'), '*am zis că înnebunesc*' ('I thought I'd go crazy'), '*bă înnebunești când auzi ce se întâmplă acolo*' ('you go crazy when you hear what's going on in there'), '*asta e realitatea cinstit*' ('that's the way things are, honestly'), '*și-asta e*' ('that's it'). Among these phrases, some have turned into clichés: '*și-asta e*' ('that's it'), '*vai de capul meu*' ('woe is me'), '*ai de:: sufletul nostru*' ('poor us'). The use of proverbs and clichés has also been signalled as story conclusions in English conversational narratives (Sacks, 1992). Other examples of formulaic story closings encountered in the literature are: 'and I lived to tell about it', 'and the rest is history', etc. (Norrick, 2000).

The fragments below point out that the teller ends her story with a formulaic phrase.

(8) Familia copilului autist/ The autistic child's family
16   Irina știe ((imită vocea)) "Andrei are nevoie de ajutor=
       Irina knows about it ((imitates her voice)) Andrei needs help
17   = o să fac și eu terapie cu Andrei o să lucrez și eu cu el" (0.5)
       I'm going to do therapy with Andrei too I'm going to work with him as well
18 M: da și-asta-i povestea cu copiii
       yes and this is the story with the children

M ends her story in line 18 with the formulaic phrase *('da și-asta-i povestea cu copiii')* ('yes and this is the story with the children'), which has the function of bringing the teller right into the present and of offering the listener, who waits for a sign of closure, an important cue that the story is over.

(9) Râde ciob de oală spartă/ The pot calls the kettle black
37C: *și ((râde)) vine asta și-i stătea ori:bil*
      and ((laughs))in she comes looking horrid
38T: *parcă te-a auzit=*
      as if she had heard you
39C: *=și toată clasa a început să râ:dă*
      and all the class started laughing
40   *și cine râdea mai tare era Cristina Pop care era oribilă săraca ea însăși=*
      and the one that laughed loudest was Cristina Pop who was horrid herself poor thing
41T: *=ea însăși ((râde))*
      herself ((laughs))
42C: *și-atunci îi zic io lu' Teo* **"râde ciob de oală spartă"** *((râde))*
      and then I tell Teo the pot calls the kettle black ((laughs))

The teller chooses to end her story in line 42 with a well-known Romanian proverb *('râde ciob de oală spartă')* ('the pot calls the kettle black') – a formulaic phrase which is meant to signal the end of the story and to point out the speaker's ironic attitude toward the outcome of the recounted event, when a teacher's hairstyle is laughed at by a student who is not very far from the object of her disdain.

Expectedly, the use of tenses is another linguistic means marking the transition from talk-in-interaction to narrative and back again.

2.2.2 Tense switching

Generally speaking, the main linguistic marker of narratives is *temporality*. Since conversation is in the present tense, the speakers' *switch to past* and more rarely to *future* is indicative of the passage from the realm of conversation to the story world. The use of *narrative present* is also an option. Therefore, we may claim that the prototypical narrative tenses are *narrative past* and *narrative future* (Ochs, 1997:189-191); (Polanyi, 1989:17). Regarding the use of the *narrative present* in conversational stories, we have to admit its occurrence in narrative discourse, even though this may not seem possible at first sight since present tense predicates are states (i.e. unbounded intervals) and are therefore inconsistent with narration, which by definition denotes a series of temporally ordered completed (bounded) events. Nevertheless, the aspectual re-categorization of the present tense in narrative discourse makes it possible for it to refer to (past) events, instead of (present) states. The present can also change its temporal reference, designating an interval which precedes the present – the *historical present* – or a moment which is posterior to the present – *the prospective present*[44] –.

In what follows, we will discuss the narrative past as indicator of the beginning of narrative discourse within the larger framework of turn-by-turn talk.

The narrative past

Each language has its own inventory of narrative tenses. The main past narrative tenses for Romanian are the *perfect simplu* and the *perfect compus*. The former is used in the written language while the latter is utilized in the spoken variant (cf. Benveniste, 1974); (Zafiu, 2000:179). These two narrative tenses represent the 'engine' that sets the narrative thread in motion. They are used to convey *narrative progression*, whereas the *imperfect* is the tense which slows down the narrative progression, creating a pause in the sequential narrative of the related processes which occasions a detailed presentation of the *spatial-temporal framework* (Zafiu, ibid:173-178); (Gramatica Limbii Române, 2005:432).

---

[44] In comparison with the historical present, the prospective present is, nevertheless, rarely used in conversational narratives.

Most of the conversational narratives in our corpus illustrate the pattern *the perfect compus + the perfect compus*, indicating a sequence of at least two temporally ordered events, and the *perfect compus + the imperfect*, presenting an event and a background state. As for the other narrative tenses in Romanian designating past events, *the mai mult ca perfect* – the Romanian tense indicating anteriority with respect to another event in the past – appears sporadically, whereas the *perfect simplu* does not occur at all in our data.

Next we will illustrate the value of the *perfect compus* in an excerpt of a conversational narrative taken from our corpus.

(10) Meci de baschet/Basketball game
1R: *hai zii cum a fost*
     come on tell me how it was
2D: *păi ne-am dus*
     well we went (there)
3   *a fost un meci întâi (0.1) înaintea noastră (0.2)*
     there was one game first before us
4   *s-a terminat meciul ăla (0.1) i-am băgat la încălzire::*
     the game ended I made them warm up.
5   *s-au încălzit ei ce s-au încălzit acolo: nu știu ce*
     they warmed up for a while and stuff
6   *a început meciul (0.2)*
     the game started
7   *bine-nțeles primele minute:? praf (0.2) praf . praf . praf*
     of course in the first minutes they were terrible (0.2) terrible terrible terrible

In the excerpt above, the narrator, D, begins his story in line 2 following a request for information on R's part regarding the result of the basketball match. In telling his story, the speaker uses the Romanian narrative past, the perfect compus, to designate a sequence of temporally ordered past events: '*ne-am dus, s-a terminat, am băgat, s-au încălzit, a început*' ('(we) went, (it) ended, (I) made, (they) warmed up, (it) started'). In this case, the perfect compus has the role of insuring the progression of the narrative in question.

We will also exemplify the pattern the *perfect compus + the imperfect* in a fragment of conversational narrative taken from our corpus.

(11) Carismă/Charisma
1F: *și de data asta tot acolo-n ultima bancă* **a stat** *[și*
     he sat in the last desk this time as well and
2G: ((*râde*)) [*ca un cățel plouat*
                                            ((laughs)) like a wet puppy
3F: *da:* **se uita** *la mine ca: ( )*

```
        yeah he looked at me like
4   parcă așa pă sub ochi pă sub sprâncene
        like eyes down under his eyebrows
5   îi era teamă că cine știe ce
        he feared lest I should
6   o să mă răzbun pe el acuma °așa:°=
        I should take revenge on him now that he
7G: și ?[adică (0.2) a parti]cipat mai mult la: ( )
        and I mean did he participate more in
8F:     [nu m-am răzbunat]
        I didn't avenge myself
```

The fragment above is part of a story in which one of speaker's F students dared to tell her she didn't have charisma. For the purpose of advancing the narrative thread, which deals with the student's and the teacher's upcoming reactions, the narrator makes use of a sequence of two temporally ordered events in the perfect compus – lines 1 (*'a stat'*) ('he sat') and 8 (*'nu m-am răzbunat'*) ('I didn't avenge myself'). The occurrence of the imperfect verb forms denoting states – lines 3 (*'se uita'*) ('he looked') and 5 (*'îi era teamă'*) ('he feared') – has the role of providing background details referring to the student's anxiety concerning the potential consequences of his reckless act.

In what follows, we will discuss the values of the narrative present in conversational narratives.

The narrative present

As already pointed out above, in the subsection dedicated to the switching of tenses, present tense predicates (which are states) may be aspectually re-categorised as events. Since it may designate events, the present may have a narrative use. Pastness is overtly expressed by means of a past framework adverbial which provides reference time (RT) for the first historical present sentence. This use of the narrative present is called the *historical (or retrospective) present*.

a). Conversational historical present/ The retrospective present

The *historical present* (HP)[45] – i.e. the use of the present tense to refer to past events – is a linguistic feature often used in colloquial language (Iordache, 2010a:284). The usage of this particular tense in narratives that are told in genuine, everyday talk-in-interaction has been referred to as *the conversational historical present* (Wolfson, 1978:215); (Schiffrin, 1981:61).

In English, both *past tense and conversational historical present (CHP)* are used alternatively by speakers to designate past events in conversational narratives (Schiffrin, 1981:45); (Wolfson, 1978:218);

---

[45] For more information, see Tannen (1980:210); Tannen (1982:7).

(Wolfson, 1979:172). In this line, the CHP has been said to convey the same referential information as the simple past. The views in the literature regarding the use of CHP in conversational narratives are diverse, if not even contradictory. Schiffrin (1981) points out that CHP is a stylistic device which is indicative of the *vivid and exciting nature of past events* in narrative. The reason why the events expressed by CHP seem to be more vivid than those expressed by past simple is that CHP 'moves past events out of their original time frame and into the moment of speaking', either because CHP gives the audience the illusion of witnessing the actual events as they are unfolding or because the teller, while narrating the events, becomes so involved in telling the story that he/she seems to relive the respective experience. 'Past events 'come alive' with the HP because it is formally equivalent to a tense which indicates events whose reference time is not the moment of the event but the moment of speaking' (p. 46). Another observation is that *CHP becomes an internal evaluation device,* enabling the storyteller to present events as if they were occurring before the very eyes of the recipients who can interpret the significance of the narrated events for the speaker's respective experience (Schiffrin, 1981:59). Wolfson (1979:222) emphasizes that the alternation between CHP and the past tense is a relevant feature, having the role of *delimiting events in the story from one another.*

Regarding conversational stories entirely produced in the CHP (from the beginning to the end), Schiffrin (1981:51-52) points out that these instances are rare and brief, their reference time being always set as prior to the speaking time, whereas Wolfson's empirical studies (1978:218); (1979:171) show no such cases.

Romanian also uses the present tense as a narrative tense, indicating past events (Zafiu, 2000:180). There is further evidence that *the historical* or *retrospective present* is often used in colloquial language instead of its past counterpart – the perfect compus – (Gramatica Limbii Române, vol. I, 2005:410). The data in our corpus of Romanian have confirmed the existence of the same values for this tense as the ones found in the English literature.

Next, we will illustrate the value of the Romanian *historical (retrospective) present* in an excerpt taken from our own corpus.

(12) *Examene auto picate*/Failed driving tests
26 A: *da' îți dai seama hai mă că parcă-i din film îți imaginezi toată faza asta*=
    fancy that come on this whole thing is like taken out of a picture
27   *îi **pică** cascheta*
    his cap falls off
28   *așa în zbor ea **încearcă** s-o prindă*
    she tries to catch it while it's still in the air
29   *îi **trage**-o palmă ((râde))*
    she slaps him ((laughs))

30 *cascheta **se duce** pe geam ((râde)) și **trece**-o mașină ((râde))(0.5)*
   the cap falls out of the window ((laughs)) and a car runs it over ((laughs))(0.5)

In the excerpt above A summarizes a story which she has just finished recounting.

Although previously in the fragment she used verbs in the perfect compus for the actual recounting of events, when it comes to evaluating the respective situation, i.e., expressing a particular attitude towards what happened, A uses verbs in the *historical* or *retrospective present* – lines 27-30 *('pică, încearcă, trage, se duce, trece')* ('falls off, tries, slaps, falls out, runs (it) over'). The first historical present utterance – line 27 is given past reference time by an implicit past adverbial (at that moment). Bringing the narrated events before the very eyes of the auditors is an occasion for the speaker to re-evaluate them – to distance herself from the events recounted in her story and to express her suspicion that things must have been exaggerated, as her hint in line 1 clearly shows it: *'hai mă că parcă-i din film'* ('come on this whole thing is like taken out of a picture').

Next we will examine an intriguing discourse phenomenon underlying conversational narratives, i.e., tense alternation between the narrative past and the conversational historical present (CHP).

Tense Alternation (the narrative past/ the CHP)

A characteristic feature of conversational narratives is that in the process of telling a story speakers may not preserve a certain tense but switch back and forth between the narrative past and the conversational historical present (henceforth, the CHP). In fact, the switch from the past to the present tense and back again has been claimed to be typical of narratives in talk-in-interaction (Fleischman, 1993:84); (Tannen, 1980:210).

In the literature, tense alternation has been regarded as a complex issue (Levey, 2006:130). It may *separate episodes in the story* (Wolfson, 1979:174); (Wolson, 1978:222), it may *emphasize the importance of a certain event in the story* (Silva-Corvalan, 1983); (Wolfson, 1978:222), or *mark the climax of the narrative* (Fludernik, 1991). Often, by slowing the pace of narration, a dramatization of the story's high point or climax is achieved (Wolfson, 1978); (Blum-Kulka (2005a:279)) as it appears that the latter is a major locus of 'linguistic turbulence' (cf. Fleischman, 1990) and strategic tense-shifting highlights dramatic narrative peaks (cf. Fleischman, 1990; Georgakopoulou, 1994; Georgakopoulou and Goutsos, 1997). Also, tense switching between the CHP and the narrative past, as a discourse feature, was shown to *organize events in a story from the storyteller's viewpoint and dramatize them*. In this sense, it is indicative of a performed story, along with direct speech, asides, repetition, expressive sounds, motion and gestures (Wolfson, 1979:216); (Schiffrin, 1981:46).

Within the macrostructure of narratives, tense-switching between the narrative past and the CHP appears to follow the subsequent general pattern: the verbs in the first segment of the complicating action are in the narrative past, then the verbs in the second part switch to the CHP. Next, possible additional switches between the two tenses may occur and finally, towards the resolution of the narrative, verbs switch back to the narrative past (Schiffrin, 1981:51). This alternation pattern between the two above-mentioned tenses has also been confirmed by the data in our corpus.

Excerpt (13) below exhibits a tense alternation which can be accounted for.

*(13) Conflicte/*Conflicts
1A: dar a zis că el a avut noroc că a prins tineri din ăștia știi?
    but he said he was lucky to come across young people like that you know?
2B: îhî
    yeah
3A: ori eu am avut numai baba<u>lâci</u>
    as for myself I only came across hags
4B: ((râde))
    ((laughs))
5A: o persoană o femeie mai bătrână (0.3)
    a person an old lady
6   **am sunat** *o dată nici* **nu am știut** *dacă* **a sunat** *sau nu știi?*
    I rang once I wasn't even sure if it rang or not you know?
7B:°îhî°
    yeah
8A: **am văzut** *că s-a uitat așa un pic pe vizor și* **am sunat** *a doua oară*
    I saw she peeped out the peephole and I rang once more
9   *când a doua oară* **iese** *nervoasă 'mă da' ce* **insistați** *atâta mi-ați trezit și copilu' nesimțiților'*
    and the second time she gets out angrily why are you insisting so much you've even awaken my child you shameless rascals
10 *mai să te* **ia la bătaie**
    almost ready to beat you up
11 *când* **am văzut** *'tuo:: doamnă gata ho:'*
    when I saw that 'ok ma'm ok'
12B: ((râde))
    ((laughs))
13A: 'da' °mă° scuzați'
    yeah excuse me
14B: ((râde))
    ((laughs))
15A: nu (0.1) sunt <u>foarte</u> (0.2) da' știi parcă parcă le-ai cere bani așa nu știu
    no they're very well you know as if you asked them for money I don't know
16B: da
    yes
17A: până la urmă e și în avantajul lor că primesc un bon valoric de treizeci de lei dacă (0.2)
    after all it's to their advantage as well cause they receive a-thirty-lei coupon if

In the fragment above, the storyteller, A, recounts an embarrassing situation, which took place while he was only trying to do his job. The event has got an amusing side to it, which is perceived by the recipient, B, who, upon hearing the story from a detached position, therefore far from direct involvement, bursts into laughter several times – lines 4, 12 and 14.

In telling his story, the speaker uses tense alternation, from the narrative past (the Romanian the perfect compus) to the conversational historical present. The narrative segment, representing the complicating action, starts with verbal forms in the perfect compus – lines 6 and 8 *('am sunat', ,nu am știut', ,a sunat', ,am văzut', ,s-a uitat', ,am sunat')* ('rang', 'wasn't sure', 'rang', 'saw', 'peeped out', 'rang') –, then switches to conversational historical present in lines 9 and 10 *('iese', ,insistați', 'ia la bătaie')* ('gets out', 'are you insisting', 'to beat up'), which stand for the climax, or high point of the story and then, towards the resolution of the narrative, verb forms switch back to the simple past – line 11 *('am văzut')* ('saw').

The tense alternation, along with the use of direct reported speech – lines 9, 11 and 13 *('mă da' ce **insistați** atâta mi-**ați trezit** și copilu' nesimțiților')* ('why are you insisting so much you've even awaken my child you shameless rascals'), *('tuo:: doamnă gata ho:')* ('ok ma'm ok'), *('da' °mă° scuzați')* ('yeah excuse me') – is meant to dramatize the climax of the story, which refers to the embarrassing position undergone by the main character in the story.

If the excerpt above illustrates the use of tense alternation marking the climax of the story, the fragment below will exemplify another value of tense variation: *separating the episodes of the story:*

(14) <u>Carismă</u>/Charisma
1 F: *și copiii au început să vorbească*
    and the children started speaking
2 *și (0.2) la un moment dat (0.2) nu știu:: ( )*
    and at one point I don't know
3 *l-am văzut pe un băiat că a vrut să zică ceva*
    I saw a boy that wanted to say something
4 *și n-a mai zis*
    and he changed his mind
5 *și i-am zis 'Adrian de ce nu vrei să ne spui părerea ta?'*
    and I told him Adrian why won't you state your opinion
6 *a zis că nu vrea*
    he said he wouldn't
7 *și-n pauză nu știu cum am nimerit eu lângă ei*
    and during the break I can't really tell how I happened to get next to them
8 *și:: (0.2) el îmi zice:: (0.2) a:*
    and he tells me oh
9 *și ei vorbeau în continuare <u>despre carismă</u>*
    and they kept on talking about charisma

10 și zic 'a: păi acum de ce vorbești? ( )
    and I say well why are you talking now
11 și:: ă: în clasă n-ai vrut să ne spui
    and um you wouldn't tell us in class
12 că ( ) ar fi fost interesant să auzim'
    cause it would have been interesting to hear
13 și el zice:: ă: 'păi eu nu vreau să:
    and he says um well I don't want to
14 să mă cert cu colegii MEI'
    to argue with my mates
15 'pentru mine carisma înseamnă altceva
    for me charisma means something else
16 după: părerea mea nu
    in my opinion no
17 de exemplu pentru toți colegii MEI dumneavoastră aveți carismă
    for example for all my mates you are charismatic
18 pentru mine nu
    for me you aren't
19G: ((râde))
    ((laughs))
20F: ((râde))
    ((laughs))

The narrative passage above may be divided into two parts or episodes. In the first part – lines 1-7, 9 –, Speaker F uses the perfect compus to present what happened in class: while all the students expressed their opinion on the topic of discussion, i.e., charisma, Adrian hesitated and eventually refused to participate. In the second part of the narrative – lines 8, 10-18 –, the storyteller switches to the conversational historical present to show the unexpected sequel of the events: Adrian finally accepts to state his opinion on the matter, which turns out to be not very flattering with respect to the teacher.

The next case that will be discussed is when the present tense designates future events. This use of the narrative present is called the *prospective present*.

b). The prospective present

In Romanian, the *prospective present* alternates or rivals with the future, especially when the speaker deems that the realization of the related processes has a greater degree of certainty than that implied by the future forms. Its modal significance is 'real, certain', a significance which is specific to the present and not 'real, possible', a feature which is typical of future forms (Gramatica Limbii Române, 2005:410-414).

Next, we will illustrate the value of the *prospective present* followed by a future time adverbial in the fragment below:

(15) Marș ecologic/Ecological march
1A: *uite sâmbătă dacă ai vrea să mergi deși nu prea cred*
    look if you'd like to come on Saturday though I don't think you would
2   *sâmbătă* **e** *un marș ecologic ă:* **e** *organizat de o tipă din PNL*
    there's an ecological march on Saturday um it's organised by a female politician from PNL
3B: *îhî*
    yeah
4A: *Alina Gorgiu (0.2) da cam așa ceva ceva de genu'*
    Alina Gorgiu or something like that
5   *și* **este** *un marș (0.1)* **se pleacă** *de la Parcu' Izvor până la Mogoșoaia*
    and it's a march they set out from Izvor Park and go up to Mogoșoaia
6   *dar* **e** *chiar linie dreaptă*
    it's a straight line
7   *deci* **se merge** *drept (0.2) la nord cinșpe kilometri jos cinșpe kilometri*
    well you go straight on for about fifteen kilometres to the north and fifteen kilometres downwards
8B: *alergat sau cu bicicleta?*
    running or by bike
9A: *cu bicicleta*
    by bike
10B: *îhî*
    yeah
11A: *și Radu mă tot întreabă: „hai mă* **mergem mergem mergem***?"*
    and Radu keeps telling me 'come on let's go shall we'
12B: *de la cât sâmbăta?*
    what time is it on Saturday
13A: *de la zece*
    ten o'clock
14B: *dacă* **nu mă duc** *la țară* **vin**
    I'm coming unless I go to the country
15A: **vii** *?*
    are you
16B: *da'* **tre'** *să plec la țară că de fapt* **e** *ziua lu' mamaia*
    but I have to go to the country cause it's my grandma's birthday
17 *dacă* **nu plec vin**
    I'm coming unless I leave
18A: *îhî că eu n-am spus nimica dacă* **merg** *sau nu (0.1) știi ?*
    yeah cause I haven't said anything yet if I'm going or not you know
19 *și încă mă mai gândesc*
    and I'm still thinking
20B: *dar eu cred că* **plec** *la țară (0.2) nu știu*
    but I think I'm going to the country I don't know

Speaker A in the excerpt above is telling B about a future ecological march, which is to take place the next Saturday. When referring to this event, he chooses the *prospective present* along with a future time adverbial ('on Saturday') – lines 1 and 2 – instead of a future verbal form as the respective event is regarded as certain and not as merely possible – value rendered by the future – lines 2, 5, 6, 7, 11, 15, 18 *('e', 'este', 'se pleacă', 'e', 'se merge', 'mergem', 'vii', 'merg')* ('is', 'set', 'out', 'is', 'go', 'are you (coming)', 'I'm going') –. Clearly under the influence of A's use of the *prospective present*, the recipient, B, joins his interlocutor in his choice of selecting the same verbal forms – lines 14, 16, 17, 20 (*'nu mă duc', 'vin', 'tre'', 'nu plec', 'vin', ,plec'*) ('(unless) I go', 'I'm coming', 'I have to', '(unless) I leave', 'I'm coming', 'I'm going') –, thus conferring his own actions a greater degree of certainty, had he used the narrative future proper.

Last but not least, we will consider the narrative future.

The narrative future

The *future* is also a narrative tense in Romanian, even though it is not used very often. There are instances in which the *narrative future* competes or, in certain contexts, even alternates with the *prospective present* – these cases are, however, rather rare and we have not found any instantiation of this aspect in our corpus of spoken Romanian. The two verbal forms are not quite synonymous, as the latter conveys a process which is deemed by the speaker to be more likely to take place than the first. The use of several verbal forms in the narrative future indicates successive processes (Gramatica Limbii Române, vol. I, 2005:445).

The next fragment is illustrative of the use of narrative future in conversational narratives.

(16) Analiză de laborator/Lab analysis
1P: *bun (0.1) înainte să le pun pe microscop* **o să pisez**
    right before I place them on the microscope I'm going to pound them
2   **o să le aplic** *într-o formă cât mai fină (0.2)*
    I'm going to lay them in the finest possible manner
3   *și bănuiesc că așa a făcut și cel care a utilizat-o*
    I suppose that's how the one who used it did it too
4   *mie-mi trebuie câteva cristale*
    I need several crystals
5   **o să mojarez** *cât mai fin ca să pot să observ (0.2) în detaliu*
    I'm going to grind them as fine as possible to be able to observe in detail
6N: *la MIcroscop optic NU am făcut acest lucru*
    I did not do that on the optical microscope
7P: *nici* **nu veți obține** *foarte multe (0.2)[informații*
    you won't obtain much information
8N: *[informații n-am]*=
    I haven't (obtained) information
9P:= *la:: microscopul (0.2) [optic*
    on the optical microscope

In the fragment above, Speaker P uses several successive verbal forms to refer to the stages of the scientific process he is going to perform – lines 1, 2, 5 and 7 *('o să pisez', ,o să aplic', 'o să mojarez', ,nu veți obține')* ('I'm going to pound', 'I'm going to lay', 'I'm going to grind', 'you won't obtain') –. The speaker uses future verbal forms denoting a colloquial style when describing the procedure he is going to use when performing the analysis – lines 1, 2, 5 –, but he switches to the standard variant when referring to the future results expected by his interlocutor – line 7(*'nu veți obține'*) ('you won't obtain') –. This switch, from a more colloquial style, to a standard one, is indicative of the social distance holding between the two interactants (the two have just met for the first time and their meeting is for professional purposes).

A few words need to be said on the issue of narrative tenses in conversational stories. Our corpus has shown a clear-cut distinction between the spoken and written language, in that the perfect simplu does not appear in our data, whereas the future verbal forms (formed from the auxiliary 'a vrea') appear scarcely. With respect to their degree of frequency, our study has revealed that, just as in English, the narrative past, the Romanian perfect[46] compus, respectively is most commonly used; second comes narrative present, and last, narrative future (cf. Parsons, 2002:690).

In what follows, we will examine the orality of narratives in talk-in-interaction.

2.3 The oral style of conversational narratives

The occurrence of narratives within the larger framework of dialogue bestows on them properties characteristic of oral, spoken language, as opposed to written language. The next section is dedicated to the discussion of the differences between the two language varieties, with emphasis on those features typical of spoken language, with the aim of pointing out the oral quality of conversational narratives.

2.3.1 Spoken vs. written language

The two language styles in question (spoken and written) have been found in the literature to differ both on the syntactic level and in point of the lexical items used (Carter & McCarthy, 2006);

---

[46] Nevertheless, the perfect simplu, the counterpart of the perfect compus for the written language does not appear in our corpus at all, whereas the mai-mult-ca-perfect, the narrative tense marking anteriority with respect to a past reference time, appears rather rarely.

(Crystal, 2003:214); (Chafe & Tannen, 1987); (Dascălu Jinga, 2002a:8-10); (Dascălu Jinga, 2002b). Several binary oppositions emphasize the differences between the two language variants, as pointed out below:

Unplanned vs. planned discourse. Sentence organization in writing is rather different from utterance structure in speech. This is due to the fact that a written message can be revised and improved until the writer is satisfied by its form and content, whereas in speech, the speaker is prone to hesitations, false starts, words on the tip of the tongue, etc. (Crystal, 2003:214); (Tannen, 1982:7); Chafe (1994:43). He/she is also likely to be interrupted, corrected by one of the interactants with whom he/she often negociates the topic of discussion or even overlap with the interlocutor in their speaking turns (Dascălu Jinga, 2002b:14), (Carter & McCarthy, 2006:164). These problems concerning message production may result in a fragmentary discourse, characterised by incomplete utterances, voiced pauses (e.g., *er, um*). Also, syntactic deviances, such as anacoluthon, ellipsis or rephrasings occur frequently in speech, mainly due to the speakers' lack of perspective on the discourse they produce (Dascălu Jinga, 2002a:8).

Interactive, face-to-face talk vs. communication at distance. Unlike the pair writer – reader(s) who, most of the times, do not meet and, what is more, the writer can guess little about the recipient and the context in which he/she will receive the message, speakers usually face one another in an interactive process, sharing the same discursive time and space (Leech & Short, 1981:257-258); (Carter & McCarthy, 2006:175). The meaning of the spoken message is generally understood by resorting to *shared knowledge* or to *the local context*. Many lexical items and syntactic structures in the spoken variant point to *the interpersonal dimension* of the ongoing talk (Carter & McCarthy, ibid.). Worthy of mention are *deictic expressions* (e.g., in here, over there, that one, right now), *ellipsis*[47] (e.g., Finished?) and *discourse markers* (e.g., *now, well, right, oh, okay, so, well, anyway*) whose role is twofold: to organize discourse or to show the recipients' involvement with what is being said. The speakers' checking of the listeners' understanding is done by means of tags (*e.g., right?, yeah?, okay?*), question tags (*have you?, didn't he?, don't you?*) and *fillers* or *phaticisms* (e.g., *you know (what I mean), you see*), whereas the recipients' providing feed-back or showing support is done by the employment of *back-channel items* (e.g., *yeah, mm, right*) (Carter & McCarthy, ibid.); (Dascălu Jinga, 2002a:8); (Dascălu Jinga, 2002b:16); (Vasilescu, 2007b:15-17). All in all, speech is characterized by simplicity and an economical character, unlike the elaboration displayed by written language which is needed to ensure the appropriate understanding of the message in a distant time and place (Carter & McCarthy, 2006:167); (Dascălu Jinga, 2002b:15-16).

---

[47]*Ellipsis* is common in speech, since the missing word may be easily recovered from the local context of communication or from the knowledge shared by interlocutors (Carter & McCarthy, 2006:167); (Dascălu Jinga, 2002b:15-16).

With respect to the vocabulary used in the two style, the speaker utilizes a rather *limited number of lexical items* (partly due to the exigencies of thinking and speaking in real-time), displaying a preference for *generic terms*, such as: *thing, stuff, fact, this, that, sort of, kind of*. At the other end of the continuum, since the writer disposes of more time to think and formulate his/her ideas, he/she will utilise *a larger amount of lexical terms,* which are *precise* and even specialised for a certain language domain. For the same reason, he/she can avoid potential mistakes, hesitations or repetitions (Dascălu Jinga, 2002a:8).

In the next section we consider those linguistic features of conversational narratives typical of spoken language, as shown in our corpus, with the aim of demonstrating that narratives acquire such properties due to the fact that they are framed by dialogue. We will begin by discussing the traits of spoken language syntax which underlie the syntax of narratives-in-interaction.

2.3.2 The orality of narratives in talk-in-interaction

A. The syntax of conversational narratives

The study of our corpus evinces all the syntactic properties of spoken language, as outlined by English and Romanian research (Carter & McCarthy, 2006); (Pridham, 2001); (Leech & Short, 1981); (Gramatica Limbii Române, 2005, vol.2); (Dascălu Jinga, 2002a); (Dascălu Jinga, 2002b); (Ionescu-Ruxăndoiu, 1999); (Irimia, 1986); (Vasilescu, 2007b).

One particular feature of conversational narratives, as representative structures of spoken discourse, is that they are characterised by brief utterances, with a low degree of subordination. Instead, they favour **co-ordination**, especially by means of the conjunction 'and' and juxtaposition (Brown & Yule, 1983:15-16); (Leech & Short, 1981:163); (Pridham, 2001:10-11); (Gramatica Limbii Române, 2005, vol.2:830-831).

Fragments (17) and (18) below are indicative of the storyteller's heavy use of *the co-ordinating conjunction 'and':*

<u>(17)Râde ciob de oală spartă/The pot calls the kettle black</u>
37C: *şi ((râde)) vine asta şi-i stătea ori:bil*
　　　and ((laughs))in she comes looking horrid
38T: *parcă te-a auzit=*
　　　as if she had heard you
39C: =*şi toată clasa a început să râ:dă*
　　　and all the class started laughing
40　*şi cine râdea mai tare era Cristina Pop care era oribilă săraca ea însăşi=*
　　　and the one that laughed loudest was Cristina Pop who was horrid herself poor thing

41T: =ea însăși ((râde))
      herself ((laughs))
42C: și-atunci îi zic io lu' Teo "râde ciob de oală spartă" ((râde))
      and then I tell Teo the pot calls the kettle black ((laughs))
43T: și și ea a zis „ce faci Cristina râ:zi" ?
      and she herself said 'laughing Cristina, are you'

<u>(18)*Familia copilului autist*</u>/The autistic child's family
8M : nu știu- îi mai băiețoasă așa ((imită vocea)) "A:ndrei ai rămas singur? vino-aici"
      I don't know –she's a bit boyish ((imitates her voice)) 'are you alone Andrei come here'
9L: ((râde))
      ((laughs))
10 M: îl lua de mână știi? (0.3)
      she would grab his hand
11   și îți dai seama că ei îi venea să plângă=
      and you can imagine that she felt like crying
12   = pentru că într-un fel și copilul va fi și frații vor fi responsabilizați
      because in a way the child will aslo be and the siblings will also be held responsible

The structure of the noun phrase in conversational narratives is rather **simple**. There are seldom epithets, few proper names and few relative clauses. This simplicity of NPs can be put down to the fact that the audience is not familiar with the characters in the stories, which makes the potential use of proper names useless from a referential or informative viewpoint. A second reason for the scarceness of proper names would be that speakers usually avoid giving names to protect the identity of the person in question and to preserve their own positive face, except for the occasions when they engage in gossiping. Therefore, when telling a story-in-interaction, the narrator usually resorts to **the use of demonstrative pronouns**, at points where one would normally expect nouns. This confers the story dynamism and a sense of immediacy, as it has the advantage of bringing the characters and events under the very eyes of the recipients (Pridham, 2001:11).

In the examples below, the storytellers switch to the demonstrative pronoun 'this' to refer to the characters in their stories. This is a way of signalling to the listeners that the climax of the story is approaching, which triggers a need for immediacy for bringing the scene closer to the audience. In our case, these linguistic devices announce that something funny is about to happen.

In excerpt (19) one would expect the teacher to look better after having had her hair done, but things turned out to be worse and, as a result, the whole class burst into laughter.

<u>(19) *Râde ciob de oală spartă*</u>/The pot calls the kettle black
*37C: și ((râde)) vine **asta** și-i stătea ori:bil*
      and ((laughs))in she comes looking horrid
38T: parcă te-a auzit=
      as if she had heard you
39C: =și toată clasa a început să râ:dă
      and all the class started laughing

In excerpt (20) the listener faces again an unexpected situation, as the bodyguard, who is supposed to be in charge of the museum and should react whenever the visitors act inappropriately, just lets the main character go after having caught her red-handed (she had used her camera to record the inside of the museum).

(20) Anna Frank/ Ann Frank
47 și da' a fost foarte drăguț adică nu:: (0.5)
    but he was very nice I mean he didn't
48 și acuma zic "what shall I do?" =
    and now I say "what shall I do?"
*49 = și **ăsta** zice "păi nimic ((râde)) că oricum ați filmat"(0.5)*
    and he says ' nothing cause ((laughs)) you've filmed anyway'

The presence of colloquial speech in narratives in talk-in-interaction is illustrated by the use of ***interjections*** and ***exclamatives,*** which denotes the subjectivity of the transmitted message (Irimia,1986:84); (Gramatica Limbii Române, 2005:828), as shown in the examples below:

interjections

*11 când am văzut '**tuo::** doamnă gata **ho:**'*
    when I saw that 'ok ma'm ok'

*68 **vai** dar el știe (.) la el să-și bage (0.1)*
    oh but he can provide for himself

*7 M: ce casă] frumoasă avea acolo **va::i** sus cu etaj*
    what a beautiful house he had up there oh my with an upstairs

*4 P: da **aoleo** ce m-am speriat [atuncea*
    yes oh my how frightened I got then

*16 P: [da' **ma::mă**] ce mă enervează*
    oh my it really annoys me

*26 ne-a udat de **fua::i** ă::: în ce hal eram de ude da' nu conta*
    we got wet oh my um we were soaked to the skin but it didn't matter

*5 =vine soțu "**oho** vine"=*
    here comes my husband oh my he comes

exclamatives

*42F: nu mi-a luat-o **slavă Domnului** că la sfârșit când m-am întors=*
    he didn't take it away from me thank God cause in the end when I got back

10 E: *auăleu* **Doamne** *și i-am spus*
oh my God and I told her

17E: *"ce* **Dumnezeu** *se întâmplă aicea" (0.2)*
what on earth is happening in here

Vocatives or **address terms** are another category of lexical items used in colloquial language. Our data confirm the presence of address terms, both at the level of communication between interlocutors and at the story level proper, when the narrator constructs the characters' speech. The class of address terms comprises *first names, endearment forms,* and *diminutives* whose role is to establish a sense of solidarity among interactants (Brown & Levinson, 1987). Colloquial Romanian uses endearments, such as *fata mea, puiu meu, copil frumos, dragă, iubita* and diminutives, such as *fetiță, puiuț, scumpica*[48] (Hornoiu, 2008:121); (Gramatica Limbii Române[49], 2005, vol.2:844). A particular feature of spoken, colloquial Romanian is the frequent use of lexical items having no descriptive content, such as *bă, băi, mă,* or *măi*, either by themselves or in combinations with *first names* or *intimate address forms,* such as *fată*, the latter being commonly used among female teenagers (Hornoiu, ibid.). Another characteristic trait of colloquial Romanian speech is the usage of common nouns indicating kinship or work relationships, such as 'frate', 'vere', 'tanti', 'tataie', 'maică', 'șefu', 'șefa'. This is generally typical of people with an average or low level of education (GLR, ibid.).

The address terms in the examples below, among which most are used at the story level proper, are illustrative of genuine, colloquial vocabulary:

37D:'**băi** *pase în doi*'
hey pass two by two

40D: '**bă** *ce cauți mă lângă el mă*'
hey what are you doing by his side

11E:,, **mă** *lasă mă duc cu: (0.1) mă duc cu trenu*'"
drop it I'm going by I'm going by train

22A: *((imită vocea))"da* **măi** *mergem cu taxiul"*
((imitates his voice)) yes we'll take the taxi

10R: **băi** *Bog[dane*
say what Bogdan

21E:*"***mă fată** *ăștia au înnebunit unde dau banii acuma"((râde))*
'these folks are mad gal whom shall I pay now'((laughs))

---

[48] This address form was added to the list by us on the basis of our own collected corpus.
[49] For conciseness reasons, we will use alternatively the abbreviated form, GLR.

13M: **'*scumpica fă ceva Maria fă ceva*'
  sweetheart do something about it Maria do something about it
*15C: și (0.2) ei ăștia i-au spus "***tanti** *noi nu avem medicamentu' ăsta (0.2)*
  and they these guys told her 'we haven't got this medicine m'am'

The spontaneous nature of oral discourse strongly influences message structure at the level of syntactic and pragmatic organization. For this reason, spoken language syntax, and implicitly that of narratives-in-interaction, is far *less structured* than that of written language and contains **fragmented verbal sequences** and/or **incomplete sentences** (often simply phrase sequences) (GLR, 2005, vol.2:830); (Dascălu Jinga, 2002:8). The reason for this is twofold: the storyteller often begins a sentence, then pauses and starts anew, rephrasing it, thus failing to finish the previous sentence. The other case is when the speaker lets his/her phrases unfinished, since he/she relies on recipients' knowledge (Dascălu Jinga, ibid.). Also, the speaker's lack of perspective over his/her ongoing speech often leads to syntactic disorder, manifested by a series of phenomena, such as *ellipsis, anacoluthon, self-corrections, false starts, followed by rephrasings and repetitions* (GLR, ibid.); (Brown & Yule, 1983:15-16); (Leech & Short, 1981:161).

In narratives-in-interaction the storyteller may leave out words, phrases, clauses, or even sentences, which the interlocutor can retrieve from the cotext. This linguistic phenomenon is known as **ellipsis** and is a frequent mark of spoken language. It is basically utilized for two reasons: for increasing the speaker's expressiveness or for economical reasons (Pridham, 2001:11); (Dicționar general de științe. Științe ale limbii, 1997:180); (Gramatica Limbii Române, 2005, vol.2:859).

In the following lines, taken from an ongoing story in our corpus, the narrator makes extensive use of ellipsis, from leaving out a word to omitting a clause and even a sentence. In line 26 the narrator leaves out a clause (we may infer that the ellipsis suppresses the clause 'she died'), most likely for economical reasons so as to prevent a possible digression from the actual story line:

26 F: și a: (5) casa ei nu e mobilată că n-au mai vrut s-o mobileze după ce: (0.3) așa
  and her house is not furnished cause they didn't want to furnish it any more after right

Line 33 contains an ellipsis of the verb ('was'), this time for emphasis purposes:

33F: și Anna Frank peste tot că erau multe poze? (0.3)
  and Anne Frank all over cause there were lots of pictures

In line 47 the teller leaves out a whole sentence (which we reconstruct as 'he didn't take my camera'), again for economical purposes so as to avoid repeating what has already been said:

47F:și da' a fost foarte drăguț adică nu:: (0.5)
    but he was very nice I mean he didn't

Another common syntactic deviation used by speakers and, implicitly, by storytellers, is **anacoluthon**. This phenomenon consists of an abrupt change in sentence construction. The speaker uses another structure which is grammatically inconsistent with the first one. Anacoluthon is mainly due to digressions, parantheses, and to the priority of the informational and communicative structure of the message over the purely syntactic one (Dicționar general de științe. Științe ale limbii, 1997:42), (Gramatica Limbii Române, 2005, vol.2:859).

The teller in the fragment below talks about a petition he filed, but then he abruptly switches to talk about the owners of some mountain chalets. Because he failed to supply the correct preposition to accompany the relative pronoun 'which', the syntactic structure he employs is all but well-formed:

*(21) O:7 a::: și-am făcut foarte multe sesizări ( ) **una** singură **care** astăzi*
and I filed many petitions only one which today
    *8 **cabanierii** de la Zănoaga și de la Bolboci trecând pe-acolo și vorbind cu ei,*
the chalet owners from Zanoaga and Bolboci passed by and as I talked to them
    *9 chiar **m-au felicitat** pentru (că) e prima sesizare*
they even congratulated me on the fact that it was the first petition

As opposed to anacoluthon, which indicates that speakers use deviant syntactic constructions, failing to perform self-correction[50], conversational narratives, as carriers of spoken language features, also display a series of interconnected phenomena involving the emergence of repair mechanisms[51]: **false starts**, followed by **rephrasings and repetitions**. These phenomena are due to the speakers' wish of using more appropriate formulas for the context in which they tell a story. That is why narrators often cut themselves off immediately after having started so as to start anew. The literature on this aspect of oral language reveals that these involuntary repetitions represent the narrators' affective hesitations, expressing various states of mind: insecurity, fear, doubt, or disturbance (Norrick, 2000); (Gramatica Limbii Române, 2005, vol.2:754).

---

[50] For further detail concerning *self-correction* see Jefferson (1974); Schegloff, Jefferson and Sacks (1977).
[51] See the section on conversation analysis in chapter 1 of the present paper.

Fragment (22) below shows that the narrator introduces her story through a false start, followed by a cut-off and a rephrase.

*(22) Pepeni/*Melons
1C:*când eram noi mici* **avea:m** *(0.3)* **tata lucra** *întru:-un sat de lângă Videle*
   when we were little we had father used to work in a village near Videle
2D: *îhî=*
   yeah
3C: = *unde erau pepenării de-astea*
      where there were melonfields

Immediately after starting her story, C restarts by changing her initial word *('avea:m')* ('we had') with a more appropriate phrase *('tata lucra')* ('father used to work'), after having paused to consider how to render verbally what she meant to say – line 1–. This initial false start or hesitation, along with the speaker's use of the time connector 'when', are indicative that a story is about to be told.

Also, in the excerpt below, the speaker starts speaking about himself but then abondons the sentence – this constitutes a false start – and constructs a new one, in which he embarks on talk about a mountain marathon. This is done by means of a rephrase:

(23) O: 1 deci **eu** *acum o lună o lună și un pic*
   so I about one month ago
      2 *aici în Bucegi* **se desfășura un maraton montan**
         there was a marathon here in the mountains of Bucegi

The orality of the spoken style is also emphasized by the storytellers' use of **voiced phrases** *('ă:')* ('er, um') and **discourse markers** *('na mă rog')* ('well') (Pridham, 2001:19), presumably with the intention of gaining time to think and avoiding being interrupted by the interlocutor at a transition relevance place:

14C: că la ei lăsasem rețeta **ă::** *mama a apărut la ei*
   cause I had left the prescription with them um Mum showed up there

22 *trebuia să o fac la dreapta* **ă:** *(0.2) aveam verde*
   I had to turn right um the traffic light was green

20C : [era] **na mă rog**
   she was well

Being located within the larger framework of dialogue and being designed by the speaker to address a particular audience, the stories in our corpus abound in **phatic elements or fillers,** used by the speaker to establish and maintain contact with the recipient (*'auzi?/uite!'*) ('listen!/look!'), (*'înțelegi?'*) ('you see?'), (*'știi?'*) ('you know (what I mean)?'), (*'nu?'/,nu-i așa?'*) ('don't you think so?'/'isn't it?') (Dascălu Jinga, 2002b:16); (Dascălu Jinga, 2002a:8); (Nicula, 2011:232).

    1 P: **fii atentă** *ți-aduci aminte când mergeam la Câmpulung? ((oftează))*
       listen do you recall when we used to go to Câmpulung ((sighs))

    2   și (0.1) am intrat într-o cameră (0.2) erau niște microfoane atârnate așa din tavan **știi?**
       and I entered a room there were microphones hanging from the ceiling you know

    *28   ***ai văzut*** că și ție când îți aduce cineva din străinătate o ciocolată ai impresia că e mai bună nu*
       you know that when someone brings you a chocolate bar from abroad you think it's better don't you

    43D: <u>băi</u> <u>nu</u> *se lipea mingea de* <u>mâinile lor</u> **tu știi cum**
       the ball wouldn't stick to their hands no way man

In turn, listeners provide feed-back or show speaker support, manifesting their interest in the tale by means of **back-channel items or back-channel signals** (*'așa, da, a...'*) (*'yeah, mm, right'*) (Carter & McCarthy, ibid.); (Dascălu Jinga, 2002b:16); (Dascălu Jinga, 2002a:8); (Vasilescu, 2007b:15-17).

    22   <u>cu nimic nimic nu venea</u>
       he wouldn't bring anything anything
    23D: **da da**
       yes yes

    23   mai aveam un pic și cădeam sub maldărul de ( )
       I was on the verge of falling under the heap of
    24P: <u>**așa**</u>
       right

    5C: mă rog (0.1) era printre primele <u>farmacii</u> (0.1) de lângă <u>casă</u>=
       well it was among the phamarcies nearest to our home
    *6A :=<u>**așa**</u>*
       right

General extenders designate a class of linguistic phrases, generally occurring at the end of a speaker's utterance. The term 'general' denotes the vague character of the expressions in point of reference, whereas 'extenders' emphasize their role of enlarging the already complete utterances to which they are attached. Their structure in English is *conjunction + NP* ('and stuff', 'and everything', 'and all', 'and blah blah blah', 'or something', 'or what', etc.) ((Overstreet, 1999) apud Hornoiu (2008:159)). The use of general extenders in genuine, everyday talk reflects the speaker's assumption concerning the interactants' *shared knowledge and experience* (Hornoiu, ibid., 160). Our corpus of Romanian conversational narratives validates this particular use of general extenders, showing that storytellers do not bother to explain a certain matter further or give extra details when he/she is aware that the audience is familiar with the issue in question. The most common general extenders occurring in our data are *'nu ştiu ce'* ('and stuff'); *'bla bla bla'* ('blah blah blah'); *'aşa'* ('and stuff'). The following excerpts are a case in point:

30 P: 'domnişoară ce se întâmplă cu viaţa dumneavoastră personală
    lady what's going on with your personal life
31 noi nu putem lăsa să ne afecteze' **bla bla bla şi bla bla bla**
    we cannot let it affect us and blah blah blah and blah blah blah

5D: s-au încălzit ei ce s-au încălzit acolo: **nu ştiu ce**
    they warmed up for a while and stuff

13M: m-am închis acolo pe (0.2) **nu ştiu ce**
    I locked myself up in there and stuff

9 M:"că uite să ieşim în parc" **sau să nu ştiu ce**
    cause we'll go out in the park or something

12P:şi zice "hai nea Ienei – era la armată – ei erau soldaţi **aşa**
    and they say come on mister Ienei – they were in the army – they were soldiers and stuff

In what follows we will discuss another recurrent linguistic feature of narratives-in-interaction which is typical of the language of conversation: the storytellers' frequent insertion of characters' words by means of direct reported speech.

Reported speech

Our investigation of the data in our corpus of conversational narratives has pinpointed that storytellers often insert reported utterances of characters into the narrative structure, either in the form of *direct* or *indirect speech*. Although in both cases the teller claims to report faithfully what was said, the semantic difference between the two variants appears to be the following: in the former, the speaker renders the characters' words verbatim, including gestures and facial expressions, whereas in the latter, he/she uses his/her own words to indicate what was said. Moreover, by employing direct speech, the teller accurately reproduces the original speaker's syntactic and lexical structure, whereas when he uses indirect speech to report the utterances of a character, he/she acts as an *interpreter* between the character in the story whose words he/she is reporting and the audience whom he/she addresses his comments (Leech and Short, 1981:318-320); (Clift and Holt, 2006:5); (Li, 1986). An even more faithful reproduction consists in the teller's attempt to mimic a character's pronunciation (voice quality, intonation, class or regional accent). This phenomenon of imitating the voice quality of the original speaker or his/her affective way of speaking (e.g., angry, whiney, exaggeratedly polite, dumb-sounding or stilted) has been called *voicing* (Couper-Kuhlen (1998) apud Niemelä (2005:197)); (Leech and Short, 1981:320-321).

Direct reported speech (henceforth, DRS) has been found to be quite frequent in conversational narratives (Niemelä, 2005:198), performing a range of functions. First of all, it plays the role of giving the auditors the *impression of authenticity* and *a feeling of immediacy*[52] as if they are witnessing the actual past events and hearing the very words of the characters (Tannen, 1986:324); (Clark and Gerrig, 1990:793); (Clift and Holt, 2006:6). This effect is conveyed through 'a combination of deictic and structural changes […]: the narrative framework replaces the situation of speaking as the central reference point – becoming the locus for time, place, and person indicators, as well as the arena within which speech acts are performed'. Indirect reports of past utterances do not create the same effect as direct quotes, as they do not involve the same deictic and structural changes (Schiffrin, 1981:58). In other words, narrators not only report *what* has been said but also use DRS to present *how* things have been said, thus constructing 'a specific representation of the original situation' and seeking 'a specific response from the recipient' (Niemelä (2005:199)). The content of direct quotes often provides an internal evaluation for the story : the use of DRS enables the storyteller to express the point of the narrative through the original utterances of the experiencer (Schiffrin, 1981:60-61).

The second function performed by DRS is highlighting and *dramatizing the key elements* in a story (Tannen, 2007); (Li, 1986); (Clift and Holt, 2006); (Chiricu, 2007:244), occurring especially at the climax of stories (Mayes (1990) apud Niemelä (2005:198)), as a punch line of an amusing story or at the peak of a complaint (Holt (2000) apud Niemelä (2005:198-199)); (cf. Drew, 1998). In Labov's view (1972), DRS is a means of internally evaluating a story. This is more effective than an external evaluation (in which the storyteller explicitly states the point of the story) as, by resorting to constructed dialogue inserted within an utterance containing an implicit assessment, the speaker offers the audience the chance to draw their own conclusions about the characters and events presented in the tale (Clift and Holt, 2006:7); Hornoiu (2008:154).

A truly revolutionary aspect concerning the *semantic interpretation* of DRS in conversational storytelling is signaled by Tannen (2007); Dubois (1989); Sams (2010) who question the traditional view of DRS as a truthful replication of the characters' actual words or utterances. The hypothesis they advance is that the so-called reported utterances are rather attributable to the storyteller who, far from actually reporting previous utterances (i.e. quoting verbatim the words of the characters in his/her

---

[52] See also Wolfson (1978:220); Hymes (1977) apud Schiffrin (1981:58).

story), in fact 'constructs' and 'animates' dialogue for reasons which relate to effective communication and the establishment of involvement among conversationalists (Tannen, 1986:313); (Tannen, 2007:112); (Hornoiu, 2008:116). The need to illustrate the real status of quotations in conversational narratives has led to the coinage of new terms meant to replace the traditional notion of DRS: *constructed dialogue* (Tannen, 2007), *pseudoquotes* (Dubois, 1989) *or fake quotes* (Sams, 2010). Tannen (1995a:202-208) and Tannen (2007:112) make an impressive inventory of the types of constructed dialogue utilized by speakers in conversational narratives. Among them, we will note the following: 'dialogue representing what wasn't said, dialogue as instantiation, summarizing dialogue, choral dialogue, dialogue as inner speech, the inner speech of others, dialogue constructed by a listener, dialogue fading from indirect to direct, dialogue including vague referents, and dialogue cast in the persona of a nonhuman speaker'.

Quotatives or introductory components of DRS may constitute further proof that the concept of constructed dialogue is a more accurate acception than the term DRS, at least in the field of narratives-in-interaction. Let aside the paradigmatic use of a pronoun and a verbum dicendi (such as 'say' or 'tell'), we have observed the use of the Romanian lexical item 'cică' as a specific quotative in colloquial language. The same holds for the use of the verb 'go' or the construction 'be + like', which are formulaic introducers[53], specific to spoken narratives (Tannen, 1986:317). One of the obvious reasons why speakers are unlikely to use genuine direct quotation is the fact that it is almost impossible for them to replicate the exact linguistic form of the characters' original utterance(s). In this sense, some speakers even acknowledge the inaccuracy of their quotations by using remarks, such as : 'ceva de genul' ('sort of'), 'cam aşa ceva' ('that sort of thing'), or hesitation markers prefacing quotes, such as 'păi' ('well') (Uchida, 1997:12).

Concerning the degree of frequence of the reporting modalities in our data, we have found that less favoured is *indirect* reported speech, whereas *direct* reported speech is preferred by speakers since it preserves the structure of spoken language. Unexpectedly, *free indirect* reported speech, which also displays the properties of orality, has been found to be absent in our data. For these reasons, we have decided to exemplify solely the use of direct reported speech in conversational narratives.

Excerpt (24) below is illustrative of the role of direct reported speech within a story.

(24) Diametral opuşi/Totally different
1 R: da deci ei sînt (0.2) cum să-ţi spun (0.3.) când îi vezi sî::nt diametrali opuşi

---

[53] For further information, see Tannen (2007); Romaine and Lange (1991); Clift and Holt (2006).

    yes so they are how should I put it when you (first) see them they're totally different
2 E: *adica el e slab*
    I mean he is thin
3 R: *cam ca mine-aşa ştii?*
    almost like me you know
4 I: *nu că io n-am văzut-o numai pe ea [pe el nu l-a]m văzut*
    no cause I only saw her I didn't see him
5 E: *[o dungă:]*
                                    a stripe
6 R: *[un schelet] de peşte aşa înţelegi?*
                                a skeleton do you get the picture
7 E: *şi ea este o imensitate=*
    and she's an immensity
8 I: *o ba[lenă]*
    a whale
9 E: *[un mas]iv*
        a massif
10 R: *te impresionează atât de tare=*
    they impress you so much
11a   = *că vezi că se iubesc*
      cause you can see they love each other
11b   *şi uite-aşa [ea*
      and just like this
12 E: *[ea îşi pune picio]rul pe el=*
                 she puts her leg on him
13   = **"*hai încalţă-mă hai spală-mi şi mie şosetele=***
      'come on put my shoes on wash my socks
14   **hai nu mă [**
      come on won't you
15   *[((R râde))]*
             ((R laughs))
16E:= **nu mă descalţi?"**
    won't you take my shoes off
17R: *şi ăsta pac o aranja aşa (0.2)*
    and this guy attended her right away
18 *((E râde))*
   ((E laughs))
19 R: *pe urmă cică*
    then she goes
20   **"*du-te mai încolo să mă-ntind*"**
      go aside I want to lie down
21 *((R şi E râd))*
   ((R and E laugh))
22 R: *ştii şi cu picioarele*
    and with her legs you know
23 E: *(0.2) în tren ((râde))*
       in the train ((laughs))
24 R: *şi cu picioarele pe uşă (0.2) aşa ştii?*
    and with her legs on the door like this you know
25 *((E râde))*
   ((E laughs))
26 R: *şi (0.3) o ţinea cu capu' (0.2)((râde))*
    and he supported her with his head ((laughs))

In the excerpt above R and E tell an amusing story about a strange couple's relationship. After having pointed out the tremendous physical difference between the two characters (lines 4-8), R and E make use of DRS to show the way the husband and wife behave on a daily basis. The wife, as quoted by the two narrators, performs directive speech acts when addressing her husband. Her requests – line 13 *('hai încalță-mă hai spală-mi și mie șosetele')* ('come on put my shoes on wash my socks') and line 20 *('du-te mai încolo să mă-ntind')* ('go aside I want to lie down') signal her authority in relation to her husband – a fact that is recognized by R and E later on in the fragment when they assert that she is the general and her husband is the executant. The wife not only gives orders, but she also reproaches her husband when she is not satisfied with his actions, as in line 16 (*'nu mă descalți?'*) ('won't you take my shoes off'). Constructed dialogue is employed here not only to report *what* has been said, but also to present *how* things have been said, thus constructing a comical representation of the original situation and seeking to arise laughter in the recipient who can vividly picture the heavy wife bossing her lean husband around.

By considering all the syntactic traits of spoken language found in conversational stories, we may conclude that narratives framed by dialogue have a high degree of oral structure. In what follows, we will discuss the vocabulary of stories in talk-in-interaction.

B. The vocabulary of conversational narratives

With respect to the vocabulary of spoken language, we may assert that it is rather *limited* (Dascălu Jinga, 2002:8). Our empirical study has shown that the lexicon of conversational narratives is characterised by a *small number* or even a *lack of synonymous terms*. Our observation is that, confronted with a pair of synonyms, the speaker chooses the informal term, rather than the formal one. In this sense, **colloquial vocabulary**, such as *idioms, slang, clichés and taboo terms* (often licentious terms), is specific to oral language and also a frequent component of conversational narratives (Pridham, 2001:19); (Irimia, 1986:84-85).

Here are several examples of *idioms* we have found in our corpus:

13 *să știu **tot ce mișcă** (0.2) **în stânga-dreapta***
    to know everything that happens there to and fro

19 I: = *e **floare la ur[eche]***
    it's a piece of cake

> 45 și când **dau nas în nas cu** un d' ăsta cu un bodyguard=
> and when I bump into one of those a bodyguard

> 2 R: **las-o baltă** (0.2) nu mai
> drop it cut it out

> 29P: dar **te** mai **fură peisajul**=
> you sometimes get lost in revery

> 12 da' Monica **n-avea nicio treabă**
> however Monica didn't have a care in the world

The following examples of *slang terms*[54] are taken from our own corpus of conversational narratives, from speakers belonging to the teenage and youth age groups. Our data confirms the conclusions formulated by Hornoiu (2008:122); Zafiu (2001:193) and Zafiu (2010:18), who point out that slang is a marker of the age variable.

> 3 am început să facem **caterincă**
> we started poking fun

> 2 o altă fază din cantonamentele mele când **eram praf**
> here's another story from my training camp days when I was loaded

> 7 bine-nțeles primele minute:? **praf** (0.2) **praf . praf . praf**
> of course in the first minutes they were terrible (0.2) terrible terrible terrible

> 11 prietena ta (0.1) da care **a fătat**
> your friend yeah who cubbed

Some of the *taboo terms*, including the *vulgar lexical items* we found in our corpus, refer to intimate relationships between people and physiological problems – these are listed under (a). Others are dysphemisms for various verbs or idiomatic expressions – they are listed under (b). Again, these terms occur in the conversational styles of both teenagers and youth, but are used with higher frequency by the former age group.

> a)20D: și pe urmă i-a zis că „da avem o relație disfuncțională
> and then she told him yes we have a dysfunctional relationship
>   21 ne certăm abia mai **facem sex**"
> we quarrel we barely have sex

> 7 și era panicat omu' (0.1) arăta că e **ȚEAva**
> and the guy panicked he meant to show it was the pipe
> 8 dar de fapt arăta că **se masturba**
> when in fact he was showing he masturbated

---

[54] For a repertoire of slang terms used in colloquial Romanian, see Zafiu (2010).

*5 iar un tip strigă tare 'fata fata ((râde)) vezi că ai: vezi că ă (0.2) ești pe **ciclu***
    and a guy shouts really loudly hey girl ((laughs)) look look you're on your period

*b)18 și eu m-am **pișat** pe mine de râs*
    and I peed my pants from laughing so hard

5P: nu știi de ce-i zice lingerică?
    don't you know why he's called butt kisser
*că-**i linge-n cur pe toți***
    cause he kisses everybody's butt

10 io io m-am dus repede să deschid ușa
    I I hurried to open the door
11 unii erau sub pat
    some of them were under the bed
*12 altul **îl durea în p___ă** ((râde))*
    someone else didn't give a shit ((laughs))

In Romanian, *words derived by diminutival or augmentative suffixes* are commonly used to express affect in spoken language (Irimia, ibid.) :

*3A: ori eu am avut numai **babalâci***
    as for myself I only came across hags

*63P: da: ce să faci (.) oricum cu **sonache** nu te pui*
    yes what can you do you can't wrangle with loony anyway

*18C: =pe bune așa **urâțică** era săraca abia mai avea păr pe cap=*
    really so ugly was the poor thing she barely had any hair left

*15 ăsta-i u::n **flecușteț** acolo ce MAre lucru*
    this is a mere trifle no big deal

Previous studies on conversation have pointed out that more often than not speakers prefer using **vague language** or **generic terms** (e.g., thing, stuff, issue, matter, fact, this, that, like this, this way, sort of, kind of), (Rom.: lucru, fapt, chestie, asta, aia, așa) instead of particular, specific words (Dascălu Jinga, ibid.); (Pridham, 2001:19). This is confirmed by our research on stories in talk-in-interaction. By far, the most frequent generic term found in our corpus of conversational narratives is ‚chestie/(pl.) chestii' (Engl. 'stuff'). Its use in the lines below illustrates its synonymy with six different lexical items: dismissal – line 22, subjects – line 10B, affairs – line 4, substances – line 59, materials – line 24. Other generic terms we found are 'fază' ('thing') – line 26 and 'minuni' ('stuff') – line 10C.

*22 și-o să-i spun „domn profesor este un șoc pentru mine dacă că am aflat **chestia** asta" (0.3)*
    and I will tell him Professor it is a shock for me to find this out

*10B: și făceam **chestiile** astea în engleză știi (0.2) ((își drege vocea))*
    and we did this stuff in English ((clears her throat))

4   ă: (0.3) instructorul a plecat avea alte **chestii**
    the driving instructor left as he had other things to do

59C: erau niște **chestii** contra coagulării sângelui (0.1) să nu formezi cheaguri
    they were some stuff against blood coagulation which impede clot formation

24F: și suntem câteva profesoare care: lucrăm după acealeași chestii în general
    and we are several teachers who basically use the same stuff for teaching

26 A: da' îți dai seama hai mă că parcă-i din film îți imaginezi toată **faza** asta=
    fancy that come on this whole thing is like taken out of a picture

10C: și:: (0.2) evident să-mi calc halate și alte **minuni**=
    and of course to iron my smocks and other stuff

Our research on stories-in-interaction has also evinced the **recurrence (repetition) of certain lexical item(s)**. The use of the repetition[55] of various lexical terms often acquires stylistic value: it pinpoints *the narrator's attitude regarding a certain aspect presented in the story* or emphasizes the story's *dramatic effect* (Norrick, 2000); (Tannen, 1983); (Iordache, 2010c:230-232).

The use of the repetition in excerpt (25) stresses the teller's perspective on the event recounted in the story.

<u>(25) Examene auto picate</u>/Failed driving tests
1.A: da da' asta (0.3) cea care a dat examen înaintea mea (0.2)
    yes but a girl who took the test before me
2   că știi ești martor=
    you are a witness you know that
3L: = da tre' să fie două perso[ane]
    yes there must be two people
4.A: [în sp]ate io-am fost martor
                              at the back I was a witness
5   tipa asta (0.2) s-a urcat pe scaun (0.3)
    this girl sat on the chair
6   și-a reglat scaunu'(0.2)
    she adjusted her chair
7   și-a-nceput să-și regleze oglinzile
    and she started adjusting the mirrors
8L: ((râde))
    ((laughs))
9.A: era-o oglindă din aia care (0.5) cum să zic?
    there was a mirror which how should I put it
10 nu se rula se putea da așa pe spate
    it didn't roll it could be turned backwards
11L: îhî
    right
12.A: se-ntorcea (0.3)

---

[55] According to Gramatica Limbii Române (2005, vol.2: 753-754) repetition is of various types: *identical repetition* (realized by repeating the same word) and *modified repetition* (realized by the repetition of different words having a nearly identical meaning), *immediate* or *at distance* (other elements intervene between a term and its repetition).

```
           it could turn
13   și-a potrivit-o pe-asta-n stânga ei(0.3)
           and she adjusted the one on her left
14   și-n dreapta ((râde))(0.5) s-a aplecat peste polițist
           and on her right ((laughs)) she leaned over the policeman
15   ((toți râd))
     ((all laugh))
16 A: măi și erau niște bărbați acolo=
           and there were several men there as well
17   = se uitau și râdea polițistu'=
           they were watching and the policeman was laughing
18   = și ăia îți dai seama își cam făceau cu ochiu'
           and you know those guys they kind of winked at each other
19   polițistu' cu ăia știi?
           the policeman and those guys you know
20 L: îhî
           yeah
21 A: discutau din priviri (0.3)
           they were exchanging glances
22   da' de fapt cică ai ai un buton acolo în stânga
           when in fact there seems to be a button on the left side
23 C: a: tot așa în spatele în[tre:]
           and also one at the back between
24 A:                         [da' nu] stai să te-ntinzi =
                              but you don't just lean do you
25   =mai ales să te-ntinzi spre polițist știi?
           and all the more lean over the policeman right
```

In the present case, the repetition (modified and at distance) of the expression ('a se apleca/a se întinde peste') ('bend/lean over'), that is, the reverbalization in different words of the situation described by A in lines 14 *('s-a aplecat peste polițist')* ('she leaned over the policeman'), 24 *('da' nu stai să te-ntinzi")* ('but you don't just lean do you') and 25 *('mai ales să te-ntinzi spre polițist știi?')* ('and all the more lean over the policeman right') has the role of highlighting the speaker's evaluation of the situation as embarrassing and preposterous in the context of an official driving test. The storyteller's attitude with respect to a certain narrative aspect can also be conveyed by a certain word which *acquires formulaic force through repetition* – immediate or at distance – and rephrasing in particular conversational contexts (Norrick, ibid.) and which can influence the recipients in adopting a similar perspective.

Excerpt (26) below illustrates that apparently unformulaic phrases may acquire formulaic force in a certain context.

```
(26) La munte/In the mountains
1 R: hai să-ți spunem (0.2)
           let us tell you
2   când am coborât noi din tren (0.3)"cum mergem"
           when we got off the train how shall we go
```

3   *"păi a : (0.2) luăm taxiurile*
    well let's take the taxi
4   *luăm taxiurile (0.2) ca să nu mai mergem pe jos și ajungem* **pân' la Crăcănel"**
    we take the taxi so as not to go on foot and we reach Crăcănel
5   *Profu' zicea ((imită vocea))* **"pân' la Crăcănel** *mă* **pân' la Crăcănel"**
    teacher said ((imitates his voice)) up to Crăcănel up to Crăcănel
6   *da' ((râde)) așa (0.2) foarte serios*
    but ((laughs)) very seriously
7   *muream de râs de parcă era o denumire normală știi?(0.2)*
    we were roaring with laughter as if it were a common name you know
8: *((imită vocea)) "da măi mergem cu taxiul"*
    ((imitates his voice)) yes we'll take the taxi
9   *((toți râd))*
    ((all laugh))
10: *((imită vocea))* **"pân' la Crăcănel"**
    ((imitates his voice)) up to Crăcănel
11 *"până unde domn' professor?"=*
    up to where teacher
12 *((imită vocea))=* **"pân' la Crăcănel"**
    ((imitates his voice)) up to Crăcănel
13 *((toți râd))*
    ((all laugh))
14: *ajungem* **la Crăcănel** *și: (0.3)*
    we reach Crăcănel and

The repeated use, at distance, of the comical word '*Crăcănel*'[56], which designates a geographical denomination – lines 4, 5, 10, 12 and 14 – acquires a formulaic character. Its function is to signal the teller's humorous and ironical attitude towards such a denomination and prompt the listener into adopting a similar perspective.

We will now go on to discuss the second stylistic value of repetition in conversational stories: *obtaining a dramatic effect*. This is achieved by means of reverbalization of the same idea through the use of different words (Norrick, 2000). Fragment (27) is a case in point.

(27) *Familia copilului autist*/ /The autistic child's family
1M: *și când mai mergeam noi așa cu toate cu toții pe pe stradă*
    and when we would walk in in the street
2   *la un moment dat a: (0.3) Andrei rămânea intenționat ultimu'*
    at a certain point Andrei stayed behind on purpose
3   *ca mama s-o facă pe Irina responsabilă pentru frățior*
    this was an occasion for the mother to hold Irina responsible for her younger brother
4   *și îi zicea 'Irina nu îl vezi pe Andrei? a rămas singur ce faci? îl lăsăm singur?"*
    by telling her 'Irina can't you see Andrei? he is alone what are you doing shall we leave him alone?'
5   *și atunci Irina se ducea așa grijulie "A:Andrei"=*
    and then Irina would go to him caringly "A:Andrei"
6 = *vorbește pe nas așa Irina*
    Irina speaks through her nose this way

---

[56] The comical nature of this word arises from the fact that the word denominating a place is a derivative of the verb 'to straddle'.

> *7L: aha*
> I see
> *8M : nu știu- îi mai băiețoasă așa ((imită vocea)) "A:ndrei ai rămas singur? vino-aici"*
> I don't know –she's a bit boyish ((imitates her voice)) 'are you alone Andrei come here'
> *9L: ((râde))*
> ((laughs))
> *10 M: îl lua de mână știi? (0.3)*
> she would grab his hand
> *11 și îți dai seama că ei îi venea să plângă=*
> and you can imagine that she felt like crying
> *12 = pentru că într-un fel și copilul va fi și frații vor fi responsabilizați*
> because in a way the child will aslo be and the siblings will also be held responsible
> *13 și va fi o greutate și pentru ei*
> and this will be a burden for them as well
> *14 L: și pentru ei da*
> for them as well yes
> *15 M: avându-l pe Andrei da pentru că și când (0.5) și ei știu de terapie*
> yes having Andrei because even when they know about the therapy as well
> *16 Irina știe ((imită vocea)) "Andrei are nevoie de ajutor=*
> Irina knows about it ((imitates her voice)) Andrei needs help

The repetition, modified and at distance, of the verbs denoting motion: (*'a alerga, a o lua la fugă, a veni, a merge'*) ('run, come, walk') and of the adverb (*'desculță'*) ('barefoot') – lines 5, 6, 10, 12 and 14 – has the role of heightening the dramatic effect of the flight scene.

All in all, the presence in our data of conversational narratives displaying lexical items which are typical of spoken language proves the orality of stories framed by dialogue.

2.4 Conclusions

The present chapter has focused on the formal, linguistic properties of conversational narratives, illustrating them with relevant excerpts extracted from our own corpus of conversational interactions. It has shown that, due to the fact that narratives are embedded within another discourse genre, the dialogue, they acquire special syntactic and lexical features, characteristic of spoken language.

Firstly, we have discussed the linguistic features marking the transition between the two types of discourse: dialogue and narrative. It has been shown that narratives are introduced in talk-in-interaction by specific *opening and closing formulas*. *Temporality* has been examined as the main linguistic marker of narratives, emphasizing the fact that speakers *switch* from the present tense of conversation *to* the *past* tense of narratives. *Future* and *narrative present* have also been pointed out to be an option. *Tense alternation* from the past to the present tense and back again has been shown to be a linguistic phenomenon characteristic of narratives in interaction, whose role is to separate episodes in the story or mark the climax of the narrative. We have also examined the ways in which stories are triggered in conversation: by means of a conversational detail (*entailed* narratives), by means of a question (*elicited* narratives), or by means of the presence of an object or person in the local environment (*environmentally cued* narratives).

Secondly, we have examined the *oral character* of conversational narratives given by their *syntactic structure* and *vocabulary*, which are characteristic of spoken language. At the syntactic level, we have noticed that conversational narratives are made up of brief utterances, usually *co-ordinated* by means of the conjunction 'and' or by juxtaposition. Also, *the structure of the noun phrase* is rather *simple*, characterized by few proper names and few relative clauses. We have also shown that the structure of conversational narratives, as an exemplification of spoken language, is less structured than that of the written language, consisting of *fragmented verbal sequences* and/or *incomplete sentences*. The syntax of interactional narratives is characterised by *syntactic disorder*, illustrated by means of *ellipsis, anacoluthon, self-correction, false starts*, followed by *rephrases and repetitions*. The use of *interjections* and *exclamatives* is characteristic of colloquial style, designating a high degree of subjectivity.

We have proved that the orality of spoken language is characteristic of conversational narratives, being indicated by means of *address terms* (such as *first names, endearment forms* and *diminutives), discourse markers, phatic elements (or fillers)* and *back-channel signals*. Also, the use of *general extenders* reflects the speaker's assumption concerning the interactants' shared knowledge and experience.

The storytellers' insertion of *reported speech*, in its direct or indirect form, has also been discussed in this chapter. The traditional semantic difference between the two types of reported speech is that in direct speech the speaker renders the characters' words verbatim, whereas in indirect speech the speaker uses his/her own words to indicate what was said. As to the *semantic interpretation* of DRS in interactional narratives, it has been pointed out that the so-called reported utterances do not belong to the characters but are in fact the storyteller's contribution, representing a positive politeness strategy meant to create involvement among interactants, which justifies the coinage of a new term for DRS: *constructed dialogue*. Direct reported speech has been shown to be favoured in conversational narratives to the detriment of indirect speech, having the role of marking the key elements of the story or of creating the impression of involvement in the narrated event.

As to the vocabulary used by storytellers in conversational narratives, it has been emphasized that it is characteristic of spoken language. Among the specific colloquial lexical items, worth mentioning are *idioms, slang* and *taboo terms,* which occur frequently in narratives in talk-in-interaction. We have also mentioned the reduced amount of synonymic terms and the high frequence of *words derived by diminutival or augmentative suffixes* used by Romanian speakers to express affect in narratives in talk-in-interaction. Last but not least, we have indicated the narrators' preference for *vague language or generic terms* and for the *repetition* of certain lexical items, which has the role of emphasizing the storyteller's attitude regarding a certain aspect presented in the story or the dramatic effect of the narrative.

CHAPTER 3.
THE FUNCTIONS OF CONVERSATIONAL NARRATIVE

3.0 Introduction

The aim of the present chapter is to discuss the pragmatic functions of conversational narratives, subsumed to the double perspective that conversational narratives are essentially a form of narrative and that they are embedded in conversation.

The theoretical framework of the analysis is that of the functions of language developed by Halliday & Hasan (1989), detailed by reference to the functions of language proposed by Roman Jakobson[57] (1960). In accordance with the principle of the *multifunctionality of language* proposed by Jakobson and the Prague School linguists and also supported by Halliday & Hasan (1989), conversational narratives will be shown to serve several functions simultaneously. For systematicity reasons, we will range the functions in a *hierarchy,* from the function dominant in a particular situation to the peripheral ones so as to point out that the same story may be seen in different ways in different situations. In the process of identifying the main function of a given interactional story we will rely on *the intention-based criterion,* which is synonymous with Grice's (1975) and Searle's (1979) idea of the purpose of a speech act. After indicating the primary function according to the main speech act structuring the conversational exchange (e.g., to entertain, to persuade the listener, etc.), we will look for the other, minor or secondary functions.

The analysis *concentrates on* the *narrative passages* rather than on the whole conversation. In fact, any narrative, whether conversational or not, could be discussed from the point of view of its *pragmatic functions.* The analysis starts with the communicative purpose of each story and continues with an analysis of the conversational narrative itself.

---

[57] This model of the functions of language will be discussed at length in the following section of this chapter.

Next, we will discuss several theoretical aspects related to the functions of language – as proposed in the literature by various scholars – which will represent the basis for the classification underlying the functions of narratives in conversational interactions.

3.1 The Functions of Language – theoretical perspectives

In the present paper, we will be using the term *function* as a synonym for the word *use* so as, when referring to the functions of language, we will mean the way people use language with a view to achieving various aims by talking (Halliday & Hasan, 1989:15). Several, usually overlapping functions of language have been put forth by researchers in the fields of linguistics, social anthropology and psychology. Our endeavour will be to reconcile the different terminologies and point out the similarity underlying them.

The view of *language as* an *instrument* for communicating with one another about things goes back to Plato whose conceptual apparatus, derived from pre-Platonic rhetorical grammar, distinguished between first person, second person, and third person, on the basis of the verbal system of Ancient Greek which was organized around a category of person, comprising first person – the speaker –, second person – the addressee –, and third person – everything else/a subject to talk about – (Halliday & Hasan, 1989:15-16); (Bühler, 2011:xxiii). It is on this basis that the Austrian psychologist Bühler (1934) devises, from the point of view of the individual[58], a schema of language functions. The name he derives for his model of language functions is the organon[59] model of language, which comprises three types of language functions corresponding to each of the three person categories: *expression*, *appeal* or *vocative*, and *representation*. The expressive function of language is oriented towards the speaker, the vocative – towards the addressee, and the representational towards the rest of the world, excepting the speaker and the addressee (Nöth, 1990:185); (Halliday & Hasan, 1989:15-16); (Newmark, 1988:39); (Butler & Taverniers, 2008); (Bühler, 2011:35); (Mulligan, 1997:194-195); (Ghiga, 1999:11). Bühler's tripartite classification was revised and extended to six functions by the Prague School of linguistics, Jakobson (1960) in particular. This series of functions is a schema of the communicative process and represents an important contribution to the functional theory of language, as it also draws attention on other three components of the speech event and their corresponding functions. Thus, not only did Jakobson rename Bühler's three functions, as follows: the representational function as the *referential* (also

---

[58] This perspective is paralleled by the cultural viewpoint adopted by Malinowski (1923). For more information, see (Halliday & Hasan, 1989).
[59] The Classical Greek word for tool or instrument.

known as the cognitive or denotative function), **the vocative function as the *conative* and t**he expressive as the *emotive*, but he also added three other communicative functions: the *phatic* (referring to the channel of communication), the *metalingual* (referring to the code being used) and the *poetic* (or the artistic, creative) function (Jakobson, 1960); (Butler & Taverniers, 2008); (Halliday & Hasan, 1989:16); (Günther, 2003:21); (Nöth, 1990:186-187); (Jaworski and Coupland, 2006:42); (Ghiga, 1999:13). It is worth noting that Jakobson's teleological or *multifunctional view of language* is a radical break-away from the Saussurian tradition, which maintained that communication had only one function – the *referential* one –, meaning that language was solely used for communicating propositional meaning (Caton, 1987:231); (Jaworski and Coupland, ibid.). This revolutionary view of language is also supported by other researchers, both in the field of linguistics and social anthropology. Thus, the social anthropologist Malinowski (1923) distinguishes, from a cultural perspective, between two language metafunctions: *pragmatic* (subdivided into *active* and *narrative*) and *magical* (related to ceremonial or religious activities) (Halliday & Hasan, 1989:15). In the same vein, discourse analysts like Brown and Yule (1983:1) point out that language serves two main functions[60]: 1) *transactional* (which conveys propositional content and which is oriented towards the transmission of information to the recipient) and *2) interactional* (which establishes or preserves social relations and expresses personal attitudes). British linguist Halliday also came up with a taxonomy of three language metafunctions: *ideational* (language serving referential goals, i.e., describing objects, events, states, presenting opinions), *interpersonal* (language dealing with the relationship between interlocutors) and *textual* (language referring to itself, as metalanguage and signaling the type of speech event a given text is) (Jaworski, 2000:113-114); (Leech, 1991:56).

All in all, in spite of the different terminologies employed by the various scholars in discussing language functions, we can conclude that they share a common ground: all of them acknowledge the fact that language is used for talking about things (representational/referential/narrative/transacttionnal/ ideational), for expressing the self (expressive/emotive/interactional/interpersonal) and persuading the interlocutors (vocative/conative/interpersonal), and, more or less, they recognize the aesthetic function of language (magical/poetic/textual) (Halliday & Hasan, 1989:16); (Brown and Yule, 1983:1).

What is especially noteworthy about the functions of language is that there is no one to one correspondence between a verbal message and a single function: in other words, language functions usually overlap in verbal communication (Jakobson, 1980:82); (Newmark, 1988:42). Tackling this issue,

---

[60] The same perspective on the functions of language is shared by Tannen (1995b:140).

Bühler talked about *the principle of dominance* – a principle adopted by Jakobson in his own model of verbal communication (Nöth, 1990:186). According to it, there is a *hierarchy* of functions operating on a given message: thus, although several functions may be present in a given message, not all of them are equally important (Jakobson, ibid.). Consequently, there is one predominant or primary function and other, secondary functions (Nöth, ibid.); (Günther, 2003:21). The way to determine the function that overrides the others is to identify the *predominant focus* of the message, which is oriented towards the corresponding factor of the communicative situation (Nöth, ibid.). For instance, the *expressive/emotive* function dominates whenever the focus of the message is on the speaker's own attitude toward the content of the message. In this sense, one has to look for interjections and emphatic speech, which are examples of language being used with a primary emotive function (e.g., *Tut! Tut!* said McGinty). The *conative* function prevails whenever the message is oriented toward the recipient. The vocative and the imperative are grammatical instantiations of this function (e.g., *Drink!*). The *referential* function overrides the others when the focus of the message is on the context of the communicative situation. The *phatic* function prevails when the focus is on the channel of communication: checking if it works, establishing or prolonging communication (e.g., *Are you listening?/ Hello, do you hear me?*). The *metalingual* function focuses on language, terminology included (e.g., *What do you mean?* or *I don't follow you*). Definitions of terms (e.g., What is sophomore? *A sophomore is a second-year student*) and spelling rules are acknowledged as metalanguage. The *poetic* function focuses on the message for its own sake (e.g., *Horrible Harry/ I like Ike*) (Jakobson, 1987); (Nöth, 1990:185-187); (Stubbs, 1983 apud Günther, 2003:21). In other words, the supremacy of one function over the others depends on the purpose of a particular speech act.

There is evidence in the literature which shows that speakers' concern for the establishment and reinforcement of human bonds (the phatic function) among conversational partners prevails over the transmittal of information (the referential function) in conversational interactions, especially in the case of *casual conversations* between social equals (Brown and Yule, 1983:3); (Stubbs, 1983 apud Günther, 2003:21).

The arguments brought in support of this hypothesis are instances of phrases and echoes of phrases found in casual conversation, which are interpreted as contributions to conversation, rather than instances of transmitting information. In this sense, sharing a common point of view or 'establishing common ground with the addressee' is deemed crucial for the maintenance of social relationships. Agreement with one's conversational partner is often achieved by means of partial or total repetition of the previous speaker's utterance (Brown and Levinson (1978) apud Brown and Yule (1983:4)).

In the next section, we will discuss the functions performed by narratives in conversation – as outlined in the literature – and propose a classification of these functions starting form the model developed by Halliday & Hasan (1989), which we will then relate to the Jakobsonian paradigm of language functions.

3.2 The Functions of narratives in conversational interactions

The interactive functions of stories have rarely been a focus of research, as the scholars' interest resided more in the narrative *structure* than in the narrative *function*. There are occasional references – van Dijk (1975); Thornborrow & Coates (2005); Küntay & Ervin-Tripp (1997) – and more systematical discussions – Mandelbaum (2003); Brewer & Lichtenstein (1982); Stein (1982); Norrick (1997). Our endeavour is to review the current stage of research regarding the functions of narratives in conversation and then, for reasons pertaining to systematicity, propose a novel classification of these functions based on the more general models of language functions developed by Halliday & Hasan (1989) and Jakobson (1960), which enable us to cover both the communicative purposes listed in the literature and part of our own findings which cannot be subsumed to the already inventoried functions.

It has been claimed that people do not tell a story without a particular reason. Moreover, the stories they tell are always *relevant* to the circumstances in which they are recounted – e.g., stories describe, explain, account for the respective circumstances (Sacks, 1992) and usually take into account the listeners' identities and the narrator's relationship with the recipients of the narrative.

Two opposite views have been put forward by conversational narrative researchers with respect to the functions of stories in conversational interactions:

1. the first view holds that the main purpose of storytelling is ***to entertain*** (Brewer & Lichtenstein (1982)).

2. according to the second view, people rarely tell a story just for the sake of *entertaining* their conversational partners. Instead, there are several functions underlying the process of storytelling, which point to various reasons underlying human behaviour (Stein (1982:487); (Mandelbaum (2003:614)). In this sense, storytelling is rather an interactive strategy for ***performing*** other ***practical activities***, such as *justifying, explaining or accounting for one's actions (or those of others)* (Thornborrow & Coates (2005),

complaining and gossiping (Harness Goodwin, 1982); (Thornborrow & Coates (ibid.). Telling stories may also function as *transmitting knowledge to the audience and illustrating a point one is advocating in the conversation*. Additionally, narratives and their recipients' response to them may represent practices through which *reality, self (or identity), and relationship* may be interactively constructed. This category comprises the following social activities: *constructing a particular social, cultural or professional identity* (Thornborrow & Coates, ibid.); Holmes & Marra (2005); Johnstone (2001); Dyer and Keller-Cohen (2000); Bucholtz and Hall (2005); Schiffrin (1996); Vasquez (2007:654)), *saving one's positive face, establishing, maintaining or transforming social relationships (ratifying group/family membership and reinforcing group norms and values, exploring the moral implications of personal experience)* (Mandelbaum, 2003:614); (van Dijk, 1975:286).

The principle of the *multifunctionality of language* advanced by Jakobson and the Prague School linguists has also proved valid for narratives-in-interaction, which have been proved to serve several functions simultaneously (Ochs, 2004:294). In the same line, we propose that there is a *hierarchy of functions* performed by stories in conversational interactions. In our analysis of the functions performed by narratives in conversation we will firstly focus on the *dominant* function and secondly, identify the presence of other *minor or peripheral* functions. For our purpose, we will rely on *the intention-based criterion* put forward by Arcand and Bourbeau (trans. of 1995:35) apud Hébert (2007), which is synonymous with Grice's (1975) and Searle's (1979) idea of the purpose of speech acts: "The dominant function is the one that answers the question, 'With what intention was this message transmitted?' and [...] the secondary functions are there to support it". For instance, the conative (or the appellative) function manifests itself directly in the message "Go answer the door" and indirectly in "The doorbell rang", where the overt function is the referential (or informative) function.

We will start our classification of the functions of storytelling in conversation with *the ideational function*.

3.3 The ideational (or referential) function

The *ideational* function of language (Halliday & Hasan, 1989), related to Jakobson's (1960) *referential*[61] function, is acknowledged to be present in all verbal messages since language is primarily designed to have an *ideational* goal, i.e. to give information (Halliday & Hasan, 1989). Thus, in their turns at talk, conversationalists make reference to the extraverbal reality (Jakobson, 1987:62); (Săftoiu,

---

[61] The *referential* function is also known as the *denotative* or *cognitive* function.

2007:11); (Dominte, 2003) or, in other words, describe reality (Duranti, 1997:63). Nevertheless, in most cases, the *referential* function does not occur independently but along with other language functions. Common examples of the referential function are: 'The earth is round', 'Water boils at 100 degrees'.

Transmitting knowledge to the audience is the most frequent subtype of the *referential* function of stories in conversational interactions.

Transmitting knowledge to the audience

Narrative turns have been shown to have a referential function in conversational interactions when the speaker's primary aim is to transmit knowledge to his/her interlocutors (Ștefănescu, 2007:198). People may transmit information to others in different forms: a story, a lesson, a proverb, an idiom, a general expression, a general truth. What makes stories different from all the other forms resides, according to Sacks (1992, vol.2:467), in the fact that stories 'make the speakers' private experiences available to the world'. In this sense, the story one hears from someone else may be passed on to others, or it may be preserved in one's memory for a longer or shorter period of time, until that experience meets the required circumstances to be told again.

Since the *referential function* has been found to be omnipresent in the conversational stories in our corpus, yet always in a secondary position in the hierarchy of functions, we will only discuss it once, in the fragment below, without mentioning it again every time we present the other subordinate functions of conversational stories.

(28) Cupa campionilor europeni/ the European cup
1 U: *când a fost la Cupa campionilor europeni (0.5) și-au ajuns acolo în finală (0.5)*
   when it came to the European cup and they made it to the final
2 *Ienei începuse să-și facă emoții pă-colo pă-colo nu știu ce (0.5)*
   Ienei had turned anxious about this and that and stuff
3 *"hai băieți (0.2) să vedem cine trage în ce ordine trage dacă e (0.3) la (0.2) meci nul"*
   come on boys let's see who shoots in one order if it comes to a draw
4 *cine cine execută*
   who who shoots
5 *și ăia "păi lasă s-ajungem" nu știu ce*
   and they (said)'let us get there first' and stuff
6 *"nu hai să stabilim înainte că" nu știu mai ce*
   no let's settle it beforehand cause and so on and so forth
7 D: *mi-a povestit și mie [cineva faza asta*
   yes I was also told this
8 U: [( ) *el știa că oricare l-ar alege să ( ) deopotrivă la el*
                              he knew that whomever he'd choose to ( ) would also
9   *și să aleagă ei între ei acolo ( )*

and they should choose among themselves there
10 P: *normal*
naturally
11 U: *și (0.2) cei mai tineri erau Lăcătuș și cu ăstălaltu' (0.2) Balint Gabi Balint a::șa*
and the youngest were Lăcătuș and the other one Balint Gabi Balint well
12 *și zice "hai nea Ienei –era la armată- ei erau soldați așa*
and they say come on mister Ienei – they were in the army – they were soldiers and stuff
13 *și ((râde)) lu' Ienei îi dăduse gradul de maior ca să poată să ia o o soldă mai mare*
and ((laughs)) Ienei had been promoted major so as to get higher wages
14 *"hai că te facem noi om (0.3) tragem noi"*
come on we'll make you rich we'll shoot ourselves
15 *el Lăcătuș și cu Balint care era [( )*
he Lăcătuș and Balint who was
16 P: [*(ce tupeu)*
what nerve they had really
17 U: ((*râde*)) *"nea Ienei te facem om"*
((laughs)) mister Ienei we'll make you rich
18 I: ((*râde*))
((laughs))
19 U: *"măi dacă" (0.2) până la urmă mă rog toată echipa*
what if eventually all the team
20 *că fiecare avea și un grad de rezervă "aoleo da' dacă ratez?"*
cause everyone was also reserved "oh my what if I fail"
21 *și te duceai acolo dădeai în minge cu (0.1) obsedat de*
and you went there kicked the ball obsessed by
22 *da' ăștia fiind cei mai tineri și cei mai ușuratici așa*
and as they were the youngest and the most careless ones and stuff
23 *"ce dacă? ratez da' nu intru în pământ"*
so what should I fail I won't die
24 D: *ha*
what
25 U: *s-au gândit ei "dacă ei s-au oferit înseamnă că ei sunt descătușați de"* =
they thought that if they volunteered they had to be released from
26 P: =*tensiuni*
tensions
27 U: *beleaua*
the pest
28 *și bineînțeles că au tras au (0.5)*
and of course they shot they
29 *a apărat ăsta (0.2) Duckadam care nu mai am loc de ardele de arădenii ăștia din cauza asta*
this one Duckadam defended and that's why these people from Ardeal from Arad keep bragging about
30 *și ăștia când au luat acolo că a apărat și ăla al lor*
and when the others scored cause their goalkeeper defended as well
31 *da' când a venit ăsta și a executat primu' șut și a și dat go:l i s-au înmuiat picioarele ălălalt de la (0.5)*
but when he came and shot first and also scored the legs of the other one (0.5) turned to jelly from
32 D: *Sevillia nu?*
(from) Sevillia wasn't it
33 U: *da*
yes

The excerpt above comprises a narrative whose main role in the interaction is *interpersonal* or phatic in Jakobson's terms, i.e. *establishing communication between speakers*.. Its secondary function, which we will insist upon, is *referential,* namely *conveying information* or *transmitting knowledge to the audience*. Prior to the storytelling, the participants engaged in making comments on the matches in the Romanian championship while watching a football programme on TV. The narrator, an old man, over 75 years old and a former navy officer by profession, presents his fellow coparticipants, his 30-year-old great-niece and her husband, with a story he assumes they could not have knowledge of since the event he makes reference to happened in 1986, a time when the recipients were just children. The narrative is an account of an *extraordinary experience* (Labov, 1966; Labov and Waletzky, 1968) and focuses on the circumstances that led to the victory of the Romanian team "Steaua – București" in its match against the Spanish team "Sevilla" – a match that decided the winner of the European Championship League (ECL).

The narrator, U, starts his narrrative abruptly in line 1 (*'când a fost la Cupa campionilor europeni (0.5) și-au ajuns acolo în finală (0.5)'*) ('when it came to the European cup and they made it to the final'), aware that the TV programme they have just watched is closely connected to what he has to say and that no story preface is needed to announce his narrative. Next, he provides background information on the time and place of the event (the final of the European Championship League (henceforth, the ECL)), on the protagonists (Ienei, the coach of the Romanian national football team and the footballers who made up the respective team) and their initial behaviour (preparing their tactics for the final) – lines 1-4 –, so as to familiarize his interlocutors with the context in which the narrated event took place. In some stories, the present one included, the speaker resorts to *direct reported speech* or *constructed dialogue*[62] with the aim of highlighting and dramatizing the key elements in a story[63]. The narrator of the current story uses *constructed dialogue* quite frequently – lines 3, 6, 12, 14, 17, 19, 20, 23, 25 – to render the characters' words in a dramatic scene when the strategies to be adopted in the upcoming decisive match – the final of the ECL – were to be decided. The *constructed dialogue* is being used in spite of the fact that the narrator is neither one of the protagonists nor a witness to the scene. The reasons for the speaker's selection of the DRS is to make the story more dynamic and entertaining and to give the audience the impression of truthfulness and credibility. Thus, according to the teller, the coach supposedly makes a request for the players to decide who will perform the penalty kicks in case the match is null – line 3. Upon the footballers' hesitation, Ienei is firm and reiterates his request – line 6. In lines 12-14 two of the youngest footballers at that time, Lăcătuș and Balint, unexpectedly perform a comissive speech act, offering to perform the penalty kicks and promising the coach to make a rich man out of him – a promise which provokes laughter in some of the participants to the conversation – lines 17-18, as they realize that the

---
[62] *Constructed dialogue* is a representation which has no claim to the truth of the characters' utterances.
[63] See Niemelä (2005:198).

two footballers may have been young, but they surely were down to earth and knew that a good result meant better remuneration for everyone. The narrator goes even further in lines 20, 23 and 25 when he quotes the characters' inner feelings and thoughts – the general sense of fear to assume one's responsibility (line 20), the two younger footballers' audacity (line 23) and the general acknowledgement that they are the best men to shoot and score (line 25).

At some point in the narrative, one of the recipients, D, recognizes the story and self-selects, remarking, by means of an assertive speech act, that someone recounted her that scene beforehand. This remark may be interpreted in two ways: as an acknowledgement of the events narrated by U, which has the role of conferring credibility to the story but also as a signal that the narrator should stop his account, as the audience is already acquainted with the story. The latter interpretation of D's comment is a threat to U's negative face as it attempts to impede U to proceed with his account.

Supposing that the narrator's interpretation of D's utterance is an invitation for him to stop, his reaction is to respond to a threat by another threat: a threat to D's positive face, as he chooses to completely ignore D's comment and go on with his story as if nothing had happened – his utterance in line 8 even overlaps the final sequence of D's remark in the preceding line. U's decision to go on with the story is supported by the other interlocutor, P, who, by affiliating with the speaker in line 10, confirms the legitimacy of the story, which seems to be new to him.

The secondary referential function we have discussed so far supports *the* main *interpersonal function*, which is related in this case to Jakobson's *phatic function*. This entails that the story is in fact a mere pretext for establishing and continuing communication between speakers of different ages, as it is well-known that old and young people share little in common. The speaker's choice of the *safe topic* of sports (namely football) for his story is a positive politeness strategy meant to claim common ground (Brown and Levinson, 1987:103-124) with a much younger audience. Also, the use of synecdoche[64] in line 29 is another means by which the teller affiliates himself with his conversational partner, his great-niece. The latter comes from the town of Arad and is addressed by the narrator by means of the general address term '*arădenii ăștia*' ('these people of the town of Arad').

The next function of stories that we will discuss is the interpersonal function occurring as a primary, dominant function in the conversational interaction.

---

[64] Synecdoche is a figure of speech in which a more generalised term is used to designate a particular term.

3.4 The interpersonal function

We started our discussion from *the interpersonal function,* since we found Halliday & Hasan's (1989) model to be closer to the pragmatic perspective of our thesis, our intention being to focus on the speaker and on the relations holding among the participants to the conversational interaction. However, since this function is very general, we preferred to discuss it in terms of the perspective described by Jakobson (1960), treating the interpersonal function in relation to the speaker (the *emotive or expressive* function), the interlocutor (the *conative or persuasive* function) and the channel of communication (the *phatic* function).

The first function we will deal with is the emotive function.

3.4.1 The emotive function

The *emotive* or *expressive* function is centred on the *speaker* and focuses on his/her attitude (i.e. anger, irony, etc.), (also feelings, thoughts, opinions, and reactions) towards the content of the message he/she is conveying (Jakobson, 1987:66-67); (Nöth, 1990:187); (Newmark, 1988:39).

In order to identify and characterize the expressive function of language, we will consider *subjective modality* – an important category encoding the speaker's attitude regarding the propositional content of the clause (Verstraete, 2001:1507); (Sokolova, 2003:123). First of all, we will focus on *deictics*. The expressive function of language may be easily identified if one follows the general orientation of the speaker's utterances: in this case, the 1st *person* prevails (Vachek, 2003:51); (Sokolova, 2003:123). Therefore, we may infer that 1st person personal pronouns and adjectives, the possessives included, (I, me, mine, my) are helpful indices in identifying utterances with an emotive contour.

Secondly, the class of *evaluatives,* for which various subclassifications have been proposed, definitely deserves our attention. In Searle (1979)[65]'s view, there is no such thing as the class of evaluative acts, and therefore they are ambiguously placed, between the assertives and the expressives. Vernant's (1997) model of illocutionary acts[66], however, integrates evaluatives as a subclass in the class

---

[65] *Expression and Meaning: Studies in the Theory of Speech Acts* (1979).

of expressive acts (acts expressing a psychological state) (Barbu, 2011:74). In the same vein, Vintilescu (2005:30-31) points out that we might consider part of the evaluative acts as expressive, since the speaker conveys an emotion (i.e. his/her psychological state) concerning a certain state of affairs. Thus, we may equate utterances like 'X is good' or 'X is bad' to exclamations, such as 'hurray' or 'puah', since both linguistic categories express the speaker's emotions. For the purpose of our study, we will discriminate within the domain of *evaluative modality* between *emotive* evaluation (the speaker's appeal to feelings) – e.g., It is good that he should be received – and *non-emotive or axiological* evaluation (the speaker's appeal to a set of values) – e.g., It is appropriate that he should be received –, though this distinction is not always clear-cut (GLR, 2005:693); (Kerbrat-Orecchioni, 1997:112). Moreover, in common, everyday talk, there is often ambiguity among assertive, evaluative and expressive speech acts (Barbu, 2011:76).

There are specific linguistic means of expressing *evaluative modality (emotive modality included)* in Romanian: verbs of evaluation, adverbial phrases, evaluative adjectives and nouns, interjections and exclamatory particles. Besides these, an important suprasegmental means, specific to the evaluative modality, is intonation.

Interjections and *emphatic speech* represent prototypical instances of the emotive function of language (Jakobson, 1987:66-67); (Nöth, 1990:187). Previous research conducted on interjections has shown that they acquire modal force, since they convey the speaker's attitude with respect to a certain event or to the propositional content (Tuțescu, 2006:45); (Świątkowska, 2006:52); (Buridant, 2006:5). Interjections (e.g., 'zău' ('really'), 'vai' ('oh, my')) go together with specific intonation, which is extremely variable and impossible to codify linguistically. In the same category fall *exclamatory words* (e.g., '*ce / ce mai...*' ('what'), '*cât de...*' ('how')) and expressions (e.g. '*Slavă Domnului*' ('Thanks God'), '*Doamne ferește*' ('God forbid')) (GLR, 2005:693).

The list below comprises evaluative and emotive verbs, adjectives, adverbs and nouns selected from GLR (2005:693), which will be helpful tools in identifying and analyzing conversational narratives with a predominantly emotive function:

Evaluative and partly emotive verbs – *a-i plăcea că... / să...* (like that), *a-i displăcea că... / să...* (dislike that) (evaluative and partially emotive), *a merita să...* (to be worth) (evaluative), *a-l durea că...* (hurt that), *a-l deprima că... / să...* (be depressed to/that), *a-l enerva că... / să...* (be annoyed to/that), *a-l îngrozi că... / să...*(be terrified to/that) (emotive, affective), *a aprecia că...* (appreciate that)(evaluative), *a detesta să...* (detest to), *a urî să...* (hate to), *a regreta că...* (regret that), *a se bucura că... / să* (rejoice that) etc. Some have an epistemic component (the surprise): *a-l uimi că...*(be astonished that), *a-l surprinde că* (be surprised that)... .

Evaluative adverbs and adverbial phrases: A). *(e) ciudat că...* (it's strange that), *(e) bine că...* (it's good that); *e rău că...* (it's bad that); *(e) de mirare că...* (it's surprising that) ' *e curios* (it's curious), *minunat* (wonderful), *surprinzător* (surprising), *regretabil* (regrettable), *trist* (sad), *util* (useful), *important* (important), *esenţial* (essential), etc.; B). *din fericire* (fortunately), *din păcate/ din nenorocire/ din nefericire* (unfortunately), *e de neiertat că / să...* (it's unforgivable to), *e de admirat că...* (it's admirable to), *e de regretat că ...* (it's regrettable that), etc.

Evaluative adjectives, usually used after a copula: *a fi (foarte) bucuros(-oasă) că... / să...* (be (very) happy that)), *a fi (destul de) mulţumit(ă) că... / să...* (be (really) pleased that), etc.

Evaluative nouns: A). with adverbial value: *noroc că...* (luckily), *păcat că...* (it's a pity that); B). *e păcat/ e o nenorocire că...* (unfortunately), *problema e că...* (the problem is that), *lucrul interesant e că...* (the interesting thing is that), *nenorocirea e că ...* (the trouble is that) etc.; C). *a avea bucuria / plăcerea să... / de a...* (be happy/delighted to), *a-i fi frică / teamă să... / că* (be afraid that).

Having set the tools for the identification of narrative passages than have an emotive function, we will now consider the most representative type of narrative where the dominant function is the expressive function, namely the narrative hosting *the construction of a particular social, cultural or professional identity*.

Constructing a particular social, cultural or professional identity

Discourse researchers consider narratives as 'the site par excellence' for examining the claims speakers make about themselves and their identities (Bamberg, 2004a:356), as well as investigating the process of construction of the speakers' identity through language. Building one's identity for the audience through the stories one chooses to recount is a means of situating oneself in society and in a group of friends/the family (Johnstone, 2001:640-641). Thus, the stories speakers choose to tell reveal the speakers' *social characteristics*, such as *class, gender* and *ethnicity*, and the role they play in rendering the narrator's unique voice (Dyer and Keller-Cohen, 2000:284). Also, narratives in talk-in-interaction have been shown to display the speakers' complex and multifaceted identities (Holmes and Marra, 2005:211) or *a particular facet of* their *personality*. Either way, the speakers' selection of a particular narrative is done considering the local context of the conversational interaction: the time and place in which the ongoing talk is set, as well as their conversational partners. For instance, the same speaker may portray himself/herself both as an expert, in a narrative addressed to an acquaintance, and as a failure in a story told to a close friend:

'In contemporary scholarship it has become commonplace to observe that speakers use the site of narratives to construct particular identities . . . the construction of identity being understood not as a single act, but as a process that is constantly active, each telling of a story offering the narrator a fresh opportunity to create a particular representation of herself . . . speakers make narrative choices in order to display a particular portrait of themselves. The self that the narrators depict is inevitably constructed for that particular context' (Keller-Cohen and Dyer (1997) apud Vasquez (2007:654)).

In fact, the value of narratives-in-interaction is not that of an objective representation of a past event but has a *subjective* character with a potential of portraying

both the storyteller as an individual and the society which shaped him/her, but which, in turn, is shaped by the narrator (Dyer and Keller-Cohen, 2000:283).

Previous linguistic studies regarding narratives in talk-in-interaction have shown that a close investigation of the linguistic resources and discursive tools used by the speakers in telling stories are indicative of the way in which they present themselves and the experiences they went through, the manner in which they situate themselves and the others as characters in the fictional world they construe, as well as the incremental way in which they shape their identities (Schiffrin (1996); de Fina (2003); Bamberg (1997); Linde (1993) apud Vásquez (2007:653); Davies and Harré (1990) apud Vásquez (2007:653)).

There are several basic strategies used by the speakers in building their identities in the stories they select to tell the audience. Building one's professional identity and expertise is mostly achieved by means of using *technical terminology*, i.e., fieldspecific concepts and terms (Heath (1979) apud Dyer and Keller-Cohen (2000:288)).

Positioning of self and other is another pervasive means of asserting one's identity by comparing oneself with other people (Shotter (1993:6) apud Dyer and Keller-Cohen (2000:289)). At this stage, we will consider the following concepts and linguistic categories which play a crucial part in determining the position adopted by the narrator with respect to the others in the storyworld:

a). the roles assigned by the narrator to the characters in the story:

'In telling a fragment of his or her autobiography a speaker assigns parts and characters in the episodes described, both to themselves and to other people.' (Davies and Harré (1990) apud Dyer and Keller-Cohen (2000:289)).

In this respect, it is worth mentioning that, in constructing one's self in relation to others in a narrative of personal experience, the storyteller often presents himself/herself 'in the best possible light' (Labov and Waletzky (1967) apud Dyer and Keller-Cohen (2000:289)). In the same line, it was shown that the speakers' identity is built relationally, on the basis of the aspects concerning the relationship between self and the other, aspects which include the following oppositions: similarity/difference, genuineness/artifice, authority/delegitimacy (Bucholtz and Hall (2005:585)).

b). pronouns and referring expressions showing alignment with or distance from others (Brown and Gilman (1968) apud Dyer and Keller-Cohen (2000:292)).

c). the concept of dual perspective, of action and consciousness, connected with the concepts of *agentive* (refers to the action and the temporal progression of the narrative) and *epistemic self* (is connected to the speaker's thoughts, feelings and beliefs) (Schiffrin (1996); Greimas and Courtes (1989) apud Dyer and Keller-Cohen (2000:288); Bruner (1990). Such analytical tools have the advantage of permitting the examination of the narrator's identity construction from a double perspective: that of the agent, of the protagonist, who is in control of the action and that of his/her epistemic self, through which the speaker has the opportunity of explaining and justifying his/her actions (Dyer and Keller-Cohen, 2000:288); Schiffrin (1996).

We have chosen to analyse the emotive function as the dominant function in the story below, which conveys *the speaker's construction of* her *professional identity*.

*(29) Metodă/*Method
1R: *Doa::mne (0.1) ce clasă mă (0.2)*
    oh God what a class
2 *acolo într-adevăr (0.5) nu puteai rezista*
    you simply couldn't make it there
3 *și mai aveam unu' (0.2) ăla GRAs așa=*
    and there was also another one the fat one and stuff
4D: *= da: (0.2) care (0.1) Mun- (0.1) Muntean sau care?*
    yes who Mun Muntean or who
5R: *cred că Muntean era [( )*
    Muntean I believe it was
6D: *[Alexandru Cătălin? ((râde))*
            Alexandru Cătălin ((laughs))
7R: *( ) nu știu dacă Muntean*
    I can't tell if it was Muntean
8D: *cum arăta?*
    what did he look like
9R: *era unu'=*
    there was one
10D: *=genu' bodyguard? ((râde))=*
    the bodyguard style ((laughs))
11R: *=ROTUND așa cu totu'*
    roundish all over and stuff
12D: *sau Alexandru ăla (0.1) blonduț (0.4) sau șaten ?*
    or Alexandru the blondish one or the brown-haired one
13R: *parcă șaten era*
    I think he was brown-haired
14D: *nu cred că (0.1) – Muntean*

I don't think that - Muntean
15R: *nu mai știu*
I can't tell
16 (   ) *vorbea (0.1) nu lucra și (0.2) găsisem io mare metodă ((râde))*
he would talk he wouldn't work and I had found a great method ((laughs))
17 *îl puse- ((râde))-sem în prima bancă (0.4) și-l puneam să deseneze (0.3)*
I had ((laughs)) placed him in the first desk and I would make him draw
18 *îl puneam să se semneze prima dată (0.2) numele și clasa*
I'd make him sign first name and class
19D: *pe (toți)?=*
everyone
20R: *=nu pe ăsta (0.2) că nu lucra*
no this one because he wouldn't work
21 *nu lucra și nici nu venea CU NICIUN MATERIAL*
he wouldn't work and he wouldn't bring any material
22 *cu nimic nimic nu venea*
he wouldn't bring anything anything
23D: *da da*
yes yes
24R: *(lua) o foaie pe care-o găsea pe-acolo și scria cu pixu'*
he'd take a sheet of paper which he found around and would write on it with the ball pen
25 *că nimic nimic n-avea (0.2) nici creion nu-și aducea*
because he had nothing nothing he brought nothing not even a pencil
26D: *da*
yes
27R: *și-atunci ce putea face în ora aia ?*
and then what could he do during that class
28 *că se plictisea vorbea făcea gălăgie=*
because he got bored he would talk he would make noise
29D: *=da*
yes
30R: *îi deranja pe ceilalți*
he woud disturb the others
31D: *normal*
naturally
32R: *și găsisem io metodă să-l pun în prima bancă (0.2) și stăteam numai lângă el (0.3)*
and I had found a method to place him in the first desk and I only stood next to him
33 *și-l puneam să se semneze (0.2) și să scrie clasa (0.2)*
and I made him sign it and write his class
34 *și strângeam toate lucrările la sfârșitul orei=*
and I would gather all the papers at the end of the class
35D: *=și-i dădeai câte-un trei*
and you'd give him a three
36R: *nu 'uite teancu' ăsta o să i-l dau doamnei diriginte ( ) să-l arate mamei tale'*
no look I'll give this pile to your headteacher to show it to your mother
37 *mare-amenințare știi ((râde))?*
great threat you know ((laughs))
38D: *și se speria măcar ?*
and would he get scared at least
39R: *se speria așa un pic da' nu prea tare (0.3) da*
he'd get scared a bit and stuff but not really yes

As we have previously pointed out, the dominant function of the present narrative in the ongoing interaction is the *emotive function,* since the story focuses on the speaker's ironic attitude toward the events presented in the story: her attempts, as an inexperienced teacher, of dealing with a naughty and reluctant pupil – lines 16 ('( ) *vorbea (0.1) nu lucra și (0.2) găsisem io mare metodă ((râde))*') ('he would talk he wouldn't work and I had found a great method ((laughs))') and 37 ('*mare-amenințare știi ((râde))?*') ('great threat you know ((laughs))'). While the word 'method' sums up what follows in the narrative, the emphatic occurrence of the prenominal adjective 'big' ('mare') represents an expressive feature which is indicative of the speaker's self-irony. The exclamatory words '*Doa::mne*' ('God') and '*ce*' ('what') accompanied by the address term '*mă*' in line 1 ('*Doa::mne (0.1) ce clasă mă*') ('oh God what a class') also play a key role in the speaker's delivery of the message concerning the teacher's difficulty in coping with such a terrible class. Finally, the use of the pronominal ('*io*' ('I') - lines 16 and 32) and verbal (*găsisem, puneam, stăteam, strângeam, o să dau*) (I had found, I made, I stood, I would gather, I'll give) first person also contributes to the general emotive contour of the story.

The speaker uses specific means to build her professional identity, that of a novice teacher in control of her class. In the analysis of the *narrator's construction of identity*, we will rely on the models elaborated by Dyer and Keller-Cohen (2000); Schiffrin (1996) and Bucholtz and Hall (2005).

The portrait sketched by the speaker is that of a novice, with little teaching experience, who, nevertheless, manages to deal with an unexpected situation: faced with naughty pupils, she proves to possess an experienced teacher's authority and creativity, as she is able to devise a method aimed at maintaining discipline during her classes by isolating the 'problem' pupil and forcing him to obey her.

The use of *professional language* represents one of the main means of a speaker's achievement of technical expertise. Although more of a novice than an expert, R frequently uses fieldspecific concepts and terms, namely lexical terms that are specific to the work a teacher does in school: *metodă, material, nu lucra, îl puneam să deseneze, să se semneze – numele și clasa –, foaie, creion, pix, strângeam lucrările, doamnei dirigintă, la sfârșitul orei, în prima bancă, clasă* (method, material, wouldn't work, I would make him draw, sign – name and class –, sheet, pencil, ball pen, I would gather the papers, headteacher, at the end of the class, in the first desk, class).

Another important strategy employed by the speaker in the discursive process of identity construction is the precise way of *positioning* her*self and others* in the ongoing story. This is revealed in a number of ways: firstly, the *roles assigned* by the narrator *to the characters in the story* may be perceived as antagonistic: the SELF might be seen as a *symbol of authority*, whereas the OTHER (the problem child) stands for *order disruption*. As a means of constructing her own professional identity (that of a teacher) in the best possible light, the speaker portrays the other *dramatis personae* (the pupils) in their narratives as being disobedient and disruptive. She establishes her superior status to the respective others by showing that the others represent a source of chaos and anarchy – lines 1-2 ('*Doa::mne (0.1) ce clasă mă (0.2)/ acolo* *într-adevăr (0.5) nu puteai rezista'*), ('oh God what a class/you simply couldn't make it there') *lines 16 ('( ) vorbea (0.1) nu lucra și (0.2) găsisem io mare metodă ((râde))'* ('he would talk he wouldn't work and I had found a great method ((laughs))'), *20-22 (' ... nu lucra/ nu lucra și nici nu venea CU NICIUN MATERIAL/ cu nimic nimic nu venea'*) ('he wouldn't work/ he wouldn't work and he wouldn't bring any material/ he wouldn't bring anything anything'), *24-25 ('(lua) o foaie pe care-o găsea pe-acolo și scria cu pixu'/ că nimic nimic n-avea (0.2) nici creion nu-și aducea'*) ('he'd take a sheet of paper which he found around and would write on it with the ball pen/because he had nothing nothing he brought nothing not even a pencil'), *28 ('se plictisea vorbea făcea gălăgie='*). ('he got bored he would talk he would make noise') *and 30 ('îi deranja pe ceilalți'*) ('he woud disturb the others').

Secondly, the analysis of the choice of *pronouns and referring expressions* in the present story shows that the narrator systematically distances herself from the others in the narrative and especially from the naughty pupil, who disrupts class order. R's identity is set out in relief against the 'problem' child – whom she refers to as *unu* (one) – lines 3 and 9, *ăsta* (this) – lines 20 and 36, *ăla* (the one) – line 3. R also portrays herself as the main agent in her narrative, making use of devices to depersonalize and/or render invisible and/or powerless the others in the narratives. R's use of the demonstrative pronouns *ăsta* and *ăla* ('this one' and 'that one') as well as of the indefinite one *unu* ('one') in the above context may be seen as *attitudinal dissociation* (Levinson, 1983:81). These deictic and referring expressions reflect emotional distance and perhaps also disrespect. Distancing is also achieved through depersonalization, as in R's choice not to give a name to the respective pupil. When it comes to naming the child, the narrator fails to identify the particular individual: – lines 5 and 7 *('cred că Muntean era [( )]'*) ('Muntean I believe it was'), *('( ) nu știu dacă Muntean'*) ('I can't tell if it was Muntean'), therefore the pupil is not assigned an identity, but he is reduced to a sketch representing the prototype of the 'naughty pupil'– lines 3 *('(0.2) ăla GRAs așa='*) ('the fat one and stuff'), *9 ('era unu'='*) ('there was one'), *11 ('=ROTUND așa cu totu'*) ('roundish all over and stuff') *and 13 ('parcă șaten era'*) ('I think he was brown-haired'). In this narrative R does not consider the identity of the other to be important for her audience. Moreover, she might realize that giving characters identities and personalities detracts the listener's attention from the main character (herself) and may even engender sympathy for the others instead of admiration for herself. Therefore, the speaker portrays herself as a teacher who manifests authority in front of the pupils by taking a firm stand when the 'problem' pupil tries to disrupt class order by speaking up and making noise.

Thirdly, the storyteller constructs her identity as a novice teacher in control of the class through *other and self evaluations* in the landscape of action. The description of her action through her agentive self when in a delicate situation is *self aggrandizing*. She emphasizes the skill that is required of her as a teacher, using verbs such as *'îl puneam să (deseneze, să se semneze)'* ('I would make him (draw, sign)') – lines 17-18, 33, *'stăteam (numai lângă el)'* ('I only stood next to him') – line 32 and *'strângeam (lucrările)'* ('I would gather (the papers)') – line 34, with claims regarding the difficulty of the situation, such as (*'Doa::mne (0.1) ce clasă mă (0.2)/acolo într-adevăr (0.5) nu puteai rezista'*) ('oh God what a class/you simply couldn't make it there') – lines 1-2. Not only does R construct her identity through positive self-evaluation but also through negatively evaluating others, using event verbs in the negative: *'nu lucra'* ('wouldn't work') – lines 20-21, *'nu venea'* ('wouldn't bring') – line 22, *'nu-și aducea'* ('brought (no pencil)') – line 25 and negative pronouns and adjectives *NICIUN MATERIAL'* ('any material') – line 21, *'nimic nimic'* ('anything anything') – lines 22 and 25, *'nici creion'* ('not even a pencil') – line 25 to display the pupil's carelessness regarding school. The narrator's self-aggrandizement is most evident in the sequence of turns in which she is shown to possess the skills that are required of her as a teacher: authority and creativity – lines 32-34 and 36. The teller's description of herself has also got a *self-effacing* side to it, which consists in using self-mockery, accompanied by laughter – lines 16 (*'găsisem io mare metodă ((râde))'*) ('I had found a great method ((laughs))') and 37 (*' mare-amenințare știi ((râde))'*) ('great threat you know ((laughs))'). This is most obvious at the beginning and at the end of the narrative when R casts herself in a less than flattering light, depicting herself as a novice, unexperimented teacher who acts on instinct, rather than expertise in devising a method meant to ensure class order and who even resorts to a threat to reach her aim.

To sum up, in the construction of herself the narrator achieves the delicate balance necessary for social acceptance between *self-aggrandizement* and *self-effacement* (Keller-Cohen and Dyer, 1997:297), as she presents herself as both a novice and a teacher who possesses authority and is in control of the class.

Beside the primary emotive function discussed above, the present narrative also performs a secondary function, namely the *phatic function*, which is meant to support the main function. This secondary function of the present narrative is given by speaker R's attempt to establish and prolong contact with the addressee, D, by means of *claiming common ground with her conversational partner* (Brown and Levinson, 1987:103) – a mechanism which consists of the speaker's use of several positive politeness strategies. In the present case, R's claim of common membership with the addressee, D, prompts her into proposing as topic for discussion a subject that the recipient is very well familiar with and which she is most likely to agree upon: the difficulty of dealing with reluctant pupils in a school both of the interlocutors used to teach. While telling the story, the speaker uses markers of phatic communion, such as the verb *știi* ('you know') – line37– and the address form *mă* – line 1, meant to promote social harmony and strengthen the friendship relationship holding between the conversational parties.

While the story in the fragment above displayed the construction of the storyteller's *professional identity*, the story we will consider below conveys the speaker's *social identity* by means of introspection regarding the moral implications of the teller's personal experience.

Telling stories is a good opportunity for speakers to assert themselves as members of a particular society by setting their experiences against a set of norms and values pertaining to the community they belong to. This is also an occasion for them to align themselves or affiliate with their conversational partners. As Ochs & Capps (1997:1-2) put it:

'The narrative visions we construe are very much guided by history, culture, and personal circumstance. One of the most important functions of narrative is precisely to situate particular events against a larger horizon of what we consider to be human passions, virtues, philosophies, actions, and relationships. As narrators, we evaluate specific events in terms of communal norms, expectations, and potentialities; communal ideas of what is rational and moral; communal senses of the appropriate and the esthetic. In this way we affiliate with other members of society. The power to interface self and society renders narrative a medium of socialization par excellence' (Ochs & Capps, 1997:1-2).

Thus, narratives function as orientation signs meant to guide people along the moral principles set by the society whose product they are, by proposing standards of what is right and what is wrong (Ochs & Capps, 2001). In this context, storytellers picture themselves as virtuous, ethical people, often morally superior to other characters in the stories they tell (Ochs, 2004:294). The recipients, friends or family members, usually request clarification, challenge perspectives, speculate about what the narrators revealed about their experiences in the stories they tell, and question the moral meaning of events, thus helping the storytellers to grasp their experiences in an adequate manner (Ochs and Taylor, 1992b).

In what follows we propose an excerpt of a conversational story which represents an instantiation of the emotive function overriding the other secondary functions in terms of the speaker's assertion of her moral values.

(30) Piele și os/ Skin and bones

1P: *aveați bagaje aveați*
   did you have any luggage you did didn't you
2E: *bagaje nu prea*
   luggage no not really
3   *stai să-ți spun acuma (0.1) altă fază (0.2)*
   now let me tell you another story
4   *acolo la sfânta Ecaterina când am ajuns (0.3) seara am stat am ajuns*
   when we got there at saint Catherine's in the evening we stayed we got there
5   *când am ajuns mă rog ne-am spălat ne-am dușulit ne-am (0.2) spovedit*
   when we got there well we had a bath a shower we confessed
6   *ne-am mă rog ce am mai făcut noi*
   we well whatever else we did
7   *seara 'hai să mâncăm'*
   in the evening let's have something to eat
8   *toată lumea avea aveam în traistă fel de fel (0.5)*
   everybody had we had in our bags all kinds of
9   *am mâncat noi (0.2) 'hai că mai mâncăm dimineață' (0.5)*
   we finished eating we'll eat some more in the morning
10 *am strâns masa și ((râde)) 'cine ((râde)) cine duce gunoiu'?*
   we cleared the table and ((laughs)) who is going ((laughs)) to take the garbage out
11 *'mă Elena ((râde)) du-te tu ((râde)) că ție nu ți-e frică'*
   you Helen ((laughs)) you go ((laughs)) cause you're not afraid
12P: *((râde)) unde trebuia să-l duceți?*
    ((laughs)) where did you have to take it
13E: *la benă (0.1) era o bena așa mai (0.2) ca de-aicea peste drum (0.5) cam așa*
   to the waste container there was a waste container about from here to there across the street
   or something like that
14P: *și ce era așa de (0.2) era groapă sau ?=*
    and what was so (special about it) was it a hole or =
15E: *=întuNERIC*
    darkness
16P: *a:: (   ) =*
    oh
17E: *= întune:ric și ă:: maicile sunt na (0.2) așa cum sun*
     darkness and um the nuns are well the way they are
18 *Gabriela era în neglije (0.5) bărbatu-su (0.3)*
    Gabriella was in her nightgown her husband
19 *'hai că-l duc io lasă' (0.5) și ies cu gunoiu': (0.7)*
    I'll take it out that's ok and I go out with the garbage
20P: (   )
21E: *era bena deschisă (0.2) capacele deschise și dau drumu' la pungă la punga cu gunoi acolo*
    the container was opened opened lids and I drop the bag the garbage bag down there
22 *când am dat drumu' la punga cu gunoi acolo (0.2) iese ceva așa (0.5) din*
   when I dropped the garbage bag down there something gets out of
23P: [*dinăuntru*
    there
24E: [*dinăuntru (0.2) ă::::::*
    there um
25P: *((râde))*
    laughs
26E: *((râde)) va::i (0.1) Doamne*
    ((laughs)) oh God
27P: *era un om acolo?*
   was there a man in there
28E: *era un om (0.2) piele (0.2) și os (0.2) un schelet (0.1) un schelet*
    there was a man skin and bones a skeleton a skeleton
29P: *ce făcea acolo?*

what was he doing in there
30 E: *căuta prin gunoaie (0.1) °săracu'° (0.7)*
he was scavenging poor thing
31 *și io când l-am văzut zic 'aoleo ce m-ai speriat' (0.5)*
and when I saw him I say oh my you scared me
32 *și (0.3) l-am întrebat că 'ce cauți'? că a a luat punga mea 'ce cauți'?*
and I asked him what are you looking for because he took my bag what are you looking for
33 *el îmi arăta că (0.2) sigur că nu înțelegeam (0.2) ° căuta ceva de mâncare °*
he showed me that of course I did not understand he was looking for something to eat
34 *vai ° rău mi s-a făcut °*
God I got sick
35 *zic 'vino-ncoace' (0.7)*
I say come here
36 *mă duc și (0.2) intru-n cameră- eram toți într-o cameră (0.7)*
I go and I enter the room –all of us stayed in one room
37 *zic 'toată lumea scoateți mâncarea' (0.5)*
I say everybody take your food out
38 P: *((râde))*
laughs
39 E: *'ce-ai înnebunit Elena'? ((râde))*
are you crazy Helen ((laughs))
40 *'veniți să vedeți ceva' (0.8)*
come and see this
41 *((oftează)) 'opriți numai câte o bucată de pâine și să-i dăm la amărâtu' ăsta'*
((sighs)) keep only one slice of bread and let us give the rest to this poor thing
42 *mai aveam salam pate ouă și ce știu io ce mai era pe-acolo fel de fel de (0.1) fructe*
we had salami, pate eggs and I don't know what else we had there all sorts of fruit
43 *am zis s-avem pe dimineață (0.5)*
we thought we should have something to eat in the morning
44 *și îți spun așa o experiență pe care n-aș mai vrea s-o mai am <u>niciodată</u> (0.4)*
and I'm telling you such an experience I wish I would never have again
45 *și în sfârșit (0.2) când l-au văzut maicile 'săracu' de el'(0.3)*
and anyway when the nuns saw him poor thing
46 ....*((râde)) 'ce pomană ai făcut și dacă ne duceam noi ori lăsam punga acolo ori' (0.2)*
((laughs)) how good of you and if we had gone there we would have either left the bag there
47 P: *ori muream pe loc*
or we died instantly
48 E: *((râde))/ ((laughs))*
49 P: *((râde))/ ((laughs))*
50 E: *și zic 'oprim cât să luăm dimineață o gură așa'*
and I say we'll just save some for a bite in the morning
51 *ele nu (0.1) erau cu mâncare așa de dimineață*
they did not eat so early in the morning
52 *și ( ) tot tot ce era- am oprit pentru noi câte ( )*
and everything everything we had we kept for us some
53 *și i-am făcut lu' amărâtu' ăla*
and we gave it to that poor soul
54 *Petre îți spun (0.1) în viața mea nu am văzut așa ceva*
Peter I am telling you I had never seen anything similar
55 *știi ce-nseamnă <u>piele și oase</u>?*
do you know what skin and bones means
56 P: *mai mai ca mine nu știu dacă se poate*
worse than me I don't know if this is possible
57 E: *nu:::*
no

```
58P: eu sunt gras
     I am fat
59E: va::i în momentu' în care i-am spus 'stai aici (0.1) așteaptă-mă' (0.4)
     oh my the moment I told him stay here wait for me
60   ele l-au văzut și-au zis 'Doa::mne'
     they saw him and said oh Lord
61   maica Gabriela s-a așezat în genunchi și a început să plângă 'Doa::mne'
     sister Gabriella went down on her knees and started crying oh Lord
62   eu i-am spus 'stai un pic aici'(    )
     I told him stay here for a moment
63   în momentu' când i-am dat plasa (0.4) știi cum?
     the moment I gave him the bag you know
64   s-a lăsat jos (0.3) în prafu' ăla vai de capu' lui și era murdar și (0.1)
     he went down in the dust woe is him and he was dirty and
65   și s-a lăsat jos și să-mi pupe picioarele
     he went down to kiss my feet
66   'vai Doamne ferește (0.2) mergi cu Dumnezeu'
     oh Lord go with God
67   sigur că i-am dat și câte un bănuț
     of course we gave him several pence
68   n-am să uit niciodată figura aia și ochii ăia
     I will never forget that face and those eyes
69   când a ieșit din benă de-acolo ă: îți dai seama am văzut albu' ochilor așa și (0.3)
     when he got out of the waste can um you see I saw the white of his eyes like that and
70P: (    )
71E: am făcut 'va::i ce m-ai speriat'
     I said oh my you scared me
72   sigur că el și-a dat seama că am spus ceva - ce-o fi înțeles el
     of course he realized I said something whatever he understood
73   spunea pe limba lui că el căuta mâncare
     he said in his language that he was looking for food
74   luase punga aia și noi ce aveam în punga aia? coji de ouă coji de salam (0.3)
     he had taken that bag and what did we have in that bag leftovers of eggs and salami
75P: da (0.1) ce =
     what
76E: =oase de (0.2) pui
     chicken bones
77   îți spun așa de bine mi-a părut că până la urmă m-am dus io ((râde)) cu gunoiu'
     I am telling you I was so glad that I ended up ((laughs)) taking out the garbage
```

The dominant function of the story in the conversational interaction above is *the emotive function*, since the narrative focuses on the storyteller's attitude (surprise, pity) with respect to the personal experience she is recounting: an unexpected encounter with a man coming from the slums of Egypt. Her story is painted with genuine emotion and abounds in expressive linguistic elements. Among these range *interjections* ('vai', 'aoleo') ('oh, my')), usually accompanied by *exclamatory words* ('ce') ('what'), ('Doamne') ('God') or *phrases* ('Doamne ferește') ('God forbid') *and expressive verbs* ('a speria') ('to scare') – lines 26 *('va::i (0.1) Doamne')* ('oh God'), 31 *('aoleo ce m-ai speriat')* ('oh my you scared me'), 66 *('vai Doamne ferește')* ('oh Lord'), 71 *('va::i ce m-ai speriat')* ('oh my you scared me'), as well as *emphatic speech*, concerning both the speaker's intonation and her inverting the word order (by placing the adjective functioning as predicate before the verb) – line 34 *('vai ° rău mi s-a făcut °')* ('God I got sick'). The ethical, axiological dimension of the speaker's message is rendered by the emotive, evaluative predicate *(a-i părea bine)* (to be glad) in line 77 *('îți spun așa de bine mi-a părut că până la urmă m-am dus io ((râde)) cu gunoiu')* ('I am telling you I was so glad that I ended up ((laughs)) taking out the garbage') and by the evaluative adjectives in lines 64 *('vai de capu' lui')* ('woe is him') and 28 *('un om (0.2) piele (0.2) și os', 'un schelet')* ('a man skin and bones a skeleton a skeleton'). Last but not least, we should mention the speaker's frequent use of the first person personal pronouns – conveyed both explicitly – lines 31 and 77 *(io)* (I), 62 *(eu)* (I) – and embedded in the person of the verb *(am dat drumu', mă duc, am făcut, etc.)* (I dropped, I go, I did, etc.), which obviously point to the general emotive orientation of the narrator's utterances.

Along with expressing a certain attitude towards her personal experience and giving voice to her emotions, the storyteller projects a positive image of herself, at times even at the expense of others. The basic strategy underlying the speaker's construction of her own portrait is *positioning of self and others*. Thus, the first step the teller takes in building her identity is to assign opposing clear-cut roles to the characters in her story by considering the similarities and differences between them: the active self versus the passive others. The speaker's *agentive self* is emphasized in an apparently objective manner, through the words of others and through her own actions. The speaker is portrayed as courageous (she is not afraid of the dark) by means of a directive speech act, a request, in line 11 *('mă Elena ((râde)) du-te tu ((râde))că ție nu ți-e frică')* ('you Helen ((laughs)) you go ((laughs)) cause you're not afraid') and by an utterance which implies that she is the opposite of the others who are given a negative characterization *('dacă ne duceam noi ori lăsam punga acolo ori')* ('if we had gone there we would have either left the bag there or') in line 46. She is also shown to be a sociable person, since she does not hesitate to communicate with a stranger whose language she can neither speak, nor understand – this is rendered by means of an expressive speech act – line 31 *('și io când l-am văzut zic 'aoleo ce m-ai speriat'')* ('and when I saw him I say oh my you scared me'), a question – line 32 *('l-am întrebat că 'ce cauți'')* ('I asked him what are you looking for') and directive speech acts, namely requests – lines 35 *('zic ',vino-ncoace'' ')* ('I say come here'), 59 *('i-am spus "stai aici (0.1) așteaptă-mă"')* ('I told him stay here wait for me') – and 62 *('eu i-am spus "stai un pic aici"')* ('I told him stay here for a moment'). The storyteller is also presented as sympathetic and generous *('vai °rău mi s-a făcut °')* ('God I got sick') – line 34 *('ce pomană ai făcut')* ('how good of you') – line 46, *('opriți numai câte o bucată de pâine și să-i dăm la amărâtu' ăsta')* ('keep only one slice of bread and let us give the rest to this poor thing') – line 41, *('oprim cât să luăm dimineață o gură așa')* ('we'll just save some for a bite in the morning') – line 50 and also modest *('vai Doamne ferește (0.2) mergi cu Dumnezeu')* ('oh Lord go with God') – line 66.

Besides the predominantly emotive function of the present story, we can also identify the *phatic* function as a secondary communicative purpose. The present story is also told for social reasons, which imply creating a sense of communion with the addressee – *the phatic function* of the narrative is hereby activated. In this sense, the speaker uses positive politeness strategies as a kind of social accelerator, indicating that she wants to establish *common ground with the addressee* (Brown and Levinson, 1987:103). One strategy used by the speaker is to *intensify the interest of* her own *contributions to the conversation to the hearer*, by 'making a good story'. This is done by *switching back and forth between past and present tenses* – as in lines 19, 21, 22, 30-37 –, the use of the *'vivid present'* having the role of pulling the hearer right into the middle of the events being discussed, increasing the immediacy and the interest of the story. The use of *directly quoted speech* – lines 7, 9-11, 19, 31-32, 35, 37, 39-40, 46, 50, 59-62, 66, 71 – is another feature of this strategy. The token tag *'ştii cum'* ('you know') in line 63 is also utilized to establish agreement and common ground with the recipient and to encourage the hearer, P, to follow the emotional trend of the story. A related technique is to exaggerate facts, to *overstate*. The exaggeration is a speaker's attempt to increase the interest of the conversational contributions by expressing them dramatically. The following expressions referring to the narrator's unusual experience and to the dreadful condition of the man she met (*'niciodată'* ('never') – lines 44 and 68 – *'în viaţa mea'* ('never') – line 54 –,*piele şi os'*, *'un schelet'* ('skin and bones', 'a skeleton') – line 28 *'piele şi oase'* ('skin and bones') – line 55) are a case in point. Another strategy used by the speaker to claim common ground with the hearer is through the use of *in-group identity markers:* in line 54 E uses an *address form*, namely the addressee's first name (*'Petre'*) to claim solidarity.

Another problem we will discuss in connection with the interpersonal function is the use of *topics* as revealing for the storyteller's socio-cultural identity, for his/her relationship with the interlocutors and for the the context/cotext of occurrence of a particular narrative. Our research has revealed that the informants in the corpus we collected talked about a large variety of **topics.** These topics make up a large inventory, illustrating events and experiences from all the stages of a human being's life. The topics we identified range from *unique events* in one's life: life stories, baptisms, weddings, funerals to *trivial, daily matters*, such as: food/cooking, clothes, buying things, sports/games, traffic, weather, women, from *private issues*, like children and family, jobs, school, foreign language acquisition, driving (tests/classes), dreams, pe(s)ts, travel accounts/visits, incidents/accidents to *matters of general interest*, as for instance, people: mentalities/habits, customs and traditions, religion, health system/medical interventions/illness, films, books, discoveries, politics (Iordache, 2009a:316).

In our opinion, a challenging aspect is the potential relation between the topic tackled by the speakers in their conversational narratives and the following factors:

a). the narrator's socio-cultural identity

b). the recipient's identity and the narrator's relationship with the recipient

c). the context/cotext of occurrence of a narrative

a). *The narrators' socio-cultural identity*

The topic chosen by a speaker in his narrative is inherently something that he/she experienced either directly (he lived/witnessed the event) or indirectly (something he/she heard from someone else). A speaker cannot recount something he has not got knowledge of. At this point we will take into account the variables related to the speakers' *social and marital status*, as well as the *educational background*. Presuppositions related to the relevance of the speakers' identity (age, sex/gender) in selecting a certain topic will be also made. In the Romanian culture there are stereotypes which argue that women and men tend to favour different topics and that young and old people have few things in common (Hornoiu, 2008).

b). *The recipient's identity and the narrator's relationship with the recipient*

When choosing a certain topic, the narrator has to take into account who he/she is addressing and to be considerate to the recipient's knowledge and interests (Polanyi (1985:200) apud Lambrou (2003:157)) or, in Sacks et al.' terms (1974:727), 'the talk by a party in a conversation is constructed or designed in ways which display an orientation and sensitivity to the particular other(s) who are the co-participants'. The teller's relationship with the interlocutor, including the degree of intimacy between them, is a decisive factor in the narrator's choice of a certain topic. Brown & Levinson's (1987) variables of *social distance*, *power* and *rank of imposition* will be taken into account when discussing the selection of a topic when taking into account the relationship between the speaker and the recipient.

c). *The context/cotext of occurrence of a narrative*

The presence in the environment of a certain object or person is likely to trigger a story related to that respective object/person or related to an item of the same kind. Likewise, a certain detail in the conversation or in a previous story is likely to entail a story on the same or on a topic similar with the previous one.

In what follows we will discuss the factors that determined the storytellers' selection of a certain topic and exemplify them in several fragments of conversational narratives that were found relevant for the present research. Special attention will be given to *the age, gender, and level of education variables*, which mark the conversational behaviour of the speakers, as attested in the literature (Hornoiu, 2008). The same variables have been found to influence the act of storytelling, as well. First, we will deal with the *age variable* as a relevant factor for topic selection.

Empirical evidence with respect to the **adults'** and **teenagers'** conversational styles comes from Hornoiu (2008). According to her data, 'as the informants reach adulthood, the percentage of *slang terms* falls significantly by fifty percent'. However, the data indicate the **adults'** predilection for *collaboratively built sentences*, which prove the recipient's ability of guessing the speaker's intention and show the conversational partners' solidarity and affiliation to the same group. The frequency of *softeners* and *compliments* in Romanian women's communal style is also indicative of the adults' adherence to their interlocutors' point of view.

On the contrary, with respect to the **teenagers'** conversational style it has been found out that it abounds in *slang terms*, which are a marker of age, rather than gender, as, according to Hornoiu's (2008) research, 'none of the *slang terms* encountered in adults' conversational style is unknown to teenagers'. Stenström et al. (2005:590) speak of "slanguage", which is extremely frequent in the teenagers' conversations. They distinguish 'slang', which is restricted to the lexicon, from 'slangy language' or 'slanguage', which refers to a style of speech that includes, beside slang, other characteristic features, as for instance various subclasses of discourse markers. The main categories of "slanguage" identified by the researchers are: '(a) proper slang, (b) dirty words, (c) vogue words, (d) vague words, (e) proxy words[67] (i.e., quotative markers), (f) small words (i.e., hedges, emphasizers, and tags)'.

The use of slang terms, along with that of *address forms,* is indicative of claiming in-group membership and shared attitudes and aim at forming emotional bonds. The occurrence of *overlapping talk* in conversations among teenagers (in the form of assessing comments and interrogatives) is not regarded as disruptive but, on the contrary, as a means of getting involved in the ongoing topic (Hornoiu, 2008).

Girls' talk (unlike women's talk) is often characterized by frequent displays of 'playful confrontation', which is expressed through name-calls, insult exchanges and teasing episodes and linguistically realized by means of lexical repetition and (partial) syntactic mirroring (Coates (1998) and

---

[67] For further information on this matters, see Stenström et al. (2005:590).

Boxer & Cortes-Conde (1997) apud Ardington (2006:92-93)). These playful practices signal affiliation, group membership, and also 'highlight the need to come to terms with individual preferences' (Heath (1998:231) apud Ardington (2006:92-93)).

With respect to the topics tackled by the teenagers in the English corpus in the literature we examined, it was revealed that in the following participant frameworks: all-teenager talk, school talk and family talk, the teenagers' favourite topics were: network talk, romance (with subsections according to sex), sex talk, partying and drinking, hobbies, 'bad' things, race relations, and the school (Stenström et al., 2005:590). As for the topics tackled by the Romanian teenagers, one may conclude that the topics found in the English corpus also apply for the Romanian corpus. However, the Romanian teenagers have been found to be also preoccupied with journeys, jobs and future perspectives.

Fragments (31) and (32) below point out that the *age variable* is a relevant factor for topic selection.

Fragment (31) shows that the topic of *funerals* is selected by an old person.

(31) La crematoriu/ Getting cremated
1 T: *mie no:: io am zis că nu vreau (0.2) să mă înmormânteze=*
    as for myself I said I didn't want to be buried
2   *=oi fi păcătoasă=*
    I might be a sinner
3   *=m-o bate Dumnezeu m-o (0.2) ce mi-o face*
    God may punish me or something
4   *da' nu vreau să mă mănânce viermii ((râde)) în pământ (0.3) nu vreau*
    but I don't want to be eaten by worms ((laughs)) in the ground I don't want that
5 I: *păi şi ce vreți? să=*
    and what do you want to
6 T: *=da:: la crematoriu ( )*
    yes to be cremated
7 I: *păi da' nu vă face slujba religioasă*
    well they won't hold the religious service there
8 T: *ba se face şi-acolo*
    yes they will
9 I: *cică numai ateii se î::*
    they said that only the atheist get cre-
10 T: *pot şi de-ăştia (0.3) nu ştiu cum (0.3) răspopiți răspo (0.2) nu ştiu cum nu răspopiți altfel*
    others can do it as well what are they calledunfrocked priests I can't tell not unfrocked priests or something else
11 *(0.5) nu ştiu ce-o fi o fi*
    I don't know what will be will be
12 *să-mi facă slujba-acasă (0.2) de-nmormântare*
    let them do the funeral service at home
13 *să-mi facă toate alea*
    to take care of everything
14 *şi-apoi să mă ducă la crematoriu dacă nu se poate să–mi facă slujba acolo*
    and then to take me to the crematorium if they cannot hold the service there

15 I: (   ) ((râde))
         ((laughs))
16 T: NU SUPORT GÂNDU' SĂ MĂ BAGE ÎN PĂMÂNT ACOLO (0.2) și ei să plece-acasă știi?
      I can't bear the thought of being placed in the ground and them going home you know
17   și să mă lase pe mine-acolo să mă mănânce viermii
      and leaving me there to be eaten by worms
((I și N râd))
((I and N laugh))
18   nu suport gândul ăsta (0.2)
      I can't bear the thought
19   mi-e *imposibil*
      I really can't
20 I: [
21 T:[și eu când ( ) PE-AI MEI ACOLO ÎMI VINE SĂ SAP PĂMÂNTUL ȘI SĂ-I SCOT
       and I when ( ) my family there I feel like digging in the ground and taking them out
22 I: da' ce vreți să vă ia cenușa acasă sau cum?
      then what do you want your family to take your ashes home or what
23 T: °s-o du::că° Simona are obligația
      Simona is bound to take them
24 I: ((râde))
      ((laughs))
25 T: s-o ducă pe digu'
      to take them to the dam
26 N: ((râde))
      ((laughs))
27 T: de la *Eforie* (0.2) Nord parcă și s-o împrăștie în mare
      in Eforie Nord I think and spread them into the sea
28   e un dig lu::ng până în mijlocu' mare-așa
      there's a long dam reaching the middle of the sea you know
29 I: ea ce zice despre asta? e de acord?=
      and what does she say about this does she agree
30 T: =da e de acord
      yes she does
31   "treaba ta ce (vrei)"
      do as you wish

The narrator of the story in the excerpt above, T, is female, aged 65, and married. She has retired, but she was a technician before that. The recipients of the story are two females, mother and daughter, both married, one aged 55, the other 29, one has retired (she was a technician before retiring) and the other is a teacher by profession. The narrator is the younger recipient's neighbour.

The topic of the story – *funerals* – is triggered by several factors. One of them is the narrator's identity: T is an old woman and old people are supposed to be more preoccupied with death and funeral preparations than young people. The story in the present fragment is characterised by the absence of slang terms in the old narrator's speech. In the excerpt above, line 5, by using a collaboratively built sentence, I proves her ability to read her interlocutor's mind, anticipating T's desire to get cremated, as confirmed by T in the following line. The absence of softeners is indicative of the speakers' preference for 'asserting their individuality within the group rather than aligning with their interlocutor's point of view' (Hornoiu, 2008). In the present excerpt, the narrator is doing just that: asserting her individuality within the group, as she sets her narrative in opposition with the preceding talk (which was about a traditional funeral) and shocks her interlocutors by asserting that she does not want to be buried but implies that she intends to be cremated instead, a statement that she will explicitly reiterate in line 6 ("*=da:: la crematoriu*").

The narrator's asymmetrical relationship with her interlocutor also influences topic selection: the social conventions and the rank of imposition between the two interlocutors (old/young) require that the narrator should tackle a decent, not a very intimate topic. The cotext also influences the selection of the present topic, as the story being narrated is an *entailed story*, which builds on a detail in the conversation, namely on the word 'funeral', as earlier in the conversation the interlocutors talked about a funeral which N was to attend the next day.

Fragment (32) shows that the topic of *conflicts* is selected by a teenager.

(32) Conflicte/Conflicts
1A: *dar a zis că el a avut noroc că a prins tineri din ăştia ştii?*
    but he said he was lucky to come across young people like that you know?
2B: *îhî*
    yeah
3A: *ori eu am avut numai babalâci*
    as for myself I only came across hags
4B: ((*râde*))
    ((laughs))
5A: *o persoană o femeie mai bătrână (0.3)*
    a person an old lady
6   **am sunat** *o dată nici* **nu am ştiut** *dacă* **a sunat** *sau nu ştii?*
    I rang once I wasn't even sure if it rang or not you know?
7B: °*îhî*°
    yeah
8A: **am văzut** *că* **s-a uitat** *aşa un pic pe vizor şi* **am sunat** *a doua oară*
    I saw she peeped out the peephole and I rang once more
9   *când a doua oară* **iese** *nervoasă 'mă da' ce* **insistaţi** *atâta* **mi-aţi trezit** *şi copilu' nesimţiţilor'*
    and the second time she gets out angrily why are you insisting so much you've even awaken my child you shameless rascals
10 *mai să te* **ia** *la bătaie*
    almost ready to beat you up
11 *când* **am văzut** *'tuo:: doamnă gata ho:'*
    when I saw that ok ma'm ok
12B: ((*râde*))
    ((laughs))
13A: *'da' °mă° scuzaţi'*
    yeah excuse me
14B: ((*râde*))
    ((laughs))
15A: *nu (0.1) sunt <u>foar</u>te (0.2) da' ştii parcă parcă le-ai cere bani aşa nu ştiu*
    no they're very well you know as if you asked them for money I don't know

The topic of the present narrative – *conflicts* – is triggered by several factors. One of them is the narrator's identity: A is a teenager and a male and it is expected that boys should be accustomed to topics such as fights and conflicts, all the more so that it is well known that there is a generation gap between teenagers and old people or even adults.

In telling his story, A uses linguistic items that are characteristic of the language adopted by teenagers: pejorative words *('babalâci')* – line3, proxy words (i.e., quotative markers) *('tuo:: doamnă gata ho:')* – line 11, *('da' ° mă ° scuzaţi')* – line 13 and vague words *('aşa un pic')* – line 8.

The narrator's symmetrical relationship with her interlocutor also influences topic selection: the lack of social distance and rank of imposition between the two interlocutors

allows the narrator to tackle any topic. The cotext also influences the selection of the present topic, as the story being narrated is an *entailed story*, which was built on a conversational sequence dealing with jobs, and in particular, with the role played by chance in being successful in one's job.

Another finding of this study reveals that the *gender* variable influences topic selection in conversational narratives.

Males are expected to be preoccupied with certain topics, among which sports, and especially football, holds a privileged place. Hornoiu (2008) notes that men's predilection for the so-called 'neutral' topics in conversation, such as sports, politics, cars, which relate to *the public world*, is 'a means of distancing themselves from their emotions and private issues proving thus that they can rise above their instinctual nature'.

At the opposite end, females' 'concern with *the private realm* and preference for topics, such as child rearing, relationships, husbands' infidelity may be related to the so-called 'emotional' part of their identity since it involves a considerable amount of self-disclosure and shared feelings'. What is more, there is a stereotype according to which women 'gossip' or 'chatter' over *trivial* matters (Hornoiu, 2008).

Men's and women's linguistic choices are seen as "communicative strategies". As "rational actors", people use linguistic structures to achieve social goals in specific circumstances (Brown (1980:113) apud Kendall and Tannen (2001:551)). In Tannen (1990) apud Kendall and Tannen's (2001:553) view, speakers 'must find a balance between seeking connection and negotiating relative status'. However, it has been found that women focus more on the connection dimension (intimacy), whereas men are more likely to focus on the status dimension (independence).

In the discourse and gender literature, men have been shown to exert control of conversation through various strategies, such as disruptive overlapping talk, securing a greater number of turns, silencing their conversational partners, etc. and to make use of verbal aggressiveness (including shouting, name-calling, insults, challenges, counter-challenges, teasing) in order to develop and strengthen their ideas (Hornoiu, 2008); (Tannen (1998:196) apud Kendall & Tannen (2001:553)). Moreover, it has been pointed out that men are likely to 'cast themselves in the role of hero in narratives about danger and violence' ((Coates, 1995); (Johnstone, 1993); (Eggins & Slade, 1997) apud Lambrou (2003:171)) and to take up the role of expertise or authority in conversation, very often engaging in monologues (which may be quite extensive) on subjects in which they claim to be experts ((Coates, 1997a); (Tannen, 1990) apud Kendall & Tannen (2001:555)).

On the other hand, **women**'s speech abounds in strategies meant to keep the flow of the conversation going (e.g., backchannel signals, completion of the other's turn, repetition, small talk, etc.), as women tend to focus on *building and maintaining a relationship*. In using backchannel signals or minimal responses (such as '*uh huh*'), the speaker displays her understanding that an extended turn is underway and shows her intention of passing the opportunity to take a turn at talk, thus *facilitating* the continuation of the respective turn (Hornoiu, 2008). It has been revealed that women are likely to recount personal stories about 'embarrassing or humiliating experiences where humour is more likely to be present as a device to regain a loss of face, so laughter is encouraged in the group' (Coates, 1995); (Eggins & Slade, 1997); Johnstone, 1993) apud Lambrou (2003:171)).

Fragments (33) and (34) below reveal that the *gender variable* is a relevant factor for topic selection.

Fragment (33) shows that the topic of *sports* is selected by a male.

<u>(33) Meci de fotbal/</u>Football match
1B: **Pleşan** *când l-a luat Dinamo de la Craiova era jucătoru' lu' Craiova*
    when Dinamo took Pleşan from Craiova he was Craiova's player
2   *ţinea echipa-n spate*
    he was the leader of the team
3P: *ţii minte când a plecat (0.2) de la U Craio:va?=*
    do you recall when he left U Craio:va
→4B: = **ţin minte şi-acuma** *c-am fost la meciu' cu Cluju'*
    I still recall that I went to the match against Cluj
5   *de conducea Cluju' cu doi-zero la pauză*
    Cluj led two-nil at the break
6   *şi i-a bătut cu trei-doi*
    and they beat them three-two
7   *ce-a făcut?*
    what did he do
8   *a dat două goluri*
    he scored two goals
9   *unu' cu capu' unu' din lovitură liberă şi-o pasă de gol (0.2) (   )*

       one by head from a free kick and a goal pass
10R: *băi Bog[dane*
       say what Bogdan
11B: *[şi-am înjurat de mi-a venit dracii*
              and I swore like a sailor
12R: (   )
13B: *da (0.1) da' traba e că dup-aia a ajuns la Dinamo şi s-a lăsat*
       yeah but the thing is that after that he went to Dinamo and he grew lazy

The narrator of the story in the excerpt above, B, is male, aged 35, married and an officer by profession. The recipients are two males, among whom one is an officer, aged 34 and divorced and one a civilian, a researcher, aged 30 and married. The narrator and his interlocutors are workmates and the 34-year-old officer is the others' boss. The conversation took place at the interlocutors' workplace, during a coffee break.

The topic of the story – *sports/games* – is triggered by several factors. One of them is the narrator's identity: B is a male and males are expected to be preoccupied with sports, especially football. In the present fragment, the male narrator, B, manages to impose himself in front of his interlocutors and hold the floor by talking across several turns – lines 4-9. His taking over the control of the conversation also manifests itself through disruptive overlapping talk – lines 10-11, as he cuts in his superior's challenging intervention in line 10 and silences him. Moreover, line 11, which refers to his swearing during the match, denotes verbal aggressiveness.

The narrator's relationship with his interlocutors is another factor that influences topic selection: the relationship between the interlocutors is asymmetrical, as there is power and rank of imposition between the interlocutors. Therefore, a neutral subject, such as football, is appropriate, taking into account the narrator's relationship with his interlocutors.

The context also influences the selection of the present topic, as the present report is an entailed narrative, being triggered by a detail in the earlier talk, as the interlocutors discussed the football matches in the Romanian championship.

Fragment (34) below shows that the topic of *cooking* is selected by a female.

(34) *Supa de găină*/Chicken soup
1T: *găina asta-i atâta de bătrână (0.3)*
       this chicken is so old
2   *nu ştiu cât timp o să-i trebuiască să se fiarbă*
       I don't know how long it will take to boil
3   *da' aşa se zice (0.2) că găina bătrână face zeama bună*
       but there's an old saying that the old chicken makes good broth
4 I: *îhî*

       yeah
5 T: *io a: am o poveste mori de râs*=
       I've got a story you're going to roar with laughter
6   =*am o*=
       I've got a
7   =*o colegă de-a mea fostă ingineră chimistă*
       a colleague of mine a former chemist engineer
8 I: *da*
       yes
9 T: *a primit o găină de-acasă de la părinții ei de la țară*
       got a chicken from her parents who lived in the country
10   *și fiind tânără căsătorită*=
       and being newly wed
11 I: =*nu știa să gătească*
       she couldn't cook
12 T: *nu știa să gătească*
       she couldn't cook
13   *da' nu numa' că nu știa să gătească (0.3)*
       and not only couldn't she cook
14   *era găina ciupilită da' mațele erau înăuntru*
       the chicken was deplumed but its entrails were inside
15 I: *a:*
       oh
16 T: *în ea și ea a luat-o*=
       and she took it
17 I:= *și a băgat-o direct*
       and she put it directly
18 T: *a băgat-o direct în apă și a fiert-o*
       she put it directly into the water and boiled it
19   *a văzut ea la maică-sa că așa se face*
       she had watched her mother doing it this way
20   *se pune găina înăuntru în apă și se lasă la fiert*
       you put the chicken in the water and leave it to boil
21   *a: (0.3) când a intrat în bucătărie tot simțea că miroase urât miroase urât*
       oh when she entered the kitchen she sensed an ugly smell that kept coming back
22   "*da' de ce oare miroase așa de urât?*"
       why on earth does it smell so bad
23   *nu și-a dat seama din ce cauză*
       she didn't realise why
24 I: *și?*
       and then what
25 T: *până când a venit soacră-sa și*
       until her mother-in-law came and
26 I: *a: ce nasol ((râde)) chiar soacră-sa*
       oh how awful is that ((laughs)) her very mother-in-law
27 T: *a venit soacră-sa și (0.3)*
       her mother-in-law came and
28   "*a:::: păi tu ce-ai făcut ?*
       oh my what have you done
29   *ai băgat găina cu mațe cu tot aicia să fiarbă o::*"
       oh you put the chicken entrails and all in here to boil
30   *ea săraca crăpa de rușine*
       she was dying of shame poor thing
31   *nu mai știa ce să mai facă*
       she didn't know what to do next
32 I: *și ce-a făcut cu ea pân' la urmă ?*
       and what did she do with it in the end

33   *a aruncat-o?*
     did she throw it away
34 T: *a cred c-au aruncat zeama aia (0.3)*
     oh I think they threw that broth away
35   *ce să mai facă nu mai putea s-o mănânce*
     what could she do about it she couldn't eat it anymore

The narrator of the story in the excerpt above, T, is female, aged 55, and married. She has retired, but she was a technician before that. The recipient of the story is a female, aged 29, married and a teacher by profession. The narrator is the recipient's mother.

The topic of the story – *food/cooking* – is triggered by several factors. One of them is the narrator's identity, as F is a woman and women are supposed to be more preoccupied with domestic activities, such as cooking, for instance, than men.

The narrator's asymmetrical relationship with her interlocutor also influences topic selection: the mother – daughter relationship is more permissive, therefore the rank of imposition between the two diminishes and the narrator can tackle a trivial topic, such as cooking, without risking that such a topic should threaten her positive face. In the present fragment, the two female speakers, T and I, manage to *keep their relationship going* by keeping the conversation flowing through backchannel signals – lines 4, 8, 46 –, completion of the other's turn – lines 11, 17 and repetition – lines 12, 18, 27, 41.

The context is also a decisive factor for the narrator's selection of the present story's topic (the story is *an environmentally cued narrative*): the presence of chicken meat in the local environment triggers in the narrator's mind an amusing story related to a chicken soup which was cooked by a former workmate of hers.

All in all, it may be concluded that the selection of topics characterize both genders in conversational and narrative discourses.

The *education* variable was also found to influence topic selection in conversational narratives.

In the case of Romanian, Iordan (1954) apud Ciolac (1999:215) identified two variants of the spoken language, which are selected by the speakers according to the content of the talk or to the speakers' knowledge, according to the circumstances in which the conversation takes place and the speakers' psychological state. These variants of the spoken language are: 'the academic language' and 'the familiar language'. The academic language is specific to the educated people's professional fields and it is utilized whenever the content of the talk is a scientific one. The familiar variant of the language is a simpler, more natural language, which abounds in expressive words and which is used by speakers when talking to their family and friends. The familiar language or the informal register is used by both educated and uneducated people, with the difference that each category speaks, in terms of lexical items and grammar, according to its own socio-cultural status. For instance, the familiar language used by uneducated speakers is characterized by particular features, such as: a set of vocabulary which is rather poor in terms of its component linguistic items and wrong or inappropriate agreement and forms. The data in our corpus verifies the findings of Ciolac (1999) and adds to the already mentioned features of the familiar language the frequent use of slang and swearing or the use of obscene words (especially in the case of men).

In the English literature, Stenström et al. (2005:591) identified a set of non-standard grammatical features, such as multiple negation ('ain't'), negative concord and pronominal forms, which are specific to the people from the lower class (Stenström et al., 2005:591).

As to the education variable on the Romanian speakers' choice of topics, the present corpus is a living proof of the difference between educated (formal) and uneducated (informal) language, topic selection being also influenced by this difference.

Fragments (35) and (36) below point out that *the education variable* is a relevant factor for topic selection.

Fragment (35) shows that the topic of *unsuccessful procedures* is selected by an educated person.

(35)Manevre nereușite/ Unsuccesful procedures
1C: *deci cum îți spuneam am avut și: manevre nereușite*
    well as I was telling you I also had a few unsuccessful procedures
2L: *° da °*
    yeah
3C: *dar am avut noroc cu colegii de pe secție*
    but luckily the colleagues in our ward were there for me
4   *care mi-au dat o mână de ajutor*
    and gave me a helping hand
5   *nu neaparat să facă ei manevra: respectivă da:r au (0.2) ă*
    not in the sense that they perform the respective procedure but they
6   *colindat prin spital și au făcut rost de instrumentele necesare*
    searched through the hospital and they got the necessary instruments
7   *ca să pot să fac (.) manevra*
    so as I could perform the procedure
8L: *îhî*
    yeah
9C: *am avut spre exemplu un pacient (0.1) de numai patruzeci de ani*
    for example I had a patient who was only forty years old
10L: *da*
    yes
11C: *cu spondilită anxilopoetică*
    with ankylosing spondilitis

12 este o <u>boală</u>: ă în care coloana vertebrală: ă devine rigidă
    it's an illness in which the spine becomes rigid
13 prin faptul că se sudează corpurile vertebrale între ele
    because the vertebral bodies join
14L: îhî
    yeah
15C: și acest pacient avea coloana <u>cervicală</u> flectată maxim
    and this patient had his cervical spine extremely flexed
16L: îhî
    yeah
17C: în consecință și pacientul a fost adus de familie în comă
    as a result the patient was brought by his family in a coma
18L: da
    yes
19C: orice (.) comă conform unei clasificări a noastre din medicină
    any coma according to a classification of ours in medicine
20 dacă are mai puțin de opt puncte în urma examenului neurologic care se face
    if it has less than eight points as a result of the neurologic examination
21L: da
    yes
22C: trebuie intubat ca să îi protejăm co- ă: calea aeriană
    must undergo intubation so as to have the airway patency protected
23L: îhî
    yeah
24C: pentru că un pacient în comă poate să verse
    cause a patient who is in a coma may throw up
25 poate sa aibe regurgitație gastrică
    he/she may have gastric regurgitation
26L: îhî
    yeah
27C: care să fie aspirată plus o serie de alte lucruri
    which needs to be sucked plus a couple of other things
28 și d'aia ca să îi proteje:::zi calea aeriană trebuie obligatoriu intubat
    and that's why in order to protect his/her airway patency he/she must undergo intubation
29 în consecință acest pacient adus în comă trebuia intubat
    as a result this patient who was brought in a coma had to undergo intubation
30 problema era că: <u>nu</u> reușeam să vedem absolut nimic în gâtul lui
    the problem was that we couldn't see anything inside his throat
31L: da
    yes
32C: nu reușeam să-i vedem orificiul traheal (0.1) pentru faptul că
    we couldn't see his tracheal orifice because
33 nu puteam să îi: facem niciun pic de extensie a <u>ca</u>pului
    we couldn't perform an extension of his head at all
34L: îhî
    yeah
35C: din cauza acelei coloane cervicale rigide
    because of that rigid cervical spine of his
36L: da
    yes
37C: am încercat inclusiv să-l intubăm nazotraheal
    we even tried to perform naso-tracheal intubation
38 nici <u>așa</u> nu ne-a ieșit manevra (0.2)
    the procedure didn't succeed this way either
39 ne gândeam că nu am mai avea decât o singură so<u>luție</u>
    we thought we had only one solution left
40 să îi facem crico-tiroidotomie

```
                to perform crico-thyroidectomy
41L: da
        yes
42C: da și să îi vârâm pe aici la nivelul membranei crico-tiroidiene un tub
        and to insert a tube at the level of the crico-thyroid membrane
43      ca să putem să îi asigurăm cât de cât calea aeriană
        so as to assure his airway patency somehow
44L: da
        yes
45C: nici eu nici un alt coleg de-al meu cu care eram de gardă
        neither I nor any of my colleagues with whom I was on that shift
46      nu mai făcusem aceasta manevră niciodată
        had ever performed this procedure
47L: îhî
        yeah
48C: exista riscul să îi tai artera tiroidiană: să aibă o hemoragie cataclismică
        I was running the risk of cutting his thyroid artery and thus to provoke a massive hemorrhage
50L: da
        yes
51C: deci ce să facem?
        so what was to be done
52L: da
        yes
53C: ce să alegi?
        what to choose
54L: da
        yes
55C: am luat legatura cu terapia intensi::vă unde ă: la noi pe terapie intensivă
        we contacted the intensive care unit where in our intensive care unit
56      se fac frecvent se pun frecvent traheostome și
        they frequently perform tracheostomies and
57L: îhî
        yeah
58C: nu era nicio problema pentru niciunul din medicii ateiști[68]=
        this posed no problem for either of the anesthetists
59L:=da
        yes
60C: le-am solicitat ajutorul măcar să stea langă noi
        we asked for their help or at least to attend us
61      și să ne învețe cum: să facem
        and teach us how to do it
62L: da
        yes
```

The narrator of the story in the above fragment, C, is female, aged 33 and single. She is a physician by profession and she works in a hospital, at the emergency section. The recipient of the story is female, aged 31, married and a teacher by profession. The two have been friends for five years.

The topic of the story, unsuccessful maneuvers, is triggered by several factors. One of them is the narrator's identity, in which the *education* variable plays an important role: being a doctor, that is, an educated person, C uses a large number of specific medical terms in talking about a dramatic experience

---

[68] This lexical item is a Romanian medical jargon, designating the anesthetists.

in her professional life – lines 11, 15, 32, 37, 40, 42, 48, 55, 56, 58 ('*spondilită anxilopoetica*', ,*coloana cervicală flectată*', ,*orificiul traheal*', ,*să-l intubăm nazotraheal*', ,*crico-tiroidotomie*', '*la nivelul membranei crico-tiroidiene*', ,*artera tiroidiană*', ,*hemoragie cataclismică*', ,*terapie intensivă*', ,*traheostome*', ,*medicii ateiști*') ('ankylosing spondilitis', 'cervical spine flexed', 'tracheal orifice', 'to perform naso-tracheal intubation', 'cricothyroidectomy', 'at the level of the crico-thyroid membrane', 'thyroid artery', 'massive hemorrhage', 'the intensive care', 'tracheostomies', 'anesthetists'). The style she adopts is not academic, but informal, familiar, as, in recounting her experience, C has in mind the circumstances in which the conversation takes place: the familiar setting, her interlocutor's identity and her relationship with her conversational partner, L, which is symmetrical, so there is no social distance, power or rank of imposition between the two interlocutors. Although being C's friend, L is not a specialist in the medical field. This is why the narrator often suspends the story to explain a set of medical terms and procedures – lines 11-13 ('*cu spondilită anxilopoetica/ este o boală: ă în care coloana vertebrală: ă devine rigidă/ prin faptul că se sudează corpurile vertebrale între ele*') ('with ankylosing spondilitis/ it's an illness in which the spine becomes rigid/ because the vertebral bodies join'), 19-20, 22, 24-25, 27-28 ('*orice comă conform unei clasificări a noastre din medicină/ dacă are mai puțin de opt puncte în urma examenului neurologic care se face/ trebuie intubat ca să îi protejăm ă: calea aeriană/ pentru că un pacient în comă poate să verse/ poate sa aibe regurgitație gastrică/ care să fie aspirată plus o serie de alte lucruri/ și d'aia ca să îi protejε::zi calea aeriană trebuie obligatoriu intubat*') ('any coma according to a classification of ours in medicine/if it has less than eight points as a result of the neurologic examination/must undergo intubation so as to have the airway patency protected/cause a patient who is in a coma may throw up/he/she may have gastric regurgitation/which needs to be sucked plus a couple of other things/and that's why in order to protect his airway patency he/she must undergo intubation'). Also, from time to time, C uses informal words, such as *('au (0.2) ă colindat prin spital', 'să îi vârâm')* ('they searched through the hospital', 'to insert') – lines 5-6, 42– to have the recipient feel 'at home' with the recounted event, which otherwise abounds in specialized terms, which are obviously new and often uncomprehensible to a non-specialist.

Last but not least, the cotext also influences the speaker's selection of the present topics, as the topic of unsuccessful manoeuvres smoothly follows a conversation on a similar topic, namely that of the serious cases a doctor has to treat in the emergency section.

Fragment (36) below shows that the topic of *women* is selected by an uneducated person.

(36) Femei/Women

1V: *vine într-o zi- două p'acolo (   )*
    he drops by that place one or two days later
2   *mă uitam așa la una*
    I was gazing at a woman
3   *patruzeci și ceva de ani arăta*
    she looked forty and something
4   *nu-i dădeai mai mult de treizeci*
    but you wouldn't say she was more than thirty
5   *zic "no bună mi-ar fi mie o dată una"*
    I say 'I'd really like a woman like this one one day'
6   *io (0.1) știi (0.2)?*
    I you know
7M: *da*
    yeah
8   *"crezi că aia se uită la tine când te vede așa slab"?*
    do you think that girl will take a shine to you when she sees you're so skinny
9   *"nu vreau să te jignesc" zice "da' (nu se uită ea la tine) când te vede așa slab"*
    I don't mean to offend you he says but she won't take a shine to you when she sees
    you're so skinny
10 *pă zic "bă: da' la aia (p____ă) -i trebe sau (p____ă)"? (0.2)*
    and I say does she need (   ) or (   )
11M: *da corect (0.2) corect*
     yeah right right
12V: *da zice (0.1) "nu vreau să te jignesc da' nu se uită aia la tine"*
     yeah he says I don't mean to offend you but she won't look at you
13M: *sau în unele cazuri bani sau de cele mai multe ori ((râde))*
     or money in some or in most cases ((laughs))
14V: *de cele mai multe ori*
     in most cases

The narrator of the story in the excerpt above, V, is male, aged 45, and divorced. He is a worker by profession. The recipient of the story is female, aged 45, divorced as well, who has retired, but who worked as a shop-assistant before that. The two have been neighbours for 20 years.

The topic of the story – *women* – is triggered by several factors. One of them is the narrator's identity: V is a middle-aged man and men are expected to be interested in women. The topic he is tackling and, especially his way of speaking, denotes his lower education. First of all, he is unable to express his message accurately. Thus, the statement he makes in line 3, namely that the woman who constitutes the object of his interest looked as if she were 40 years old *('patruzeci și ceva de ani arăta')* (she looked forty and something) is utterly contradicted in the following line, as what he actually asserts is that the respective woman looked at least ten years younger *('nu-i dădeai mai mult de treizeci')* ('but you wouldn't say she was more than thirty'). Next, he obsessively repeats the offense he took – line 8 (*',crezi că aia se uită la tine când te vede așa slab"?)* ("do you think that girl will take a shine to you when she sees you're so skinny") in lines 9 (' *'nu vreau să te jignesc" zice "da' (nu se uită ea la tine) când te vede așa slab"')* ("I don't mean to offend you he says but she won't take a shine to you when she sees you're so skinny") and 12 (*',da zice (0.1) "nu vreau să te jignesc da' nu se uită aia la tine"*) ("yeah he says I don't mean to offend you but she won't look at you") – only with a slight change. Furthermore, not only does V use obscene words when challenged by another male in the story he is narrating, which is a sign of weakness, but he also repeats them to his female interlocutor ad litteram, without even bothering to paraphrase them so that their salacious and insulting nature would wear off.

Another factor is the narrator's relationship with his interlocutor, which is symmetrical, so there is no social distance, power, or rank of imposition between the two.

Therefore any topic, no matter how trivial, can be tackled among people of the same age who have known each other for a lifetime. The cotext is also a decisive factor for the narrator's selection of the topic of the present narrative: the present report is an entailed narrative, as it builds on a detail in the previous conversation, namely on the proper noun 'Mihai', which was mentioned earlier by the speaker and which also designates one of the characters in the present report.

To sum up, our research confirms the fact that the data in our Romanian corpus of conversational narratives verify the hypotheses advanced on the three variables characterizing any speaker's socio-cultural identity: age, sex/gender, and level of education.

The next function of stories in conversation we will put forth is the *persuasive* function.

3.4.2 The persuasive function

The *persuasive*[69] *function* of language covered by Halliday & Hasan's interpersonal function goes back to Jakobson's *conative* function (1987 [1960]), which focuses on the addressee and finds its linguistic expression in the *vocative* (e.g., Tom!), the *imperative* (e.g., Go away!), the *pronominal and/or verbal second person* and the *exclamatory intonation* (Jakobson, 1987:67-68); (Săftoiu, 2007:10); (Dominte, 2003). This function was shown to enable the speaker to determine the addressee to do something by issuing orders, giving advice or making suggestions, conative utterances presupposing not only the presence of a recipient but also reactions (linguistic ones included) on his/her part (Vachek, 2003:51).

Currently, the persuasive or argumentative function of language has been studied in detail in the *pragma-dialectical theory*[70] – an argumentation theory developed by Frans H. van Eemeren and Rob

---

[69] See also Kinneavy (1971).
[70] This theory is also called *pragma-dialectics*.

Grootendorst (1984, 1992, 2004) for the analysis and evaluation of argumentation in actual discourse. Pragma-dialectics[71] defines standpoints and argumentation as (complex) speech acts that are 'characterized by the commitments assumed by the speaker when performing a speech act' (van Eemeren, 2002).

A reference point of any argumentative dispute is the ***ideal model of a critical discussion*** put forward by pragma-dialecticians. This model represents a system of norms permitting the resolution of differences of opinion holding between reasonable disputants by means of a regulated exchange of speech acts (Cosoreci-Mazilu, 2010:18). In accordance with this model, a dispute comprises four ***stages of discussion***: the *confrontation stage*, the *opening stage*, the *argumentation stage* and the *concluding stage)* (van Eemeren and Grootendorst 1992:35); (van Eemeren, 2002); (Cosoreci-Mazilu, 2010:19); (Sălăvăstru, 2003:396-397). Although in actual argumentative discourse participants do not usually go through the four stages of the ideal model in the order mentioned above, they are bound to comply, either explicitly or implicitly, with the stipulations made in each stage in order to resolve their differences of opinion. In the *confrontation stage* one party ('the protagonist') presents a standpoint which is doubted or contradicted by another party ('the antagonist'). In the *opening stage* the disputants determine the common starting point of the discussion. Next, in the *argumentation stage*, the protagonist advances argumentation to defend his/her standpoint against the criticisms put forward by the antagonist. Finally, in the *concluding stage* the parties consider if their difference of opinion has been resolved and if so, in whose favour: if, following the argumentative exchange, the antagonist comes to accept the protagonist's standpoint, the latter wins, whereas if the protagonist withdraws his/her standpoint as a result of the antagonist's criticism, the latter is the winner.

The ideal model of a critical discussion is extremely useful in analyzing and evaluating disputes, since it provides a list of *speech acts* which can lead to resolving the difference of opinion holding between the disputants (van Eemeren and Grootendorst, 1984 apud Cosoreci-Mazilu, 2010:20). Among the five types of speech acts advanced by Searle (1979), four (*assertives, directives, commissives, declaratives*) have been found relevant to a critical discussion. Thus, *assertives* are used by speakers to convey standpoints, to advance argumentation in favor of or against a standpoint, to make statements, suppositions or claims and to draw a conclusion. *Directives* – requesting, prohibiting, forbidding, recommending, begging and challenging – are usually used by disputants to challenge the opponent to

---

[71] It draws on pragmatic elements put forward by 'ordinary language philosophers', such as Austin (1962), Searle (1969, 1979) and Grice (1975), as well as on the work of critical rationalists, such as Crawshay-Williams (1957), Popper (1972, 1974) and Barth and Krabbe (1982). For more details on the matter see van Eemeren (2002); Cosoreci-Mazilu (2010).

defend a standpoint, to request argumentation and clarification. Orders and threats are not favoured in a critical discussion, since their use might impede the resolution of the dispute. *Commissives* – promising, accepting, agreeing – are used by speakers to accept (or not) a standpoint, to agree on premises and starting points, to decide to start a discussion. *Usage declaratives* – a subtype of declaratives, comprising definitions, precizations, explanations or specifications – are utilized with the purpose of clarifying how a particular speech act is to be interpreted. They can be used in any stages of a critical discussion, contributing to resolving the difference of opinions. *Expressives* – congratulations, condolences, and expressions of joy, disappointment, anger, or regret – convey a speaker's attitude and feelings towards a particular event or state of affairs and are not relevant to the resolution of a dispute. Nevertheless, they may be considered as indirect speech acts through which primary speech acts are expressed (van Eemeren and Grootendorst, 1992:37-40); (Cosoreci-Mazilu, 2010:20); (Sălăvăstru, 2003:396-397).

In this section we turn to stories whose main function is persuasive or argumentative, related to Jakobson's conative function. Firstly, we will discuss a subtype of the persuasive function which we have identified in our Romanian corpus of narratives-in-interaction, namely illustrating a point one is advocating in the conversation.

Illustrating a point one is advocating in the conversation

Stories may also function as *rhetorical tools* for making a point or a claim. This is the case of narratives which are concrete representations of the speaker's claim and are meant to persuade the hearers of the validity of the speaker's assertion by providing clear evidence that supports his/her point (Bamberg, 2004a:357-358). This is an efficient way for the speakers to prove themselves right and gain a certain status within the group (Ochs, 1997:187-188).

The narrative in the excerpt below was introduced by the speaker in the conversation with an argumentative function: the intention of persuading the recipient that the point she is advocating is valid.

(37) *Examene auto picate*/Failed driving tests
( )1C: *măi Ali Alina ((râde)) când am auzi:t (0.1)*
    Ali Alina ((laughs)) when I heard (0.1)
2A: *ce ? ((râde))*
    what ((laughs))
3C: *ce-ai făcu:t (0.2)*
    what you did
4A: *ce ((râde)) ce chestia asta ?*

          what ((laughs)) this thing
5C: *da*
          yes
6A: *eh lasă c-am auzit mai rău=*
          oh I've heard something worse
7C: *=da hai zii*
          have you come on tell me
8 A: *o prietenă de-a mea era să dea peste unu' la trecerea de pietoni (0.3)*
          a friend of mine nearly hit a man on the zebra crossing
9   *și p'ormă a intrat în refugiu'din stația de tramvai*
          and then she hit the waiting shed at the tram stop
10 C: *cu polițistu' în mașină?*
          the policeman inside and all
11 A: *da (0.2) a intrat și i-a zdrobit roata la mașină*
          yes she hit it and crushed the car's wheel
12 C: *deci un prieten de-a lu' frate-[miu']*
          well a friend of my brother's
13 A:*[deci mai] bine-așa ca mine cel puțin=*
          whereas I at least
14 C: *=a dat peste-un polițist (0.5)*
          hit a policeman

The above conversational fragment is a *dispute*, since the two interlocutors, A and C, have a difference of opinion with respect to speaker A's failing her driving test.

The claim A makes by means of an assertive speech act in line 6 (" *'eh lasă c-am auzit mai rău=*") ('oh I've heard something worse') that her performance in the driving test, which resulted in failure, was not as bad as others', casts doubt on C's previous statetement, advancing another standpoint: that her failure was decent and far from blunder. This exchange of turns between the two interlocutors expressing contradictory viewpoints concerning a particular aspect of A's life occurs in the *confrontation stage* of the dispute. C's agreement to listen to A's arguments in defense of her own standpoint – line 7 (*',=da hai zii"*) ('have you come on tell me') marks the *opening stage* of the dispute between the two participants to the conversational interaction. The argumentation A advances in support of her standpoint takes the form of a narrative, a brief report, to be exact. This concise narrative, realised by assertive speech acts, tells of a protagonist's practically catastrophic mistake and technically consists of three errors: hitting a man on the zebra crossing, entering a safety island, and crushing the car's wheel – lines 8-9 and 11. This illustration of a serious blunder occurs in the *argumentation stage* of the discussion and is clear evidence supporting A's standpoint – line 6 (*'eh lasă c-am auzit mai rău'*) ('oh I've heard something worse') and justifying her claim of superiority. A's storytelling also constitutes *a face-saving act,* a remedial work directed toward her own positive face. Her failure experience constitutes a licence for her passing judgements on others' failure and asserting her superiority over others, as is illustrated by her evaluative utterances in lines 6 (*'eh lasă c-am auzit mai rău'*) ('oh I've heard something worse') and 13 (*'deci mai bine-așa ca mine cel puțin'*) ('whereas I at least').

Finally, the dispute between the two parties is resolved implicitly in the *concluding stage* of the discussion. C's assertive act – lines 12 and 14, which tells of another tremendous blunder, suggests that she has accepted her interlocutor's standpoint and agrees with A by acknowledging her superior driving and therefore softening the threat to A's positive face. A's argumentation thus proves an efficient way for the speaker to prove herself right and gain a certain status within the group.

The secondary function performed by the above narrative in conversation is *the emotive function*. The emotive function is meant to convey the storyteller's superior attitude towards the events presented in the narrative. This becomes most obvious with the speaker's use of evaluative predicates in lines 6 (*'am auzit mai rău'*) ('I've heard something worse') and 13 (*'mai bine-așa'*) ('whereas I at least').

We will now examine another subtype of the persuasive function performed by conversational narratives through *justifying, explaining or accounting for one's actions (or those of others)*.

Justifying, explaining or accounting for one's actions (or those of others)

The literature on conversational narratives has revealed that narratives may function as *accounts* when storytellers recount past events with the primary goal of defending their conduct. In this case, the teller is in position of offering explanations, whereas the recipient holds a less active role in interaction. Among the various perspectives on accounting, two deserve our attention. Firstly, accounting is 'strongly related to remediating social wrongs, especially as this activity relates to matters of face preservation' (cf. Goffman, 1967). Secondly, accounts are meant to provide an explanation of everyday activities without focussing on remediating social wrongs (Buttny (1993) apud Mandelbaum (2003:617).

Next, we will consider an excerpt in which the given narrative functions in conversational interaction as *accounting for the teller's actions* and is meant to persuade the listener to accept the explanations and justifications provided by the speaker.

(38)Vizită anulată/ Cancelled visit
1M: *rămăsese să vin joi la tine (0.1) știi?*
    I was going to come to your place on Thursday you know
2L: *îhî*
    yeah
3M: *măi și parcă joi (0.1) că spusesem io că trec pe la tine=*

```
           I think it was on Thursday cause I said I was going to drop by
4L:    =  da  da da
          yes yes yes
5M:   şi mama copilului "hai da' nu rămâi ?
          and the child's mother come on won't you stay
6     ce faci azi : d'auzi n-ai putea să rămâi până (0.1) toată zIUA ?"
         what are you doing today couldn't you stay until all day long
7     îţi spun toată ziua '=
         I'm telling you all day long
8L:   =îhî
         yeah
9 M: "că uite să ieşim în parc" sau să nu ştiu ce
         cause we'll go out in the park or something
10    " da hai că rămân toată ziua"=
          yes ok I'll stay all day long
11L:  = îhî
         yeah
12M:  deci am rămas toată ziua (0.2)
         so I stayed all day long
13    m-am închis acolo pe (0.2) nu ştiu ce
         I locked myself up in there and stuff
14    după care a doua zi (0.1) iarăşi "auzi da' ce faci azi" ?
         after which the next day again  listen what are you doing today
15    ((râde)) vineri cre' că era asta
         ((laughs)) on Friday I think it was
16L:  d'ai dormit acolo?=
         did you sleep there
17 M:="n-ai putea să rămâi toată ziua ?"
          couldn't you stay all day long
18    deci asta era vineri şi zic
          I mean that was on Friday and I say
19    "n-aş putea că vreau să mă duc şi eu pe la o prietenă că (0.1) o să fie ziua ei şi na na na
         I couldn't cause I want to go toy a friend of mine cause it'll be her birthday and blah blah blah
20    " bine atuncea da' (0.1) vii la cinci (0.1) şi "da' să vii la cinci "
         ok then but be here by five and make sure you'll be here by five
21    a::(0.2) stau io  şi mă gândesc că până ajung acasă şi să vin la Laura că n-am niciun timp
         uhm I stand and ponder that there's no time to get home and come to Laura's
22    în două ore să vin la Laura să mă duc să mă-ntorc nu se poate=
         coming to Laura's going coming back is impossible in two hours' time
23L:  = da da da
         yes yes yes
24M:  deci era două şi la cinci trebuia să vin ce: în trei ore da' n-ai timp
          so it was two o'clock and by five I had to come back wha:t in three hours you don't have time
25L:  nu
         no
26M:  da' n-ai timp clar
         definitely there's no time
27    numai două ore faci pe drum şi (0.1) nu (0.2) e o prostie
         it takes you two hours only to get there and no it's silly
```

The narrative in the fragment above has been introduced in the conversational interaction with the purpose of accounting for one's actions. The purpose for which the narrator, M, introduces her narrative as an account for her action is to remediate a social wrong, namely having failed to pay a visit to the listener, as promised. The arguments supporting her case revolve around two main reasons: the unexpected request of her employer to stay after hours – lines 5-6, 14, 17, 20 – and the large distance to her friend's place as compared to her brief break – lines 21-22, 24, 26-27. Since the act of apologising may constitute a face threat directed to the speaker's own positive face, M makes sure to provide the appropriate arguments to persuade her interlocutor that she was not to blame for what happened, thus redressing her positive face.

The present narrative also performs a secondary function which supports the dominant, persuasive one: *the emotive function*. Speaker M indicates her revolting attitude toward the events she is presenting by means of expressive features, such as the use of emphatic speech – line 6 *('zIUA')('day')*, the utilisation of the evaluative predicate *('e o prostie')* ('it's silly') – line 27 and of the evaluative adverb *('clar')* ('definitely') – line 26. Finally, the storyteller presents an exaggeration of the facts by means of specific linguistic units, such as the quantifiers 'toată (ziua)' ('all day long') – lines 6, 7, 10, 12, 17 – and 'niciun (timp)' ('no time') in line 21. Last but not least, the abundance of the use of the first person personal pronouns, conveyed both explicitly – lines 3, 21 *(io)* (I) and 19 *(eu)* (I) – and embedded in the person of the verb (*să vin, spusesem, trec, spun, rămân, am rămas, m-am închis, n-aș putea, vreau, să mă duc, să mă-ntorc* (come, said, drop, say, stay, I stayed, I locked myself up, I couldn't, I want, to go, coming back) is a proof of the general emotive contour of the teller's utterances.

Next, we will deal with the phatic function of conversational narratives as overruling the other, secondary functions.

3.4.3 The phatic function

The *phatic* function, related to Halliday & Hasan's interpersonal function, focusses on the channel of communication and has the role of establishing and maintaining contact between conversational partners (Jakobson, 1987:68-69). This language function has its roots in the term *phatic communion* – a term coined by social anthropologist Malinowski (1923) to acknowledge the role of language in creating unity and establishing human bonds: "[...] a type of speech in which ties of union are created by a mere exchange of words" – (Malinowski, 1923:478 apud Padilla Cruz, 2005:228)); (Dinneen, 1995:317); (Nöth, 1990:187); (Coupland et al., 1992:208); (Coupland, 2000:2). This was quite a revolutionary idea, since, at the time, it was thought that communication primarily served the purpose of expressing meaning *(referential (cognitive/denotative) function* in Jakobson's terms) (Malinowski, 1972 apud

Coupland, 2000:2); (Malinowski, 1960 [1923] apud Gellner, 1998:148); (Dinneen, ibid.). This social function, which emphasises *language as a mode of action*, is considered in fact to be the primitive function of language (Malinowski, 1960 [1923] apud Gellner, 1998:147-148). Jakobson adopted the term 'phatic' in his model of verbal communication and emphasized the role of language in establishing, prolonging, or interrupting communication to check if the channel works ('Hello, do you hear me?') or to see if the listener pays attention to the ongoing talk ('Are you listening?') (Jakobson, 1980:84); (Nöth, ibid.). In post-Malinowskian studies, 'phatic communion' gained a negative evaluation, being considered phony, dull and semantically empty (Wolfson, 1981; Leech, 1974; Turner, 1973 apud Coupland, 2000:3).

Among the most prominent 'phaticisms'[72] we would mention greetings, questions about the interlocutors' health, well-being, family, remarks on commonplace, even trivial topics, such as the weather, tellings about apparently irrelevant events and even uninteresting, aimless talk (Padilla Cruz, 2005:228); (Coupland, 2000:3). The basic reasons for which conversationalists use phatic language are: avoiding silence, which could lead to an unpleasant tension between the interlocutors and negatively influence social interaction (Padilla Cruz, 2005:228) and creating a sense of solidarity, involvement and social well-being among interlocutors (Lyons (1968:417); (van Dijk, 1975:286); Hudson (1980:109); Silva (1980) apud Padilla Cruz (2005:229); (Coupland, 2000:3).

A very important issue with respect to the phatic function of language is how to account for the *phatic interpretation* of utterances. Two directions have been proposed in this sense: some researchers consider as phatic those utterances which occur *in specific conversational phases* (especially at the beginning or at the end of conversational interactions) (Padilla Cruz, 2005:229-230); (Coupland, 2000:5). Others believe that an utterance is phatic depending on the interlocutor *activating* and processing *particular mental structures* (Padilla Cruz, 2005:229-230). With respect to the first case mentioned above, it is noteworthy that phatic communion is conveyed by a series of linguistic sequences (e.g., greetings, questions and answers), usually arranged in *adjacency pairs,* which are frozen pairs characterized by little variability and high predictability (Hoey, 1991 apud Padilla Cruz, 2005:230). The interlocutor's selection of the *preferred* element of the adjacency pair favours the interpretation of such utterances as phatic, i.e. as oriented toward the relational aspect of communication (as in example (a.) below), whereas the use of a *dispreffered* element triggers the interpretation that the utterance was not understood as phatic (as in example (b.) below) (Padilla Cruz, 2005:230):

---

[72] Phaticisms are utterances and fragments of discourse aimed at avoiding silence and establishing/keeping contact with the interlocutor (Padilla Cruz, 2005:229).

(a.) A: How are you doing?
    B: Fine, thanks.

(b.) A: How are you doing?
    B: Well, I've got a terrible headache today and my legs ...

With respect to spoken Romanian, previous research has shown that the most frequent phaticisms used by the speaker to attract the listener's attention are: substitutes of the second person personal pronoun you ('mă', 'măi', 'bă', 'bre'); nominal appellatives, which are often semantically empty ('dom(nu)le') ('mister'); syntagms made up of pronouns + nouns ('măi frate') ('bro') or nominal syntagms ('mama dracu(lui)') ('the devil'); frozen verbs with a pragmatic use ('uite', 'știi', 'să știți') ('look', 'you know'); deictics ('iată', 'iacă') ('look'); complex forms ('măi uite-acuma') ('look here now'). Along with the above-mentioned phaticisms, there are also certain frozen questions ('așa că vin și te întreb' ('so I ask you'), 'ce-mi spui?' ('what do you think'), 'acuma ce să vezi?' ('what do you think happened'), 'ce-a făcut?' ('what did he do') aimed at raising the audience's interest (Pop, 2006:26).

We will now go on by considering one of the most pervasive phatic subfunctions of stories in talk-in-interaction: *entertaining the audience*.

Entertaining the audience

As we have shown earlier, all researchers admit that entertaining the audience is a function of conversational narratives, although some claim that this function is always subordinate to some other functions. However, when the storytelling's purpose appears to be solely that of entertainment, and the storyteller does not intend to perform another practical activity by means of storytelling (e.g., complaining, accounting, etc.), on most occasions the storyteller's undertaking goes beyond entertaining. Entertaining constitutes just a plea the speaker uses to establish or maintain social relationship with his/her interlocutors (Constantinescu, 2007:175). This is often accomplished by means of positive politeness strategies, which are oriented toward solidarity and affiliation through establishing common ground (Brown and Levinson, 1987). Moreover, laughter may be used in the interactive construction of intimacy (Jefferson, Sacks, and Schegloff, 1987) and collaborative or 'joint' joking (cf. Davies, 1984) is often 'the ultimate locus of conversational involvement' (Davies, 2003:1362).

Norrick (2003:1339) classifies the various forms of *conversational humour* (jokes, puns, personal anecdotes and irony), enlarging our perspective of the differences and similarities holding among these categories in terms of humor mechanisms, their internal structure, and integration into discourse. In point of humor mechanisms, jokes, puns, and irony differ, since *jokes* end in a punchline, which complies with the relevance maxim but violates the graded informativeness condition, as it determines the recipient to switch the first, unmarked interpretation with the subsequent second, marked interpretation. *Puns* violate both the relevance and the graded informativeness requirements, forcing the recipient to look for a second, unmarked interpretation. *Irony* is in accordance with the relevance maxim but violates the graded informativeness condition, thus forcing the recipient to look for a marked interpretation that represents the negation of what has been asserted. *Personal anecdotes* are similar to jokes, with the difference that the proposition (or the propositions) which violate(s) the graded informativeness requirement do(es) not necessarily end the text: personal anecdotes elicit laughter by means of several humorous propositions, unlike jokes, which end in a humorous line. Personal anecdotes represent true reports of the speaker's funny experiences and they usually open with a preface, such as 'the funniest thing happened to me' or 'I remember when I was five or six', whereas jokes deal with caricatures or types of people (i.e. 'this traveling salesman' or 'this guy') and are introduced through prefaces, like 'have you heard the one about . . . ?' Personal anecdotes are relevant to the surrounding conversation, as they offer new information about the narrator and encourage active participation from recipients, whereas jokes are 'disconnected from surrounding conversation', as the information about a fictional character becomes irrelevant when the joke has come to an end, and limit the listeners' involvement through laughter at key points. Stories told about mutual acquaintances are set midway between narrative jokes and personal anecdotes. As opposed to jokes and personal anecdotes, which are clearly delimited from turn-to-turn talk by being introduced through story openers, punning is unannounced and is therefore disruptive of topical conversation, violating the relevance maxim.

Conversational humour is meant to stir laughter. Among the various linguistic strategies used by the speaker to elicit laughter from the interlocutor, we consider *constructed dialogue* and *repetition*[73] to be especially noteworthy, since both devices are essential in persuading the recipient to adopt the speaker's attitude towards the recounted events, thus avoiding disagreement between conversational parties (Hornoiu, 2008:146).

Our empirical study has revealed that stories told for apparently entertainment purposes are usually funny, personal experiences, which abound in details (these, joined by the recipient like in a

---

[73] For more details concerning constructed dialogue and repetition, see chapter 2 of the present paper.

puzzle game, make up the picture of the amusing situation) or secondhand stories taking a shorter, anecdotal form. Both the above-mentioned types of conversational narratives present characters that find themselves in unusual, humorous situations, the storyteller's role consisting in seeking to provoke laughter in the co-participants to the conversation, thus achieving to create a cheerful atmosphere, favourable to establishing contact with his/her interlocutors.

The following excerpt is an example of a story meant to entertain the audience:

(39) Cascheta/The cap

8 A: *hai să-ți mai povestesc ceva ((râde))*
let me tell you another story ((laughs))

9 *mi-a povestit-o profu' de franceză că eram io foarte necăjită că n-am luat examenu'*
the French teacher told it to me cause I was very upset for not having passed my driving test

10 =*zice "da' din ce cauză?"*
he asks why not

11 *'a mi-e și rușine am plecat cu frâna trasă'*
oh I'm so ashamed I drove with the brake on

12 *a zice "lasă că-ți spun ce-a făcut o prietenă"*
oh he says don't worry I'll tell you what a friend did

13 *cică prietena fiicei lui tot așa a dat examenu' și a pornit cu frâna trasă (0.5)*
it appears that his daughter's friend also took the test and drove with the brake on

14 *și a pornit mașina îți dai seama*
and the car started imagine that

15 *s-a oprit brusc așa știi cum e te hățână puțin*
it stopped suddenly you know what it's like it shakes you a bit

16 *și polițistu' avea cascheta ((râde)) din aia pe cap și ((râde)) i-a zburat cascheta*
and the policeman had his cap ((laughs)) on and ((laughs)) his cap flew away

17 *asta a vrut să-i prindă cascheta ((râde)) și i-a tras o palmă ((râde)) (0.3)*
she wanted to catch his cap and ((laughs)) she slapped him ((laughs))

18 *și cascheta a ieșit pe geam ((râde)) că era geamu' deschis ((râde)) (0.5)*
and the cap got out of the window ((laughs)) cause the window was open ((laughs))

19 *și a trecut o mașină ((râde)) (0.5)*
and a car ran it over ((laughs))

20 C: *((râde))*
((laughs))

21 A: *și i-a făcut praf cascheta ((râde)) (0.5)*
and crushed his cap ((laughs))

22 C: *((râde))*
((laughs))

23 A: *și ea s-a panicat și ăla a zis că (0.3) dacă mai dă cu (0.2) el în veci n-o să mai ia carnetu'*
and she panicked and the chap said that if she takes her test with him again she won't pass it ever

24 *"afară"*
get out

25 C: *și ăla săracu' n-avea simțu' umorului*
the poor chap didn't have a sense of humour

26 A: *da' îți dai seama hai mă că parcă-i din film îți imaginezi toată faza asta=*
fancy that come on this whole thing is like taken out of a picture

27 *îi **pică** cascheta*
his cap falls off

28 *așa în zbor ea **încearcă** s-o prindă*
she tries to catch it while it's still in the air

29 *îi **trage**-o palmă ((râde))*
    she slaps him ((laughs))
30 *cascheta **se duce** pe geam ((râde)) și **trece**-o mașină ((râde))(0.5)*
    the cap falls out of the window ((laughs)) and a car runs it over ((laughs))(0.5)

The fragment above relates a comical situation, meant to provoke laughter in the participants to the conversation and thereby amuse the audience with the main purpose of creating intimacy and maintaining the social relationship between the narrator and her interlocutor.

The present story comes from a second-hand source and takes a shorter, anecdotal form: the comical situation does not concern the narrator but a total stranger (the story was told to A by one of her colleagues, as a consolation to the situation she was in after failing her driving test – line 9). The present narrative-in-interaction presents characters that find themselves in unusual, humorous situations: the protagonist of the comical happenings in lines 13-24 is a friend's of A's colleague's daughter who, during her driving test, starts the car with its brake on. As a result of this, the car stops, the policeman's cap flies out of the car's open window and is run over by another car. Meanwhile, in an attempt to catch the policeman's cap, the girl slaps him on the face. She then panics and the angry policeman promises her she will never pass her driving test, if he is to examine her again. The present anecdote contains several humorous propositions intended to elicit laughter – lines 16-19 and 21 –; thus differing crucially from jokes, which characteristically aim at a single response (preferably laughter) precisely at their conclusion.

By means of the humorous situations presented in the narrative, the storyteller, A, seeks to provoke laughter in her conversational partner, thus creating a cheerful atmosphere and constructing intimacy between the interlocutors. Thus, the repetition of the key-word ('cascheta') ('the cap') – lines 16-18, 21, 27, 30 – goes hand in hand with the brief instance of constructed dialogue ('afară'), representing the climax of the story in order to provoke laughter, which constitutes evidence that the recipient is indeed entertained by the comical events presented in the story. Involvement with the recipient is also sought by *claiming common ground* with the addressee (Brown and Levinson, 1987:103-124). This is achieved through a series of positive politeness strategies. One of them is the use of *in-group identity markers:* A's use of *address forms* – namely the lexical item, '*mă*' – line 26. Another strategy of claiming solidarity with the hearer is through the use of expressions that draw the hearer as a participant into the conversation, also known as token tags, (such as '*îți dai seama*' ('imagine/fancy') – lines 14 and 26 –, *'știi cum e'* ('you know what it's like') – line 15 – and *'îți imaginezi'* ('fancy that') – line 26, which claim the hearer's knowledge of that kind of situation in general and not of the particular details which the speaker refers to in the story). The speaker's use of proximal, rather than distal demonstratives ('here, this', rather than 'there, that'), where either of them would be acceptable, seems to convey increased involvement or empathy. The use of 'this' (instead of 'that') when referring to the protagonist of the story and to the comical situation presented in the anecdote – lines 17 and 26 – is a case in point. The use of the 'vivid present' when recapitulating the sequence of events just presented in the anecdote – lines 27-30 –, a tense shift from past to present tense, represents another positive politeness device which functions to increase the immediacy and therefore the interest of the recounted story.

In addition to the phatic function, the story is also *persuasive*, since it can be regarded as an argument, a strategy used by an able storyteller with a view to convincing her interlocutor that her own mistake was infinitely smaller as compared to the protagonist's blunder in the recounted story. On this occasion, the narrator uses the story to build a positive public image for herself to the detriment of the main character in the narrative. Thus, her own error is played down, whereas that of the main character in the story she is telling is insisted upon at length and described in minute details – lines 13-19, 21 and 23-24.

Next, we will consider another aspect of the phatic function performed by a narrative in conversational interaction: gossip.

Gossip

It has been generally acknowledged that the boundaries between the various types of talk are not clear-cut. With respect to labeling *gossip*, two main directions have been identified by the researchers in the field of conversational interactions. Some scholars consider that *gossip* is a component of the wider class of *small talk*, which also comprises various other forms of talk, like *chat* and *time-out talk* (Coupland, 2000:1), whereas others refer to *gossip* as a rough equivalent of the term *small talk* (Coates, 2000; Jaworski, 2000). In the latter case, nevertheless, several terminological clarifications have been made. Thus, the term *gossip* basically points to 'sequences of talk about certain types of interpersonal relationships or events', whereas *small talk* is usually associated with conversational openings and closings, which comprise 'greetings, self-introductions, recollections of previous meetings, expressions of concern for members of the addressee's family, etc.'. However, there are instances in which the two social activities above overlap: thus, gossip during a coffee break may be a form of small talk, whereas enquiring about the health of one's family at the beginning of a conversation may count as a form of gossip, as it is talk about relationships (Jaworski, 2000:111-112). In reviewing several studies on gossip, Jaworski & Coupland (2005:668) point out that there is a negative side to it, as the latter is associated with *highly critical talk about absent third parties* and is even regarded as immoral (cf. Bergmann (1993) apud Mandelbaum (2003:620)). A surprising aspect, however, is represented by the claim that there is also a positive side to gossip: talking about others is seen as "humanizing", in that 'it is part of our experience of *building relationships, sharing with others*, and ultimately becoming and being human', or, in other words, gossiping creates bonds between people engaged in such activities, representing an important component of social life (Malinowski, 1972 apud Coupland, 2000:2), (Bergmann (1993) apud Mandelbaum (2003:620)). In the present paper, we will be using the term *gossip* in the sense defined by Jaworski & Coupland (2005) as 'talk about people and their personal lives that involves some kind of newsworthy element and some form of (usually) pejorative evaluation'.

Gossip as a form of talk has been shown to evince a set of prerequisite features: a). both conversational partners (gossipers) need to be familiar with the subject of gossip; b). the main character (or 'the gossipee' in Jaworski & Coupland's (2005) terms) is not present at the ongoing talk between gossipers or gossip participants; c.) he/she performs actions directed toward someone else; d). the actions performed can be considered offenses; e). the hearer is the recipient of the offenses (this last feature is characteristic for instigating gossip stories); e). the gossipers strengthen their social relationship but engage in a tacit conflict with the gossippee (Harness Goodwin, 1982:804); (Bergmann (1993) apud Mandelbaum (2003:620)); (Coupland & Jaworski, 2003:86), whom they portray as ' the other' (Dedaić, 2005:673).

Regarding the functions performed by gossip sequences in turn-by-turn talk, it is worth noting that two metafunctions were identified in the literature, as follows: the phatic and the referential functions. The *phatic* function relates to the fact that gossip establishes rapport between conversationalists and reinforces group-solidarity (Coupland, 2000:2); (Besnier, 1989) by means of emphasizing the common ground between gossipers (i.e. common concerns, common attitudes) (Brown & Levinson, 1987:118), as well as sanctions morally problematic behaviour (Bergmann (1993) apud Mandelbaum (2003:620)). The *referential* function points to the role of gossip in conveying information and establishing norms of acceptable moral conduct in a community (Jaworski, 2000:114); (Jaworski & Coupland, 2005); (Dunbar, 1996:7). Besides acknowledging the contribution of gossip in strengthening group cohesion, Besnier (1989) and Jaworski & Coupland (2005) also touch upon a less exploited aspect, namely that gossip may serve as a tool for forging for oneself a positive public image at the expense of others (the gossipees), whose actions, opinions and beliefs are criticized in their absence (Dedaić, 2005:680). This relates in our opinion to the *emotive* function of language.

One linguistic strategy often used by gossipers for discrediting an absent third[74] party is *irony*. By using ironic utterances, speakers engage upon the task of attacking the gossipee by implicitly denying what they state (Kotthoff, 2003:1390). As an indirect speech act, the mechanism of irony relies on the background information shared by interactants (Hutcheon, 2005:94). In this sense, the hearer is expected to perceive the ironic utterance as a violation of Grice's quality maxim and arrive at the offensive meaning of the utterance indirectly, by means of conversational implicature (Leech, 1983: 82). Using irony is therefore advantageous for the speaker, in that he/she can perform a face threatening act (FTA) (e.g., a criticism) by means of an off-the-record strategy, whose social goal is avoiding responsibility (Dedaić, 2005:681); (Culpeper et al., 2003:1553).

The narrative in excerpt below was introduced into the conversation with the purpose of maintaining the social relationship between the two participants to the conversation, by means of gossiping.

*(40) Savantul/*The scholar
1P: *ce mai face sonache*
    how is loony
2A: *ă: ce să facă*
    uhm well
3   *uite mâine mă duc pă la el (0.1) că: (0.2)*
    well I'm going to see him tomorrow because
4   *deși:: (0.2) m-a: (0.2) m-a angajat acum câteva luni*
    though he hired me a few months ago
5   *totuși ă: (0.3) și-a dat seama că: nu sunt atât de bun precum se aștepta el*
    however he realised I was not as good as he had expected
6   *și-a căutat oameni specialiști și serioși*
    he looked for specialists and serious people
7   *nu ca mine (0.1) care: (0.1) lucrez cu (0.2) ă: respectând toate standardele (0.2) de protecție*
    not like me who: I work uhm observing all protection standards
8   *pentru că (0.1) în comparație cu mine acei specialiști la care el apelează*
    because as compared to me those specialists whom he calls on
9   *fac (0.1) lucruri miNOre ca de exemplu umblă cu sânge contaminat*
    do minor things such as for instance handle contaminated blood
10 *și pe urmă pune mâna pe clanță (.) de trebuiesc de trebuiesc dezinfectate toate clanțele (0.3) lucruri=*
    and then touch the door handle so that all door handles need disinfection
11P: *=specialiști în concepția lui=*
    specialists in his opinon
12A: *=da lu- lucruri din acestea mărunte îți dai seama care nu: nu:*
    yes minor things like this you do realise which are not not
13 *trebuiesc trecute cu vederea*

---

[74] For other linguistic strategies concerning the negative evaluation of a third party, see Ionescu Ruxăndoiu (2010:65-68).

they must be overlooked

14 așa ceva mai ales că se pot dacă se întâmplă să iei o hepatită
   something like this especially if one happens to catch hepatitis
15 asta-i u::n flecuștet acolo ce MAre lucru
   this is a mere trifle no big deal
16 nu nu trebuie să ne supărăm
   we mustn't make a fuss
17 eu sunt neserios [dacă]
   I am unserious if
18P: [( )]
19A: dacă respect ă: dacă respect toate standardele
    if I observe uhm if I observe all standards
20 e și: ă mă duc mâine
   well and uhm I'm going tomorrow
21 probabil a nu știu câta oară o să-mi spună că (.) m-a concediat
   he will probably tell me for the umpteenth time that he has fired me
22 și-o să-i spun „domn profesor este un șoc pentru mine dacă că am aflat chestia asta" (0.3)
   and I will tell him Professor it is a shock for me to find this out
23 ca și când eu n-aș ști ce de ce-i în stare (0.2)
   as if I didn't know what he could do
24 da și (0.2) ă (0.2) iar și-a luat și jumate di:n ă (0.2) statul de plată
   yes and uhm he once again took half of the payroll
25 adică vreo (0.3) trei mii de lei pe lună ăh ((oftează))
   that is about three thousand lei a month ((sighs))
26P: a înfășcat partea leului
    he grabbed the lion's share
27A: da iar celorlalți nu vrea să le dea: (0.1) nimica
    yes and he will not give anything to the others
28 pentru că nu mai bine bine numai cui vrea el (0.5) [pentru că]
   because no it's better to give only to whom he wants because
29P: [aha aha]
                                                     I see
30A: secretarei lui îi dă (0.1) îi dă bani deci nu: nu e o problemă
    he gives money to his secretary I mean that's no problem
31 numai altora dacă se poate să lucreze pe gratis și cu materialele lor
   only to others if they can work for free and with their own materials
32 și să facă și descoperiri ar fi ok
   and to make discoveries as well that would be ok
33P: da așa sunt unii oameni numai ( ) numai
    yes some people are like that only for only
34A: da ce să facem asta este
    yes what can we do that's the way things are
35 eu o să-i spun de acum încolo
   I will tell him that from now on
36 dacă vrea să mă plătească foarte bine
   if he wants to pay me very well
37 nu am nimic împotrivă dar în condițiile mele (0.2)
   I have nothing against it but on my terms
38 deci fără: cu stai să vezi că de fapt nu e și e și (0.2)
   I mean without wait and see that in fact there is not and there is and
39 îmi vrea bine nu:
   if he agrees ok if not
40P: acuma așa se obișnuiește să muncești pe gratis
    now it's customary to work for free
41A: ă: da pentru unii dar: el dacă era om de știință
    uhm yes for some but he if he was a scientist
42 și într-adevăr savant cum se: (0.2) cum se consideră a fi

  and a real scholar as he claims to be
43 *trebuia să dea și celorlalți chiar dacă nu dă atât de mult*
  he should have given to the others too even if it isn't much
44 *dar măcar puținul ăla pe care îl dă să-l dea constant*
  and that small sum he gives he should at least give it constantly
45 *cum să spun chiar dacă era nimic*
  how should I put it even if it weren't much
46 *că-i nimic (0.2) acea sumă (0.1) sub (.)*
  because that sum is nothing (it's) under
47 *undeva sub salariul minim pe economie se află suma respectivă*
  the respective sum is somewhere under the minimum wage
48 P: *se crede darul lui Dumnezeu pe pământ*
  he thinks of himself as God's gift on earth
49 A: *ă da: ă: (0.1) un fel nu: se crede foarte specialist în ceea ce face*
  uhm yes in a way no he thinks of himself as a real specialist in what he does
50 *deși: descoperirile lui nu se (0.2) ă nu (0.1)*
  although his discoveries aren't uhm don't
51 *nu au ă: (0.1) rezonanță internațională ca să zic așa*
  don't have high international visibility so to speak
52 *sunt doar niște faze incipiente doar*
  are only incipient phases only
53 P: *în primul rând nu au finalizare*
  first of all they have no finality
54 *uite unde era Einstein de Dâmbovița*
  look where the Einstein of Dâmbovița was
55 A: *da și își închipuie că el face un studiu în câteva luni și dă lovitura (0.1)*
  yes and he imagines he will conduct a study in a few months and hit the jackpot
56 *păi sunt alții care studiază (0.2) zeci zece ani cinsprezece ani douăzeci de ani și [nu reușesc]*
  well there are others who study for tens ten years fifteen years twenty years and they don't manage
57 P: [*douăzeci*] *de ani*
                             twenty years
58 A: *și nu reușesc să facă ceva*
  and they don't manage to do anything
59 *și el așa în câteva luni nimic nici măcar cu aparatură*
  and he in a few months nothing not even with equipment
60 *că hai să zicem că dacă ar fi avut aparatură super performantă*
  cause let's suppose if he had had a high-performance equipment
61 *ar fi zis că mai era cum mai era da' nici măcar așa*
  he would have said it was possible but not even so
62 *să dai lovitura pe ș pe nimic și fără aparatură și fără bani și nu se poate (0.1)*
  hitting the jackpot on nothing without equipment and money and it is impossible
63 P: *da: ce să faci (.) oricum cu sonache nu te pui*
  yes what can you do you can't wrangle with loony anyway
64 A: *ă (0.2) da (0.2) el (0.2) știe să (0.2) se protejeze pe el*
  uhm yes he can protect himself
65 *numai la alții e prost*
  only when it comes to others is he stupid
66 *când e vorba să le dea altora atunci este (0.1) prost*
  when it comes to giving to others then he is stupid
67 *nu știe e (0.2) nu știe cum să facă statele de plată*
  he doesn't know he is he doesn't know how to do the payrolls
68 *vai dar el știe (.) la el să-și bage (0.1)*
  oh but he can provide for himself
69 P: *milioane*
  several million
70 A: *zeci de milioane pe lună*
  tens of milion a month

The fragment above is an instance of a conversational narrative introduced in interaction for social reasons (relating to the *phatic function*), i.e., with the purpose of attending to the social relationship between the two interactants, through the practical activity of gossiping.

The gossip is triggered by one of the parties', P's, eliciting question regarding a news-update of the gossipee (an absent third-party whom both the interlocutors are familiar with). A's engagement in an extensive response in the next turn shows his willingness to gossip, thus revealing the inappropriate conduct of the main character in his story (the gossipee), which obviously breeches well-established social norms regarding the respect for other people's work. According to A, the gossipee, A's University Professor, favours and employs certain people that are incompetent and therefore unqualified for the job and also takes lots of money for himself to the detriment of other young employees, whom he exploits and refuses to pay according to their efforts.

In the process of gossiping, the two interlocutors achieve rapport and strengthen their solidarity as a group. This is done by appealing to several strategies which make up the mechanism of *claiming common ground with the addressee* (Brown and Levinson, 1987:103-124), among which, the utilisation of *constructed dialogue* – line 22 (*'și-o să-i spun „domn profesor este un șoc pentru mine dacă că am aflat chestia asta"'*) ('and I will tell him Professor it is a shock for me to find this out') and the use of the *token tag* (*'îți dai seama'*) ('you do realise') – line 12 (*'=da lu- lucruri din acestea mărunte îți dai seama care nu: nu:'*) ('yes minor things like this you do realise which are not not'), whose function is to invite the addressee's involvement (by encouraging the hearer, P, to follow the emotional trend of the story) and thus to establish agreement and common ground. Another important strategy used by the two converastionalists to achieve affinity is the use of *in-group terminology*, i.e., the use of *slang*: the term 'sonache' devised by P as a nickname for A's Professor – lines 1 and 63 – evokes associations and attitutes that the speaker, P, and the recipient, A, share with respect to the term used: a person afflicted with madness. Another category of in-group terminology includes ironic terms, such as '*Einstein de Dâmbovița*' ('Einstein of Dâmbovița') – line 54, „*darul lui Dumnezeu pe pământ*' ('God's gift on earth') – line 48 and „*specialiști*' ('specialists') – lines 6 and 8, which are being used in order to mock at the hyperbolic status claimed by the gossipee.

A's utilisation of a plethora of ironic utterances (by which the speaker implicitly denies what he states) is meant to attack the positive face of the gossipee, that of a well-reputed scholar – lines 6, 9, 10, 12-16 (*'și-a căutat oameni specialiști și serioși/fac (0.1) lucruri mi<u>NO</u>re ca de exemplu umblă cu sânge contaminat/ și pe urmă pune mâna pe clanță (.) de trebuiesc de trebuiesc dezinfectate toate clanțele (0.3) lucruri=/ =da lu- lucruri din* *acestea mărunte îți dai seama care nu: nu:/trebuiesc trecute cu vederea/așa ceva mai ales că se pot dacă se întâmplă să iei o hepatită/ asta-i u::n flecuștet acolo ce MAre lucru/ nu nu trebuie să ne supărăm')* ('he looked for specialists and serious people/[they] do minor things such as for instance handle contaminated blood/and then touch the door handle so that all door handles need disinfection/yes minor things like this you do realise which are not not/they must be overlooked/ something like this especially if one happens to catch hepatitis/this is a mere trifle no big deal/we mustn't make a fuss'). The speaker's ironic use of the diminutive *flecuștet* ('trifle') conveys a depreciation of the quality of the work performed by the Professor's new employees. Also, the occurrence of the demonstrative determiner *acei* ('those') accompanying a human entity *specialiști* ('specialists') – line 8 *('acei specialiști la care el apelează')* ('those specialists whom he calls on') acquires an ironic contour in the present speech situation. By means of an implicature, the recipient interprets her interlocutor's ironic utterances as a violation of Grice's quality maxim and assigns them the exact opposite meaning of what has been contended. Evidence of the recipient's recovering the intended meaning of the speaker's utterance and his contemptuous attitude toward the gossipee comes in line 11, where P acknowledges the doubtful competence of the new employees *('=specialiști în concepția lui=')* ('specialists in his opinon').

Besides the dominant phatic function outlined above, the present narrative also performs a *referential function* in conversation: transmitting information about the professional life of an absent third-party (a University Professor) and establishing norms concerning moral conduct in society: one should be fair to one's employees: treat them respectfully and pay them adequately, according to the amount of work they carry out.

Another seconday function performed by the present gossipy account in conversational interaction is the *emotive function,* since the speaker's goal is to persuade his interlocutor that he is a genuine researcher. Thus, A embarks upon building a positive professional identiy for himself to the detriment of others, namely the gossipees: the Professor and his newly employed specialists, whom he undermines[75], as we have shown above, through the use of irony.

Next, we will discuss the phatic function performed by narratives in conversation through establishing, maintaining or transforming social relationship, in particular, ratifying group or family membership and reinforcing group norms and values.

---

[75] For the strategies used by the speaker in constructing his/her identity, see the section on the emotive function.

Small talk:
Establishing, maintaining or transforming social relationship.
Ratifying group/family membership and reinforcing group norms and values

Small talk as a communicative mode goes back to Malinowski's (1923) coinage of the term *phatic communion* which designates the establishment of social bonding 'merely' by talking. Although this mode of discourse has been dismissed by some as marginal, it has been pointed out to be central to conversation analysis and sociolinguistics, whose data rely on everyday language. The main role of small talk is, no doubt, the achievement of *solidarity* or *intimacy* between interactants by means of particular encoding choices[76] (Coupland, 2000:2-6); (Ghiga, 1999:18); (Săftoiu, 2009:49).

Storytelling may also represent an opportunity for the speaker to *establish rapport*[77] with the recipient, i.e., to *ratify group/family membership and reinforce group norms and values*:

> storytelling is very common in casual conversation. It provides conversationalists with a resource for assessing and confirming affiliations with others... (Eggins & Slade (1997) apud Coupland & Jaworski (2003:87)).

The literature on narratives-in-interaction, as well as our own research have revealed that telling a story is often prompted by the speaker's desire to satisfy his/her positive face want – the desire to belong to a group, to assert that his/her values are the same with those of the group, to show that his or her wants are shared by others, as well, to emphasize that both interlocutors want the same thing, and that they share a common goal. This is especially the case of collaborative narratives where interlocutors ask questions and make comments, concurring to the development of the narrative (Goodwin, C., 1984; Goodwin, M. H., 1990; Jefferson, 1978; Ochs et al., 1992). In this case, story content need not be newsworthy nor should the story make a new point if co-narration holds the promise of high-involvement, as for instance when conversational parties indulge in reliving pleasant moments (Norrick, 1997:203; (Norrick, 2000).

The narrative in the excerpt below was introduced in conversation with the purpose of *ratifying group/family membership and reinforcing group norms and values*.

---

[76] See also Brown & Levinson's politeness strategies (1987) [1978].
[77] See Norrick (1997:203) for a more detailed account of the term.

*(41) Vijelia/*Thunderstorm

1 P: *fii atentă ți-aduci aminte când mergeam la Câmpulung?* ((*oftează*))
   listen do you recall when we used to go to Câmpulung ((sighs))
2 M: *da ce frumos erea și bine și erea și (0.2)*
   yes how beautiful and well it was and
3   *da' ți-aduci aminte când ne-a prins ploaia?*
   and do you recall when we got caught in the rain
4 P: *da aoleo ce m-am speriat* [*atuncea*
   yes oh my how frightened I got then
5 M: [*la tata lu' Aurica ce*
                                 at Aurica's father what
6 P: *eram mică*]
   I was little
7 M: *ce casă*] *frumoasă avea acolo va::i sus cu etaj*
   what a beautiful house he had up there oh my with an upstairs
8   *și ne-a prins ploaia și erea într-o zonă:: cu o vale* **așa** *era cu fructe cu multe legume*
   and we got caught in the rain and we were in an area with a valley **and stuff** with fruit and many vegetables
9   *și toate le-au fost inundate de apă*
   and everything was flooded by water
10   *a venit* **așa** *o vijelie mare o ploaie o*
   such a great thunderstorm a rainstorm came
11   *așa și noi de fri::că am plecat acasă la noi pe (0.3) acolo unde ședeam și::=*
   well and we were afraid so we left for home for the place where we stayed and
12 P: =*cum se numea? nu pe Mălin*
   what was its name not Mălin
13   *cum se numea? va::i (0.2) nu Bughea ă::: (0.5) unde stătea Nelu*
   what was its name oh my not Bughea uhm where Nelu used to live
14   *hai zii*
   come on tell (me)
15 M: [*așa și*
      well and
16 P: [*da' ma::mă] ce mă enervează*
   oh my it really annoys me
17 M: *așa și trebuia să ne ducem acolo și eream și cu Nae după no::i*
   well and we had to go there and Nae was with us as well
18   *și Nae ce vesel erea ce fericit erea și cu ă:: așa și fata lu' ă:: și Petre erea acolo*
   and how merry and happy was Nae and with uhm well and the daughter of uhm and Petre was there
19   *și fata lu' Petre te-a luat pe tine-n câ::rcă*
   and Petre's daughter gave you a piggyback
20   *io am pus o pelerină pe ti::ne că totuși ploua afa:ră*
   I put a raincoat on you cause it rained outside
21   *ea și-a luat niște cizme înalte la fel a facut și: (0.2) Petre*
   she put on a pair of high boots and so did Petre
22   *și Nae zicea 'Petrișo:r Petrișo:r' și erea mic parcă-l văd ce frumos erea și scump*
   and Nae said Petrișor Petrișor and he was little I almost see him how cute and sweet he was
23   *și se urca pe umerii lui și-am mers încet-încet pe lângă apă bineînțeles*
   and he climbed on his shoulders and we walked slowly-slowly by the water naturally
24   *am traversat a::pa*
   we crossed the water
25   *io și cu mama am traversat apa*
   I and my mother crossed the water
26   *ne-a udat de fua::i ă::: în ce hal eream de ude da' nu conta*
   we got wet oh my uhm we were soaked to the skin but it didn't matter
27   *nimeni nu s-a îmbolnăvit nimeni n-a răcit nimeni n-a avut nimic*
   no one got ill no one caught a cold no one had anything
28   *și-am mers noi pe jos și-am mers și-am mers și-am mers și pe locuri uscate*

bineînțele::s
and we walked and walked and walked and walked in dry places as well naturally
29 *când am ajuns acolo ploua totuși pe Carpați (0.5) pe strada Carpați când am ajuns la Ne::lu=*
when we got there it rained on Carpați street on Carpați street when we get to Ne::lu's
30 P: = *da va::i strada Carpați era va::i da*
yes oh my Carpați street it was oh my yes
31 M: *am (0.2) când am ajuns aproape de târg am mers acolo*
we when we arrived near the fair we went there
32 *ne-am schimbat am pus hainele alea și nimeni n-a răcit nimeni n-a pățit nimic*
we changed we put those clothes away and no one caught a cold nothing happened to anyone

The present story deals with events that were shared by the two interlocutors (Georgakopoulou, 2006b) and represents a *collaborative accomplishment* whose structure emerges online and is negotiated by the participants. The narrative is not told so much for its informational content but rather for solidarity purposes: to ratify family membership. P is the initiator of the narrative, as her question in line *1 ('fii atentă ți-aduci aminte când mergeam la Câmpulung? ((oftează))')* ('listen do you recall when we used to go to Câmpulung ((sighs))') could count as a request or an invitation for her interlocutor to participate in joint-storytelling. As P was only a little girl when the events in the story took place and therefore cannot remember much, M takes on the role of the main narrator. It is her who takes most of the turns in telling the story, whereas P's subsequent interventions (which are only four) represent her personal contributions to the narrative. Line 4 constitutes an evaluation of her own feelings *('da aoleo ce m-am speriat [atuncea')* ('yes oh my how frightened I got then'), which is rendered by means of an expressive speech act –, whereas the utterance in line 6 *('eram mică]')* ('I was little') – a representative speech act – is meant to offer an explanation for the speaker's fright, which she has previously mentioned in line 4. P's *high involvement* with the story (Blum-Kulka, 1997:108) is also marked by her request for information/clarification – lines 12-13 *('= cum se numea? nu pe Mălin/ cum se numea? va::i (0.2) nu Bughea ă::: (0.5) unde stătea Nelu')* ('what was its name not Mălin/what was its name oh my not Bughea uhm where Nelu used to live') –, by her frustration at her inability to remember a certain detail, which is rendered by means of an expressive speech act in line 16 *('[da' ma::mă] ce mă enervează')* ('oh my it really annoys me'), by her eagerness to find out what happened next, which prompts her into eliciting the continuation of the story from her interlocutor – through a directive speech act – line 14 *('hai zii')* ('come on tell (me)'), and finally, by her relief and joy when learning that forgotten detail – line 30 *('= da va::i strada Carpați era va::i da')* ('yes oh my Carpați street it was oh my yes').

The norms and values which are being reinforced and praised in the present narrative are family values. Belonging to a family and joining one another for better and for worse is seen by the speakers as a source of harmony, peace, happiness, health, beauty, tenderness, and welfare – line 2 *('da ce frumos erea și bine și erea și (0.2)')* ('yes how beautiful and well it was and'). Children, as the youngest members of the family, are considered as a source of joy and blessing – lines 18-19, 22 and 23 *('și Nae ce vesel erea ce fericit erea/ și fata lu' Petre te-a luat pe tine-n câ::rcă/ și Nae zicea "Petrișo:r Petrișo:r " și erea mic parcă-l văd ce frumos erea și scump')* *('și se urca pe umerii lui')*, ('and how merry and happy was Nae/and Petre's daughter gave you a piggyback/and Nae said Petrișor Petrișor and he was little I almost see him how cute and sweet he was') ('and he climbed on his shoulders') and family bonds are so strong that not even the rough weather conditions could alter them – lines 26-27 *('ne-a udat de fua::i a::: în ce hal eram de ude da' nu conta/ nimeni nu s-a îmbolnăvit nimeni n-a răcit nimeni n-a avut nimic')* ('we got wet oh my uhm we were soaked to the skin but it didn't matter/no one got ill no one caught a cold no one had anything').

The two interlocutors' use of positive politeness forms, emphasizing closeness between them, can be seen as a solidarity strategy (Yule, 1996:65). Linguistically, such a strategy includes personal information – the story told by the main narrator relates a thunderstorm they experienced at a certain moment in their youth, childhood respectively – and it is marked through inclusive terms, such as 'we' – lines 1,11, 17, 23, 24, 28, 29, 31, 32 and 'us' – lines 3, 8, which in Romanian are not rendered explicitly but can be deduced implicitly, as the grammatical categories of person and number of the pronouns are included in the verb desinence. The strategies of positive politeness employed by the two participants to the conversation concern the mechanism of *claiming common ground with the addressee* (Brown and Levinson, 1987:103-124). One such strategy is exaggerating interest, approval, sympathy with the hearer. This is done with exaggerated intonation and stress, as well as with intensifying modifiers, as in lines 2 *('da ce frumos erea și bine și erea')* ('yes how beautiful and well it was and'), 7 *('ce casă] frumoasă avea acolo va::i sus cu etaj')* ('what a beautiful house he had up there oh my with an upstairs'), 18 *('și Nae ce vesel erea ce fericit erea')* ('and how merry and happy was Nae'), and 22 *('ce frumos erea și scump')* ('how cute and sweet he was'). Another strategy is intensifying interest to the hearer, which is a way for the speaker to communicate to the addressee that he shares some of his wants. In the present fragment this is done through the use of directly quoted speech, as in line 22 *('și Nae zicea 'Petrișo:r Petrișo:r')* ('and Nae said Petrișor Petrișor'). Another characteristic way of claiming common ground with the addressee is to seek ways in which it is possible to agree with him/her. The raising of 'safe topics' allows the speaker to stress his/her agreement with the hearer and therefore to 'satisfy' the hearer's desire to be 'right' or to be corroborated in his/her opinion. The 'safe topic' adopted by both interlocutors in their conversation is the beauty of the holidays they used to spend in Câmpulung. Agreement may also be stressed by repeating part or all of what the preceding speaker has said in a conversation. In addition to demonstrating that one has heard correctly what was said (satisfying the hearer's need to be noticed and attended to), repeating is used to stress emotional agreement with the utterance or to stress interest and surprise. P's utterance in line 30 is a case in point. Another strategy of claiming common ground with the hearer is to make only the minimal adjustment in point of view when reporting. This entails the use of directly quoted speech along with the use of names and references without explanation, as is the case of the characters' names *(Aurica – line 5, Nelu – line 13, Nae – line 17, Petre – lines 18, 19, 21)* and of places *(Mălin – line 12, Bughea – line 13, Carpați – lines 29 and 30)* in the fragment above. The preference for extremes on value scales which is also a feature of positive politeness derives part of its impact from the tacit claim that the speaker and the hearer have the same values with respect to the relevant predicate, the same definition of what the scale is, of what constitutes beauty or goodness (as in *'frumos și bine'* ('beautiful and well') – line 2, *'casă frumoasă'* ('beautiful house') – line 7, *'o vijelie mare'* ('a great thunderstorm') – line 10). The sequencing of statements conjoined with 'and/but' also may reveal shared values and may be used to stress them, as in lines 8, 9, 18, 19, 22, 23 and 28.

Besides the main phatic function performed by the present narrative in conversation, one may assert that it also performs a secondary function: the *emotive function*, as the story clearly expresses the speakers' genuine emotion regarding a particular shared event they experienced at a certain point in their lives. Among the expresssive elements used by the two co-narrators range *interjections (aoleo, va::i, fua::i)* (oh, my, wow), usually accompanied by *exclamatory words (ce)* (how/what), *(ma::mă)* (oh my) *and emotive verbs (a se speria)* (to get scared), or *evaluative adjectives (frumos)* (nice/beautiful), *(vesel/fericit)* (happy), *(scump)* (adorable) – lines 2 (*'da ce frumos'*) ('yes how beautiful'), 4 (*'aoleo ce m-am speriat'*) ('oh my how frightened I got'), 7 (*'ce casă frumoasă'*) ('what a beautiful house'), 16 (*'[ma::mă]'*) ('oh my'), 18 (*'ce vesel ... ce fericit'*) ('how merry ... happy'), 22 (*'ce frumos ... și scump'*) ('how cute and sweet'), 7, 13, 30 (*'va::i'*) ('my') and 26 (*'fua::i'*) ('wow'). The use of *emphatic speech*, which relates either to the speakers' specific, prolonged intonation – lines 7, 13 and 30 *('va::i')* ('my'), 11 *('fri::că')* ('afraid'), 17 *('no::i')* ('us'), 19 *('câ::rcă')* ('piggyback'), 20 *('ti::ne', 'afa:ră')* ('you', 'outside'), 22 *(Petrișo:r Petrișo:r)* ('Petrișor Petrișor'), 24 *('a::pa')* ('water'), 28 *('bineînțele::s')* ('naturally'), 29 *('Ne::lu=')* ('Nelu'), or to certain particular features pertaining to message construction, such as the use of repetition, conjoined with syntactic parallelism – lines 27 *('nimeni nu s-a îmbolnăvit nimeni n-a răcit nimeni n-a avut nimic')* ('no one got ill no one caught a cold no one had anything') and 32 *('nimeni n-a răcit nimeni n-a pățit nimic')* ('no one caught a cold nothing happened to anyone'), as well as the use of a high degree of *intensification* – lines 2, 7 and 22 *(ce frumos/frumoasă)* ('how cute'), 18 *('ce vesel ... ce fericit')* ('how merry and happy'), 26 *('în ce hal eram de ude')* ('we were soaked to the skin') also convey the co-tellers' enthusiastic attitude towards the past related events. Last but not least, the plethora of first person personal pronouns *((noi)* (we)), *((io)* (I)) utilised by the speakers throughout the narrative also emphasizes the general emotive orientation of their utterances.

Next, we will deal with the textual function of conversational narratives.

3.5 The textual function

The *internal structure* is a textual property of the narrative as a complete text, in the sense defined by Halliday & Hasan (1989). From this perspective, we have distinguished between *canonical* and *non-canonical narratives*.

Canonical/conventional narratives[78] deal with *personal, past experience of non-shared events* (Georgakopoulou, 2006b). Prototypical stories are explicitly introduced into the ongoing conversation with a preface like 'do you remember when...' or 'did I tell you about...' or are elicited by instructions to tell a story (Ervin-Tripp and Küntay, 1997). They are fully-fledged stories which take long pages of transcript and represent

'a coherent temporal progression of events that may be reordered for rhetorical purposes and that is typically located in some past time and place, a plotline that encompasses a beginning, a middle, and an end, conveys a particular perspective and is designed for a particular audience who apprehend and shape its meaning' (Ochs and Capps, 2001:57).

They have a well-defined internal structure, containing all of the following *invariant structural units* (Labov and Waletzky (1967): *an abstract/a preface* anticipating the topic, the *orientation* (containing data on the characters' identity, their initial behaviour and on the story's space and temporal background), the *complicating action*, the *evaluation* –representing the protagonist's thoughts and feelings which interrupt the complicating action, underlying what is of interest for the narrator/recipient –, the *resolution*, and the *coda* – representing the final comment on the narrated events or the narrator's present perspective, with a possible evaluative tinge.

The second factor which defines the canonicity of a story is the storyteller's use of the canonical *past tense* as a narrative tense.

---

[78] Canonical narratives are generally synonymous with the term *stories*. For further details on stories, see chapter 1.

Fragment (42) below is an instance of a canonical narrative.

(42) Nuntă la Biserica Rusă/Wedding at the Russian church
1M: *am fost la nuntă la Geta*
    I was at Geta's weddding
2D: *da? cum a fost?*
    yes how was it
3 M: *frumos drăguț*
    nice cute
4   *mâncarea (0.2) nu*
    not the food though
5 D: *unde au făcut?*
    where was it
6 M: *la un restaurtant frumos la*
    at a nice restaurant at
7D: *nu (0.2) unde au făcut la biserică?*
    I mean what church
8   *până la urmă [cine a câștigat? ((râde))*
    who won in the end ((laughs))
9 M: *[a:: aicea la Rusă au făcut*
    oh here at the Russian church
10 D: *la Rusă?*
    at the Russian church
11 M: *a zis părintele Vasile că (0.2)*
    father Vasile said that
12   *părintele Vasile e duhovnicul lor da' mai mult a lu' Geta*
    father Vasile is their confessor well he's more of Geta's confessor
13 D: *aha*
    I see
14 M: *și la sfârșit a zis cică "ei și la anu' o să scoatem ă:: schelele astea*
    and in the end he said well next year when we take this scaffold out
15   *când o să fie bebele o să scoatem schelele astea*
    when the baby is born we'll take this scaffold out
16 D: *[((surâde))*
    ((smiles))
17 M:*[și o să fie frumos"=*
    and it'll be nice
18   *= "și acuma recunoașteți dacă nu aveam schelele astea nu mai putea să se suie cameramanul"*
    and now you have to admit that unless we had had this scaffold the cameraman couldn't have climbed on it
19   *că în timpul slujbei s-a sona s-a suit un <u>sonat</u>*
    cause during the service a crazy cameraman climbed (on the scaffold)
20 D: *((râde))*
    ((laughs))
21 M: *de <u>came-ra-</u>man care avea vreo cincizeci spre șaizeci de ani de'ăsta așa*
    the cameraman was about fifty or sixty years old or so
22 D: *[aha*
    I see
23 M: *[hazliu și cu și cu poante și cu toate chestiile ((surâde))=*
    funny and prankish and experienced ((smiles))
24   *= s-a suit pe schelele alea ca să*
    he climbed that scaffold in order to
25 D: *de ce?*
    Why
26 M: *ca să-i filmeze și era în timpul slujbei și-ți dai seama că-ți venea râsu'*

```
              to film them and it was during the service so you felt like laughing you know
27 D: da
       yes
28 M: pe de altă parte te uitai să vezi și ce reacție are părintele=
       on the other hand you were watching for Father's reaction
29     = și te gândeai că părintele-ar zice ce caută =
       and thinking that the Father would wonder what he was up to up there
30     =paznicu' s-a urcat după el știi?
       the guard climbed up as well you know
31     parcă erai în filme[ cu comici
       as if it were in a comedy
32 D:                  [va::i
                       oh my God
33 M: taram-taram-taram-tara=
       taram-taram-taram-tara
34 D: =pantera roz
       the pink panther
35 M: nanam știi? deci în timpul slujbei=
       nanam during the service you know
36     = nu era suficient că s-a suit ăla cu camera? s-a suit și paznicu'=
       wasn't it enough that the cameraman climbed up the guard climbed up too
37     = deci dacă cădeau amândoi de-acolo? dacă-o pățeau știi?
       I mean what if they had fallen down what if they had got hurt you know
38 D: parcă erau detectivi știi? ((râde))
       as if they were detectives you know ((laughs))
39 M: ce situație (0.5)
       what a situation
40     și cică "și recunoașteți acuma că dacă nu s-ar fi urcat n-ați fi avut așa o imagine globală"
       and he goes you have to admit that if he hadn't climbed up there you wouldn't have had such an overall picture
41 D: ((râde))
       ((laughs))
42 M: ar fi trebuit să aduceți avionu' (   ) sau ceva așa o imagine din avion=
       you should have brought a plane or something (to get) such a bird's eye view'
43 D := e și spontan
       he's quite spontaneous
44 M: Doamne deci îți dai seama ? supertare ((râde))
       oh my God can you believe that supercool ((laughs))
```

The story in the excerpt above is an illustration of a *conventional story*, as it deals with a personal, past experience of a non-shared event (Georgakopoulou, 2006b): an unusual event which took place during a wedding ceremony which the narrator attended. The present narrative's canonicity also draws on the story preface – the initial clause signalling the beginning of the story – in fact an *abstract* summarizing the story that is about to come – line 1 ('*am fost la nuntă la Geta*') ('I was at Geta's weddding') .

The narrative is also canonical through its considerable length and its well-defined internal structure, comprising all the invariant structural units. While the story *preface* has the role of announcing the topic – line 1–, the *orientation* provides background information on the protagonists (Geta, the bride, Father Vasile, the priest, a cameraman and a watchman) and on the place of the events taking place in the narrative (The Russian church, whose interior is being refurbished and therefore is full of wood scaffolding) – lines 9-14, 18 and 30 –. *The complicating action* is marked by the 50/60- year-old cameraman's unexpected move to get on the scaffolding to film the wedding from above, followed shortly by the watchman – lines 21, 24, 26, 30. This creates a scene which seems torn off a comedy (line 31) or a Pink Panther cartoon (line 33-34), or even a detective film (line 38). The *resolution* is rendered by Father Vasile's speech, who concludes that the scaffolding in the church proved to be extremely useful to the newly-weds, who would surely have a splendid bird's eye view of their wedding – lines 11, 18, 40. Lines 36-37, 39 and 44 represent the *evaluation* part of the story, as M interrupts the main action to express her thoughts and feelings. By means of three successive questions in lines 36 *('nu era suficient că s-a suit ăla cu camera?')* ("wasn't it enough that the cameraman climbed up") and 37 *('deci dacă cădeau amândoi de-acolo? dacă-o păţeau ştii?')* ('I mean what if they had fallen down what if they had got hurt you know'), M expresses her concern for the two men who could have injured themselves, should they have fallen off the scaffold. By means of two expressive speech acts in lines 39 *('ce situaţie')* ('what a situation') and 44 *('supertare')* ('supercool'), she also expresses her bewilderment at the strange situation nobody would have imagined or thought to be happening in a church, during a religious service. M's use of a phatic element or of a filler to check her interlocutor's understanding *('Doamne deci îţi dai seama ?')* ('oh my God can you believe that') – line 44 – also has the role of highlighting the seriousness of the facts and of determining the listener to align with her point of view. This last utterance may also function as a *coda*, since it signals the end of the story and represents the narrator's present perspective on the events contained in the conversational narrative.

The second factor determining the canonical character of the present story is the narrator's use of the *past tense*, which is a typical linguistic feature marking the passage from conversational discourse to narrative discourse.

Non-canonical narratives[79] are spontaneous, often ambiguous conversational events. According to Georgakopoulou (2006b), they do not always fit the traditional narrative-internal criteria, such as 'the presence of a protagonist and events creating conflict, reference to events in the past, presence of a climactic complicating action, or closure of the storyline with a resolution'. Further, the onset of conversational stories does not always clearly demarcate the narrative segment from the preceding talk (Ervin-Tripp and Küntay, 1997). Georgakopoulou (2006b) names non-canonical

---

[79] The category of non-canonical narratives includes, in our opinion, a particular type of narratives called *reports*, which are those narratives lacking events creating conflict, reaching a climax, or ending with a resolution but which are nevertheless told in the past tense. For further details on the literature on reports, see chapter 1.

narratives *small stories* – a term which covers 'a gamut of underrepresented narrative activities, such as tellings of ongoing events, future or hypothetical events, shared (known) events, but also allusions to tellings, deferrals of tellings, and refusals to tell'. These tellings are typically small when compared to the seemingly endless pages of transcript of conversational narratives. Small stories may be more or less connected with the narrative canon: some of them may fulfill prototypical definitional criteria (e.g., temporal ordering of events) but still may not sit well with the canon (e.g., stories of projected events, given that the emphasis of the literature has undoubtedly been on past events).

The use of narrative tenses which are an alternative to the conventional past tense is another characteristic of non-canonical narratives. Among the tenses used in the unconventional narratives, worth mentioning are the *narrative future* and the *narrative present* (whether the conversational historical present or the prospective present).

Fragment (43) below is an instance of a non-canonical narrative.

*(43) Imnu' Mălăiești/*The Mălăiești hymn
1 E: *da' ia spune-i mă cum a fost cu imnu' Mălăiești?*
  come on tell her about the Mălăiești hymn
2 R: *las-o baltă (0.2) nu mai*
  drop it cut it out
3 I: *((râde))*
  ((laughs))
4 R: *te rog io mult*
  pretty please
5 *i-ai mai spus și Cristinei și mi-a mai trimis și pe mail*
  you've also told Cristina and she even sent it to me by e-mail
6 *nu nu da' oricum e aiurea*
  no no it's silly anyway
7 *lasă nu mai nu (0.5)*
  drop it cut it out
8 E: *((râde)) și dacă ți-a trimis ce mă?*
  ((laughs)) so what if she sent it to you
9 R: *da: (0.3) nu știu (0.5)*
  well I don't know
10 *dacă nu-mi place (0.2) și oricum i-o prostie*
  I dislike it and it's silly anyway
11 E: *păi da' ăsta-i imnu'*
  but this is the hymn
12 I: *da'cine l-a inventat?[*
  who invented it anyway
13 E: *[ce l-am inventat io? ((râde))*
        it's not as if I have invented it or something ((laughs))
14 R:*((râde)) ( ) l-a inventat*
  ((laughs)) ( ) invented it
15 I: *hai zii*
  come on tell us
16 R: *eram în mijlocu' focului acolo și ne bălăngăneam*

```
                we were there around the fire and we were swinging
        17 E: mai ales tu Roxana io nu=
                especially you Roxana I wasn't
        18 R: =((cântă)) ta na na na na și strofa
                ((sings)) ta na na na na and the stanza
        19      ((râde)) (      ) cu aceleași mișcări da:r (0.5)
                ((laughs))with the same movements but
        20 I: din ce în ce mai  [(    )
                more and more
        21 R:                   [da' nu-mi venea să cred
                                 and I couldn't believe my ears
        22      și tot repetau și tot repetau
                and they kept repeating it on and on
        23      oricum nu știu cui i-am mai zis
                anyway I don't know whom I've also told about it
        24 I: da' cine-l cânta?
                but who sang it
        25 R: și zice "doamne ce prostie (0.2) de"=
                and she says oh my God what a silly (  )
        26 I: = cine-l cânta?
                who sang it
        27 R: era niște ((râde)) erau niște copii=
                there was ((laughs)) there were some children
        28 E: =Dumnezeu știe cine
                God knows who
        29 I: cine?
                who
        30 R: erau copiii ăștia de la cabană și aveau ei la telefon
                there were some children from the chalet and they played it on the phone
        31 I: a:: aveau înregistra:t?[
                did they have it recorded
32 R:                           [da înregistrat da da
                                 yeah recorded yeah yeah
        33 I: a::
                oh
        34 R: și:: foa:rte  (0.5)
                and very
        35 E: când a zis mă că-i Floare de Colț?=
                when did they say Edelweiss was going to be
        36     = pe cinșpe august nu? sau când?(0.3)
                on August fifteenth right or when
        37 R: da ((surâde))
                yes ((smiles))
        38 I: ce festivalu'?=
                what do you mean the festival
        39 R: =da festivalu' da
                yes the festival
```

The story in the excerpt above is an illustration of a non-canonical narrative. Its unconventional nature is rendered by the following features: the events referred to in this narrative are *shared* by two of the participants to the conversation, the narrative is *typically small* and it represents a *marginal* case: the storyteller's *refusal/deferral of recounting* the events. Moreover, the story *lacks* events creating conflict, *a climactic complicating action* and *closure* of the storyline *with a resolution*: the story ends with a third party's evaluation of the hymn, who also dismisses it as nonsense – line 25 *('şi zice "doamne ce prostie (0.2) de"')* ('and she says "oh my God what a silly" ( )') .

Fragment (44) below represents another instance of a non-canonical narrative.

(44) Din nou la munte/Back in the mountains
1 E: *păi io m-aş mai duce la Mălăieşti*
    well I'd like to go to Mălăieşti again
2   *putem să organizăm noi ceva?*
    can we organize anything
       (0.5)
3 R: *da*
    yes
4 E: *cu băieţii (0.2)*
    with the boys
5   *de la Braşov ceva nu ştiu cum*=
    something from Braşov
6   =*nu e greu*
    it's not difficult
7   *Crăcănel (0.2)*
    Crăcănel
8 R: ((*râde*))
    ((laughs))
9 I: *care Crăcănel?*
    which Crăcănel
10 R: ((*râde*))
    ((laughs))
11 E: *de la Crăcănel*
    from Crăcănel
12 I: *ce mai e şi ăsta?*
    what's that
13 R: ((*râde*)) *hai că zicea profu' când am luat [taxi]*
    ((laughs)) when we took the taxi the Teacher said
14 E: [*da] putem să ajungem mai încolo la izvoru' ăla*
                     yes we can get farther to that spring
15   *că de-acolo chiar că ştim*
    cause we know (the route) from there
16 R: *da*
    yes
    (0.2)
17 E: *nu?*
    dont't we
18 R: *da a:: **vine** şi ursu'*=
    yeah the bear is coming too
19 I: = *e floare la ur[eche]*
    it's a piece of cake
20 E: [*haide] mă:*
             come on
21   **trecem** *prin trei poie- poieniţe*
    we're passing through three clear- clearings.
22 R: *e:: da' (0.3) **mergem** şi noi cu cineva care ştie*
    no way we're going with someone who knows the way
23 I: [*hai mă ziceţi-mi şi mie ce e cu*] *Crăcănel ăsta*
    come on tell me what this Crăcănel is all about
24 E:[*să organizăm şi noi ( ) la Mălăieşti*]

let's organise (a trip) to Mălăiești ourselves

The conversational narrative in the fragment above is another instance of a non-canonical narrative, since it is typically *small* and the onset of the story – line 4 – does not clearly demarcate the narrative segment from the preceding talk. Moreover, the story lacks events creating conflict, a climactic complicating action and closure of the storyline with a resolution: E's plans of going to the mountains have been eventually shattered, as shown by her request in line 24.

Another reason why the present narrative does not sit well with the canon is that it deals with a *marginal* case: *future/ hypothetical events*. At some point in the conversation E expresses her desire to go again to the mountains and requests R's approval with a view to organizing a trip to Mălăiești – line 2. When R agrees, E starts envisaging the future/ hypothetical trip and her plans turn into a narrative presenting future events – lines 4-7, 14-21. The projected events are expressed by verbs in the prospective present (lines 14, 18, 21, 22 – 'ajungem, vine, trecem, mergem') ('get, is coming, we're passing, we're going'). The storyteller's choice of *the narrative present* (the prospective present) over the future tense forms is indicative of the fact that the speaker deems the realization of the recounted events as having a greater degree of certainty than that implied by the future forms.

Finally, the narrative's unconventional character is also given by the fact that it is a *collaborative accomplishment*: R and I intervene in lines 18-19, apparently concurring with E's arrangements but in fact ironically subverting them, aiming at putting E down to earth. Line 22 works exacly in the same direction.

3.5.1 The metalingual function

Halliday & Hasan's (1989) *textual function* covers Jakobson's (1960) *metalingual* and *poetic* functions. The *metalingual* function of language refers to the capacity of language to reflect upon or talk about itself (Duranti, 1997:7), to describe and analyse itself (e.g., "a 'cat' is a three letter word") (ibid., p.199). This function focuses on the linguistic code and plays an important role in common, everyday talk, as for instance, when the speaker or addressee needs to check whether they use the same code. For this purpose, linguistic items are usually isolated to examine their meaning and/or function in discourse (ibid., p. 200). Such are the cases when conversationalists need to clarify definitions of terms ('What is to be fluncked?' 'To be fluncked is to fail in an exam'), spelling rules (Jakobson, 1987:69); (Dominte, 2003), and, we would add, even the reference of a term ('Who are you speaking of, X or Y?'). This function is typical of the language learning process, including a child's acquisition of his/her mother tongue (Jakobson, 1987:69) and permits dictionaries and grammars to be written (Duranti, 1997:200).

Now we will examine the *metalingual function* of a conversational narrative that is introduced in the ongoing talk with the purpose of *clarifying a linguistic term*, which is obviously unknown to the recipient.

Clarifying a linguistic term

(45) La munte/In the mountains
1 E: de la **Crăcănel**
    from Crăcănel
2 I: **ce mai e și ăsta?**
    what's that
3 R: ((râde)) hai că zicea profu' când am luat [taxi]
    ((laughs)) when we took the taxi the Teacher said
4 E: [da] putem să ajungem mai încolo la izvoru' ăla
                                   yes we can get farther to that spring
5   că de-acolo chiar că știm
      cause we know (the route) from there
6 R: da
    yes
    (0.2)
7 E: nu?
    dont't we
8 R: da a:: vine și ursu'=
    yeah the bear is coming too
9 I: = e floare la ur[eche]
    it's a piece of cake
10 E: [haide] mă:
                    come on
11   trecem prin trei poie- poienițe
      we're passing through three clear- clearings.
12 R: e:: da' (0.3) mergem și noi cu cineva care știe
      no way we're going with someone who knows the way
13 I: [hai mă ziceți-mi și mie ce e cu]**Crăcănel ăsta**
      come on tell me what this Crăcănel is all about
14 E: [să organizăm și noi ( ) la Mălăiești]
      let's organise (a trip) to Mălăiești ourselves
15 R: **hai să-ți spunem** (0.2)
      let us tell you
16   când am coborât noi din tren (0.3) "cum mergem"
      when we got off the train how shall we go
17   "păi a : (0.2) luăm taxiurile
      well let's take the taxi
18   luăm taxiurile (0.2) ca să nu mai mergem pe jos și ajungem pân' la **Crăcănel**"
      we take the taxi so as not to go on foot and we reach Crăcănel
19   Profu' zicea ((imită vocea)) **"pân' la Crăcănel mă pân' la Crăcănel"**
      Teacher said ((imitates his voice)) up to Crăcănel up to Crăcănel
20   da' ((râde)) așa (0.2) foarte serios
      but ((laughs)) very seriously

21 *muream de râs* **de parcă era o denumire normală** *știi?(0.2)*
   we were roaring with laughter as if it were a common name you know
22 *((imită vocea))* "*da măi mergem cu taxiul*"
   ((imitates his voice)) yes we'll take the taxi
23 *((toți râd))*
   ((all laugh))
24 *((imită vocea))* "**pân' la Crăcănel**"
   ((imitates his voice)) up to Crăcănel
25 "*până unde domn' profesor?*"=
   up to where teacher
26 *((imită vocea))*= "**pân' la Crăcănel**"
   ((imitates his voice)) up to Crăcănel
27 *((toți râd))*
   ((all laugh))
28 *ajungem la* **Crăcănel** *și: (0.3)*
   we reach Crăcănel and

The story began by R in line 15 is meant to decode or shed light on a term which is both ambiguous and funny *('Crăcănel*[80]*)*. Previously in the ongoing talk, upon hearing an unfamiliar term, one of the conversationalists, I, asks to be informed about its meaning. Her first request, made by means of an indirect speech act – line 2 – *('ce mai e și ăsta'?)* ('what's that') is ignored by her fellow conversationalists, so she reiterates it a few turns later, this time in the form of a direct speech act – line 13 *('[hai mă ziceți-mi și mie ce e cu]Crăcănel ăsta')* ('come on tell me what this Crăcănel is all about'). As a further failure to respond to I's request would have equated a threat to her positive face, one of the participants to conversation, R, decides to oblige I and clarify the respective word for her. However, the term is not given a definition by the speaker, as one might have expected, but pointed out implicitly, by means of a story related to it. The meaning of the term (a strange and funny geographical denomination of a place in the mountains) can be inferred from line 21 *('muream de râs* **de parcă era o denumire normală** *știi?')* ('we were roaring with laughter as if it were a common name you know'). This 'explanation' is revealed gradually from the narrative recounted by the storyteller, who makes sure to create some tension and present the events dramatically by *alternating between past and present tenses* – lines 16-19, 21-22, 28 – and by resorting to *constructed dialogue* and *voicing* (i.e., mimicking the voice quality of the characters altogether) – lines 19, 22, 24, 26 – a narrative strategy which provokes laughter and a cheerful disposition among the conversationalists, meant to *reinforce in-group solidarity*. In the same vein, the speaker uses the token tag '*știi*' ('you know') – line 21 with a view to seeking agreement and establishing common ground with the recipient. This brings us to identify a secondary function fulfilled by the present narrative, namely the *phatic* function.

Finally, we shall now turn to the poetic function of conversational stories.

---

[80] The term is derived from the verb to sprawl, or straddle one's legs.

3.5.2 The poetic function

The *poetic* function of language is not restricted to poetic or literary language. It may occur in an utterance pertaining to any type of language or verbal activity but *exclusively as an additional function*, everytime discourse displays such qualities as creativity, playfulness or self-awareness (Jakobson, 1987:69-71); (Săftoiu, 2007:12-13); (Jaworski and Coupland, 2006:42). Symptomatic of the poetic function are the use of *paronomasia*[81] or *punning* and the utilization of *assonance* or *alliteration* (e.g., 'I like Ike', 'the horrible Harry'). The poetic function was pointed out to rely on the *selection* (from a paradigm) of verbal elements and on their *combination* (in syntagms). The selection of linguistic items is based on equivalence, whereas their combination relies on contiguity. For instance, the speaker selects one linguistic element from a series of equivalent terms (e.g., child, kid, youngster, tot), then selects another from a list of partially synonymic verbs (e.g., sleeps, naps, dozes, nods) and finally combines them in speech (Jakobson, ibid.); (Săftoiu, ibid.).

Achieving dramatic effect

As pointed out in the theoretical framework, the poetic function of language occurs in common, everyday speech only as a subsidiary function. The previous chapter has shown that there are two categories of storytellers: average and exquisite, the latter category coming really close to theatrical performers or entertainers in point of *achieving dramatic effect*. Good narrators know how to organize the content of their stories by means of:

– the *selection of lexical items* providing the details of the story;

– the use of *repetition;*

– the use of *humour* by means of *punning, irony, banter*

– the use of *constructed dialogue*

– *tense alternation* (from the past tense to *the conversational historical present*)

---

[81] The use of a word with different meanings or of words similar in sound to achieve a particular effect.

We will not insist upon these linguistic means of achiving dramatic effect, since we have discussed them in detail in the previous chapters of our thesis. Instead, we chose to illustrate the poetic function of stories-in-talk-in-interaction by several, brief fragments:

(a) 25 *"până unde domn' profesor?"*=
       up to where teacher
    26 ((*imită vocea*))= *"**pân' la Crăcănel**"*
       ((imitates his voice)) up to Crăcănel

The humourous nature of the above narrative sequence relies on the pun '*Crăcănel*', which has two different meanings: the first points to a person who straddles, whereas the second meaning refers to a geographical denomination.

(b) 6 *a început meciul (0.2)*
       the game started
    7 *bine-nțeles primele minute:?* **praf** *(0.2)* **praf . praf . praf**
       of course in the first minutes they were terrible (0.2) terrible terrible terrible

(c) 14 *adică* **cum prindeau mingea poc** *cu ea la coș*
       I mean whenever they caught the ball they popped it to the basket
    15 **cum . prindeau mingea poc.**
       whenever they caught the ball they popped it

(d) 19 **un singur coș** *la un moment dat au mai dat și ei .* **un amărât . de coș**
       they hardly scored a single lousy basket at a certain point
    20 *a: au egalat ăia la* <u>unu</u>
       the others drew one - one
    21 *s-a făcut* <u>unu</u> <u>unu</u> *(0.1)*
       it turned one to one
    22 *după care au reușit și ei să dea* **un amărât de coș** *î:n când mai era un minut*
       after which they managed to score a lousy basket when there was only one minute left

(e) 21 *nu lucra și nici nu venea* **CU NICIUN** *MATERIAL*
       he wouldn't work and he wouldn't bring any material
    22 **cu nimic nimic** *nu venea*
       he wouldn't bring anything anything
    23 D: *da da*
       yes yes
    24 R: *(lua) o foaie pe care-o găsea pe-acolo și scria cu pixu'*
       he'd take a sheet of paper which he found around and would write on it with the ball pen
    25   *că* **nimic nimic** *n-avea (0.2)* **nici** *creion nu-și aducea*
       because he had nothing nothing he brought nothing not even a pencil

In the examples above, the repetition of certain key words (marked in bold) at the level of narrative sequence emphasizes the speakers' critical attitude towards the narrated events (the weak performance of the basketball team, the reluctance of the pupil in class, respectively), adding to the dramatism of the story.

3.6 Conclusions

Many of the aspects we have described in this chapter are similar to those found in the English literature on conversational narratives, showing the validity of the proposed model concerning the functions of language (Halliday & Hasan, 1989). The problem of the pragmatic purpose (i.e., of the communicative purpose of conversation) can be found in the literature. For instance, Sacks (1992) claims that people do not tell a story just for the sake of telling it and that there must be another reason underlying people's urge of introducing a story in the conversational interaction they are engaged in : to offer something that is relevant now, i.e., describe, explain, account for the current circumstances. Thinking over the functions describing the communicative purpose of conversational narratives, we have found that they are expectedly general functions of the language. Therefore, we have proposed to deal with the problem of the communicative purpose in the functions of conversational narratives also in relation to the proposal advanced by Jakobson (1960).

We started from certain communicative purposes in the literature, but since we observed that the perspective was incomplete, i.e. we could not subsume part of our findings (i.e., the metalinguistic and the poetic functions) to the functions proposed in the previous studies on the functions of conversational narratives, we enlarged the respective perspective, talking about functions characterizing language serving referential goals (*the ideational function*), the narrator and the interlocutor (*the interpersonal function*) and functions characterizing the text (*the textual function*). In other words, we started from Halliday & Hasan's (1989) more abstract description of the language functions, which stipulates the co-presence of the language functions. In a similar way, Jakobson (1960) and the Prague School linguists advanced the principle of the *multifunctionality of language* and the idea of a *hierarchy of functions*, ranging from the dominant function to secondary, minor, or peripheral ones. For us, the dominant function gives the purpose of the speech act. Relying on *the intention-based criterion*, which is synonymous with Grice's (1975) and Searle's (1979) idea of the purpose of a speech act, we tried to guess which was the storyteller's actual intention in telling a story and, listing the entire repertoire of possible functions, we identified the dominant function according to the main speech act structuring the conversational exchange.

The present chapter has revealed that speakers manifest a particular predilection in terms of the intention with which they introduce their stories in conversation. Halliday & Hasan's (1989) ***ideational function,*** comprising language as a system of signs, being omnipresent in every verbal message, is therefore always present in every conversational narrative.

The function which has been pointed out to dominate by far in the hierarchical structure of the main functions performed by narratives in conversation is **the interpersonal function**. Since this function, proposed by Halliday & Hasan (1989) is very general, we preferred to discuss it in terms of the perspective described by Jakobson (1960), treating the interpersonal function in relation to the speaker (the emotive or expressive function), the interlocutor (the conative or persuasive function) and the channel of communication (the phatic function). Thus, we have found out that the favoured function is *the phatic function*. The most common situations in which it occurs are, according to the literature and the present research, the following: entertaining the audience, gossiping, and establishing, maintaining or transforming social relationship, ratifying group/family membership and reinforcing group norms and values. The *emotive function* has been found to overrule the other, peripheral functions when the storyteller constructs a certain identity for himself/herself and when he/she explores the moral implications of personal experience, whereas the *persuasive function* is dominant when the speaker uses a story to illustrate a point he/she is advocating in conversation and to justify or account for his/her actions.

The other functions, namely *the referential, the metalingual and the poetic functions* (the last two functions being related to Halliday & Hasan's (1989) **textual function**) have been shown to occur more rarely or not at all as dominant functions. *The metalingual function* was found to be on top of the hierarchy whenever the storyteller engages upon telling a story in order to clarify a particular linguistic term. With respect to *the poetic function*, it is noteworthy that it solely occurs as a secondary function in narratives embedded in freely occurring conversations, in cases where the storytellers seek to achieve a certain dramatic effect on the audience. This was shown to be achieved by means of various linguistic devices, such as the *selection of lexical items* providing the details of the story, the use of *repetition,* the use of *humour (punning, irony, banter),* of *constructed dialogue* and of *tense alternation* (from the past tense to *the conversational historical present*). Last but not least, *the referential function* was shown to occur always as a peripheral or secondary function, supporting all dominant functions.

A few additional aspects have been considered in connection with the functions of narratives in conversation. A problem we have discussed in connection with the interpersonal function, under the heading of identity construction, is the use of *topics* as revealing for the storyteller's socio-cultural identity, for his/her relationship with the interlocutors and for the the context/cotext of occurrence of a particular narrative. It has been shown that the sociolinguistic variables of *age, gender, and level of education* are determinant factors for topic selection in narratives embedded in conversation.

The textual function of narratives has been found to have an explanatory role as to the conversational narrative as a finalised text or product, emerging as a result of the conversation between the interlocutors. That is why we have decided to discuss here the *internal structure*[82] of conversational narratives. From this perspective, we have distinguished between *canonical* and *non-canonical narratives*. The former category has been pointed out to have a complete internal structure, displaying all the obligatory and optional elements in the Labovian model[83] (1972) and to use the canonical past tense as a narrative tense. The latter category has been shown to stand in opposition to the first category, since it has an incomplete structure, lacking the optional elements in Labov's paradigm (1972) and uses narrative tenses other than the conventional past tense, namely the narrative future or the narrative present (whether the conversational historical present or the prospective present).

All in all, the present chapter has demonstrated that all the functions of narratives in conversation proposed in the literature have been found in the corpus we collected[84] and that we added two more functions to the ones existing in the previous research in the field. We have also pointed out that, very often, conversational narratives perform various different functions simultaneously.

---

[82] This issue could also have been discussed in chapter 2, where we talked about the linguistic features of conversational narratives.
[83] See also Labov & Waletzky (1967).
[84] Our corpus comprises both formal and informal conversations, having subjects ranging from all social classes, ages (except childhood) and gender distinctions.

CHAPTER 4.
INTERACTIONAL FEATURES OF CONVERSATIONAL NARRATIVES

4.0 Introduction

In this chapter, conversational narratives will be considered in the light of *conversation analysis*, as developed by Sacks, Schegloff and Jefferson (1974). Recall that conversation analysis views **conversation** as a *characteristic mode of behaviour*. Similarly, **narratives** represent *typical modes of organizing experience*. Narratives will fit into the pattern of behaviour that is described as conversation. The embedding of narratives in conversation gives rise to characteristic problems. We have studied these problems under the name of *interactional features*. Interactional features are also the product of the sociological variables of age, gender and level of education of speakers, since these bear on conversational behaviour. The same variables influence the discursive strategies of positive and negative politeness (Brown and Levinson, 1987 [1978]) and positive and negative impoliteness (Culpeper, 1996); (Culpeper et al., 2003).

The interactional features we will examine in the present chapter are *the speakers' right of telling stories*, which is secured by *the speakers' right of telling them*, the interactive, often *polyphonic nature* of conversational narratives, their *unfolding across several turns of talk*, and the *fragmentary nature* of stories across extended and interrupted discourse.

Other aspects related to the production of specific narrative forms engendered by the intersection of narrative with conversation will also be examined. The typical narrative forms we will consider are *rounds of narratives* or *story sequences* and *collaborative stories*. Both forms will be shown to promote a sense of solidarity and harmony among speakers, either by the recurrence, in close proximity, of the same story pattern or by the joint production of the same story.

4.1 Interactional Features of Conversational Narratives

One important interactional feature of narratives in talk-in-interaction is *the speakers' right of telling stories*. This is secured by the stories being *relevant* in the interactional context in which they are embedded. Other manifestations of conversational narratives refer to the interactive, often *polyphonic nature* of conversational narratives, their *unfolding across several turns of talk*, and, last but not least, the *fragmentary nature* of stories across extended and interrupted discourse.

The first interactional feature which we will consider is story relevance.

4.1.1 Story Relevance

As stipulated by the turn-taking principle, which is central in conversation analysis, every party has the right to talk in a conversational interaction. The fact that a story represents a breach in the common turn-taking script, hindering the interactants from alternating the speaker – recipient roles and imposing the role of the speaker to a party for a longer time interval, entails a negotiation between the interlocutors. This represents a redressive action in accordance with the requirements of negative politeness: the potential narrator needs to compensate for taking up the other participants' right to talk, so that his/her action might not be perceived as an imposition or threat to the other participants' negative face (e.g., the desire to be free in one's actions, not to be hindered or imposed upon) (Ionescu-Ruxăndoiu, 1991:39); (Brown and Levinson, 1987 [1978]).

This negotiation is instantiated in the form of a *story preface*, whose role is to present

the upcoming story as relevant to the local context of the ongoing interaction, so as to grant the potential storyteller an extended right to speak.

Several terms have been employed in the literature to designate the speaker's

need to justify his conversational move of engaging into the telling of a story, which, as shown above, entails taking up a larger amount of time than that required by a common conversational turn: *tellability*[85] (Sacks, 1992); (Norrick, 2000); (Norrick, 2005), *newsworthiness* (Coupland & Jaworski, 2003:88)

---

[85] and [86] are terms designating the newsworthy character of a narrative.

and *reportability*[86] (Gűllich & Quasthoff, 1986:224); (Labov, 2011:547). To add to the list, we propose the term *relevance*. In our opinion, the relevance of a story consists of two elements: its *novel content* and the *interactants' involvement* in the act of narration. We will discuss the relevance of stories in point of content first.

A) Story relevance in point of the novelty of the content

In order to get and hold the floor longer in a conversation, as well as not to get sanctioned by the audience at the end of the story, a potential narrator must, first of all, present his/her story as *relevant* and *interesting* ('tellable' in Sacks' terms (1992) or reportable) from the point of view of the *novelty* of its content (Norrick, 2000); (Iordache, 2008:240); (Iordache, 2010b:79). This is usually done by means of a *story preface*, whose role is to announce the *newsworthiness* of the upcoming narrative and to signal the sort of evaluative – appreciative response expected from the audience when the story is over.

There are several types of events which count as worthy of being told in a story. Conversational stories often focus on *unusual, unexpected* events or on events that are considered *exceptional* by the community in which they are told (Blum-Kulka, 2005:276); (Georgakopoulou, 1997:3). A subclass of exceptional events are *transgressive* events, in the sense that they tackle topics conventionally regarded as rude (Coupland & Jaworski, 2003:88); (Norrick, 2005). *Local news*, pointing out a *new* or *unexpected* event (Sacks, 1992), is also worth mentioning as reportable in point of content. Last but not least, the relevance of a story resides in its *expression of the universality and commonality of human condition*:

'it is the task of a narrator to justify taking up airtime by making the story that of Everyman – what any reasonable person would do in similar circumstances' (Goffman (1981) apud Linde (2001:525)).

Regardless of the various types of reportable events, the *relevance* of a story *is locally dependent upon the context* in which the story is told (Norrick, 2000:105): thus, the events recounted in the narrative need to be unknown to the recipients, since telling a story without a currently or locally relevant point constitutes a loss of face for the teller (Polanyi, 1979); (Sacks, 1992); (Norrick, 2000).

Fragment (46) below points out that the relevance of a story resides in its newsworthy character.

(46) La Betleem/ At Bethlehem

1E: *ha::i să-ți spun o întâmplare ((râde))*
   let me tell you a story ((laughs))

2P: *ziceți*
    please do

3E: *apropo de arabi ((râde))*
    speaking of Arabs ((laughs))

4 *am mers cu încă o prietenă c-o prietenă de-a mea la Betleem (0.3)*
   I went with a friend a friend of mine to Bethlehem

5 *mergem la Betleem (0.2) intrăm*
   we went to Bethlehem we went in

6 *"mă mi-e foame"*
   I'm hungry

7 *"și mie (.) leșin de foame"*
    me too I'm starving

8 *"hai să mâncăm ceva"(.)*
   let's eat something

9 *mergem acolo-i aglomerat acolo-i aglomerat*
   we go it's crowded in here it's crowded in there

10 *găsim o (0.2) dugheană așa un restaurant mai (.) mai liber*
    we find a pub a less crowded restaurant

11 *unde erau și mese libere (.) intrăm noi înăuntru (.)*
    where there were spare tables as well we go in

12 *ne așezăm la bar (.) comandăm noi ce comandăm*
    we sit at the bar we order something

13 *ne-a servit acolo (0.2)*
    they served us something

14 *la un moment dat (.) văd că pleacă unu' doi trei (0.2)*
    at a certain point I see people leaving one two three

15 <u>*am rămas numai noi*</u> *(.) s-a golit tot localul*
    we were the only ones left (.) the whole restaurant got empty

16P: *((râde)) ( ) 'ce se întâmplă aici'*
    ((laughs)) what's happening in here

17E: *"ce Dumnezeu se întâmplă aicea" (0.2)*
    what on earth is happening in here

18 *ieșim și chelnerii ăia ospătarii ăia ce erau (0.3)*
    we get out and the waiters or whatever they were

19 *aveau dugheană și afară unde vindeau și la ghișeu*
    there was also a kiosk outside where they sold over the counter

20 *nu erau nici ăla*
    the other chap wasn't there either

21 *"mă fată ăștia au înnebunit unde dau banii acuma"((râde))*
    'these folks are mad gal whom shall I pay now'((laughs))

22P: *erau la rugăciune ce făceau?*
    were they praying or what

23E: *ne ducem la ălalalt că sunt una lângă alta acolo și-l întreb pe ăla*
    we go over to the other chap cause over there the kiosks are one next to the other and I ask him

24 *zic "unde este (0.1) trebuie să (plătesc)"(0.2)*
    I say 'where is I have to (pay)'

25 *și zice "stai un pic" se uită el și strigă*
    and he says 'wait a bit' he looks around and calls out

26 *zic "*<u>*unde ai dispărut? să-ți dăm banii*</u>*"*
    I say 'where have you gone let us pay'

27 *a luat banii a plecat ((râde)) asta era ziua (0.2)*
    he took the money he left ((laughs)) this happened during the day

28 <u>*seara*</u> *nu a doua seară ne ducem (.) la Betleem din nou (0.3) cu gașca noastră*
    in the evening no the next evening we go to Bethlehem again with our group

29 *că era (0.2) ă: ajunul Crăciunului noaptea de Ajun*
    cause it was Christmas Eve at night
30P: (   )
31E: *să sărbătorim (0.2) și: ne-am dus ne-am închinat*
    to celebrate and we went (there) we prayed
32 *mă rog unii mai erau rătăciți pe acolo (0.2)*
    well some seemed quite at a loss there
33 *zic "hai să acu' e ajunul Crăciunului hai să mergem să mâncăm ceva"*
    I say 'come on it's Christmas Eve let's go somewhere and eat something'
34 *că postisem toată ziua*
    cause we had fasted all day long
35   *ne ducem la restaurant*
    we go to the restaurant
36P: *tot acolo sau la*
    to the same place or
37E: <u>*la altul*</u> *la altul mai mai select mai așa (.)*
    to another one to a more exclusive one
38 *și povestim ((râde)) la prietene "auzi ce-am pățit noi" asta asta*
    and we tell ((laughs)) our friends 'look what's happened to us' and so on and so forth
39 *cum au ieșit toți mă frate nu aveam unde să dăm banii*
    how everyone got out and we had nowhere to pay
40 *zice "păi cine-a fost"*
    she says 'who went there'
41 *zic "io și Cristina noi amîndouă"*
    I say 'I and Cristina the both of us'
42 *zice "(știi) de ce au plecat ăștia"*
    she says 'do you know why they left'
43 *"nu"*
    no I don't
44 *"femeile n-au voie în restaurant și pleacă ei" ((râde))*
    women are not allowed in the restaurant so they leave ((laughs))
45P: *exact la asta m-am gândit și eu bă ori că n-are voie*=
    this is exactly what I thought of either she isn't allowed
46E: =<u>*stai*</u> *stai stai c-am uitat*
    wait wait a minute I forgot to
47 *stăm noi acolo la masă (.) am văzut că încep să plece*
    we sat there at the table we saw they started to leave
48 *zic "mă ăștia sunt nebuni (.) au început să plece"*
    I say 'these folks are nuts they started to leave
49 *mai erau niște francezi două-trei mese mai în-* =
    there were also some French people two or three tables away
50P: =*erau bărbați mă gândesc*
    they were men I reckon
51E: *nu erau și femei*
    no there were women as well
52 *mai erau niște chinezi sau ce or fi fost japonezi așa și restul toți*
    there were also some Chinese or Japanese or whatever they were and the rest of them
53   *zic "ăștia au înnebunit unde ne ducem noi pleacă"*
    I say 'these folks are nuts wherever we go they leave'
54P: (   )
55E: *cine?*
    who
56P: *femeia n-are voie să intre singură*
    women aren't allowed to go in alone
57E: *n-au voie bărbații să stea la un loc cu femeile*
    men are not allowed to be in the same place as the women
58   *decât cu nevestele lor (.) n-au voie*

```
           except with their wives they aren't allowed
59P: a și ăia or fi fost
           oh and those folks must have been
60E: plecau ei afară
           it was them who left
61   a plecat toată lumea (.) din crâșmă și noi am rămas
           everyone left the pub and we stayed
62   nu ne-a zis nici du-te mai încolo
           they didn't even say a word
63   ne-a servit și ne-au lăsat și au plecat
           they waited on us and they left
```

The storyteller in the fragment above, E, marks her story as relevant in point of the novelty of its content, thus arousing the recipient's interest through the introduction, in line 1, of a story preface accompanied by laughter (*'ha::i să-ți spun o întâmplare ((râde))'*) ('let me tell you a story ((laughs))'). This strategy is meant as a clue for the recipient that he should expect the unfolding narrative to be an amusing one.

The story acquires a puzzling character since it is based on a series of cultural differences between two peoples, the Arabs and the Romanians. The script a common European has in mind for having lunch in a restaurant involves entering the place, sitting at a table, being waited on, the actual process of eating, and finally paying the bill. With the Arabs, things seem to be slightly different. For a person who is unaware of such cultural differences, things may appear enigmatic. The narrator exploits the hearer's lack of knowledge in this matter to increase the suspense and keep the recipient's interest alert, as well as to prompt him into guessing the reason underlying the Arabs' strange reaction and behaviour when faced with what a European would normally consider a common situation.

Upon having found out that all the Arabs in the restaurant left shortly after the narrator and her friend had entered the restaurant, the recipient's first guess is that they may have left to say their prayers – line 22 *('erau la rugăciune ce făceau?')* ('were they praying or what'), but it is not until the end of E's performance that P learns the real reason for the Arabs' leaving: their cultural rules forbid females to walk unaccompanied by a male in their family and males to be in the same place with females, unless they are married – things which P began to suspect, as he confesses in line 45 *('exact la asta m-am gândit și eu bă ori că n-are voie=')* ('this is exactly what I thought of either she isn't allowed') .

To conclude, this story is relevant since it grants the recipient access to a new culture and its mentality.

A typical effect of embedding stories in conversation is the emergence of *rounds of stories* or *story sequences*. These terms designate narratives occurring in clusters or sequences of narratives, which are linked by the same topic and are contiguous (appear in proximity) to one another: in many conversational settings, stories do not appear isolated but implicitly invite related stories from other participants: 'an illustrative story by one participant provides a ticket another participant can use to allow the matching of that experience with a story from his repertoire' (Goffman, 1974:510). The first story of such sequences is known as *first story*, whereas the upcoming stories are called *second stories* or *response stories* (Sacks, 1992, vol.2:4); (Norrick, 2000:28); (Coates, 2003:83).

In compliance with previous research in the field, it appears that there are *similarities* between first and second stories regarding their *topic* and *characters*. The second story is carefully designed as almost a replica of the first story: thus, the *topic* tackled by the recipient of the first story in his/her own story involves a consideration of the model provided by the first speaker as a bridge onto one own's contribution (Coates, ibid.), so that the second story will develop into either an *emulation* (an almost exact repetition of the prior story with little variation or elaboration) or an *elaboration* (a repetition of the subsequent story containing some variation and elaboration) of the first story (Kŭntay and Şenay, 2003). Moreover, the second storyteller organises his/her story around a *character* which plays a similar part to the one played by the character in the first story. Finally, some of the linguistic units (i.e., words/phrases/sounds) used by the first speaker in building his/her story may also occur in the second story, as the recipient is utterly sensitive to the way the first story was told and this prompts him to use some of the words he/she heard in the preceding story (Sacks, ibid.); (Tannen, 1987:575). A particular feature of second stories is that they preserve part of the features from first stories without being framed again. That is why second stories in story sequences are characterized by *ellipsis of presupposed information* or are based on the information from previous stories.

Story sequences are made up of at least 2 stories, but they can even go up to seven or more, depending on the conversationalists' ability and disposition of producing new stories. The longest round of stories in our data consists of seven stories, but we have also encountered two rounds of five stories.

As demonstrated by previous studies in the field of conversational narratives, our thesis confirms that rounds of narrative play an essentially social part in conversational interactions: *creating or maintaining friendship or social bonds* among interlocutors *by aligning with one's conversational partner*, which counts as a positive politeness strategy in Brown and Levinson's Politeness Theory (1987) [1978].

Fragment (47) below illustrates a round of narratives whose components are locally relevant, enabling the interlocutors to achieve a sense of solidarity and intimacy with one another.

(47) Examene auto picate/ Failed driving tests
1 A: *o prietenă de-a mea era să dea peste unu' la trecerea de pietoni (0.3)*
    a friend of mine nearly hit a man on the zebra crossing
2   *și p'ormă a intrat în refugiu'din stația de tramvai*
    and then she hit the waiting shed at the tram stop
3 C: *cu polițistu' în mașină?*
    the policeman inside and all
4 A: *da (0.2) a intrat și i-a zdrobit roata la mașină*
    yes she hit it and crushed the car's wheel
5 C: *deci un prieten de-a lu' frate-[miu']*
    well a friend of my brother's
6 A:*[deci mai] bine-așa ca mine cel puțin*=
    whereas I at least
7 C: =*a dat peste-un polițist (0.5)*
    hit a policeman
8 A: *hai să-ți mai povestesc ceva ((râde))*
    let me tell you another story ((laughs))
9   *mi-a povestit-o profu' de franceză că eram io foarte necăjită că n-am luat examenu'*
    the French teacher told it to me cause I was very upset for not having passed my driving test
10   =*zice "da' din ce cauză?"*
    he asks why not
11   *'a mi-e și rușine am plecat cu frâna trasă'*
    oh I'm so ashamed I drove with the brake on
12   *a zice "lasă că-ți spun ce-a făcut o prietenă"*
    oh he says don't worry I'll tell you what a friend did
13   *cică prietena fiicei lui tot așa a dat examenu' și a pornit cu frâna trasă (0.5)*
    it appears that his daughter's friend also took the test and drove with the brake on
14   *și a pornit mașina îți dai seama*
    and the car started you ca imagine that
15   *s-a oprit brusc așa știi cum e te hâțână puțin*
    it stopped suddenly you know what it's like it shakes you a bit
16   *și polițistu' avea cascheta ((râde)) din aia pe cap și ((râde)) i-a zburat cascheta*
    and the policeman had his cap ((laughs)) on and ((laughs)) his cap flew away
17   *asta a vrut să-i prindă cascheta ((râde)) și i-a tras o palmă ((râde)) (0.3)*
    she wanted to catch his cap and ((laughs)) she slapped him ((laughs))
18   *și cascheta a ieșit pe geam ((râde)) că era geamu' deschis ((râde)) (0.5)*
    and the cap got out of the window ((laughs)) cause the window was open ((laughs))
19   *și a trecut o mașină ((râde)) (0.5)*
    and a car ran it over ((laughs))
20 C: *((râde))*
    ((laughs))
21 A: *și i-a făcut praf cascheta ((râde)) (0.5)*
    and crushed his cap ((laughs))
22 C: *((râde))*
    ((laughs))
23 A: *și ea s-a panicat și ăla a zis că (0.3) dacă mai dă cu (0.2) el în veci n-o să mai ia carnetu'*
    and she panicked and the chap said that if she takes her test with him again she won't pass it ever
24   *"afară"*
    get out
25 C: *și ăla săracu' n-avea simțu' umorului*
    the poor chap didn't have a sense of humour
26 A: *da' îți dai seama hai mă că parcă-i din film îți imaginezi toată faza asta*=
    fancy that come on this whole thing is like taken out of a picture
27   *îi **pică** cascheta*
    his cap falls off
28   *așa în zbor ea **încearcă** s-o prindă*
    she tries to catch it while it's still in the air

29　　*îi **trage**-o palmă ((râde))*
　　　she slaps him ((laughs))
30　　*cascheta **se duce** pe geam ((râde)) și **trece**-o mașină ((râde))(0.5)*
　　　the cap falls out of the window ((laughs)) and a car runs it over ((laughs))(0.5)
31 C: *da a: (0.5) și frate-mio a picat la traseu prima dată*
　　　yes oh my brother failed the route the first time as well
32　　*deci frate-mio e i-am zis Schumacher-repetistu'*
　　　I mean my brother is I nicknamed him the Schumacher-repeating man

The fragment above consists of a five story-sequence. The first story (lines 1-2, 4) briefly reports an amusing story. The second one (lines 5, 7), just like the first narrative, also relates a comical situation by reference to the story's climax. The third story (line 6) and the fifth one (lines 31-32), which are extremely elliptical, are allusions[87] to a previous telling of the events, while the fourth story (lines 8-24) is a fully-fledged story.

All five stories are related to one another and to the background of the conversation, as they share the same topic (failing driving tests) and have similar characters (playing similar parts: they all fail their driving tests in a more or less comical manner). C, the narrator of the second story, picks up some information from the first story and introduces it into her ongoing story without bothering to frame her story anew. She only mentions the element which makes her story top the first narrative, told by A: in A's story the driver nearly hit a pedestrian, whereas in her story, the driver actually hit a policeman. She also makes use of ellipsis, leaving out presupposed information, such as the circumstances that led to the actual happening of the event. The third story, related by A, stands in opposition to the previous two stories, as we may deduce from the allusion A makes in line 6 that her mistake was not that catastrophic as those of the characters in the first and second stories. The fourth narrative is in the line of the first two stories, though it is not so briefly recounted. It presents a fully-fledged comical situation, which provokes laughter in the participants to the conversation. Finally, the fifth story relates to the third one, since it mentions the character of the narrative having failed the practical test in his first driving test, which is exactly the same situation A hinted at in her story (line 6).

The present excerpt is indicative of the social role played by story sequences in talk-in-interaction as the two interlocutors constantly align with each other by means of positive signals, such as laughter, thus fostering their friendship.

A second factor accounting for the tellability of an ongoing narrative will be examined below.

---

[87] Allusions to stories qualify as a type of non-canonical narratives. For more information, see chapter 3, the section on the distinction between *canonical* and *non-canonical* narratives.

B) Story relevance in point of the interlocutors' involvement in the ongoing narrative

So far we have seen that the novelty of a story is a basic ingredient which ensures the storyteller's hold of the floor by capturing the auditors' attention. However, the relevance of a story does not only reside in its newsworthy content or, in other words, it is not restricted to *contextual factors*. The tellability of a narrative may also be dependent on *social factors*, since it may refer to the *dynamics* of the recounted event (Norrick, 2000); (Iordache, 2010b:80). This is the case of *familiar stories*, often introduced by prefaces marking them as known, which are told or even *co-told*, in spite of their being familiar to (almost) everybody present, since the emphasis is this time on the *interactants' high involvement* with the narrated event and the relationship holding between the interlocutors (Iordache, 2009b:223).

Collaborative narratives are the result of the contribution of two or more people who share knowledge of the event they are recounting, 'either through experiencing the event together or having knowledge of a past event' (Coates (2005) apud Leung (2009:1342)). The authors of the narratives are not just the ones that introduce them, but also the interlocutors who influence their unfolding, namely the recipients, who are not, as one might think, just passive listeners, but active co-tellers (Goodwin, 1981); (Coates, 2001 apud Lambrou (2003:155-157)). Co-narrators participate to the development of the story not only by providing minimal back-channeling but also by 'adding events, providing details about the setting or characters, telling the point of the story, or adding other narrative elements' (Coates (1996, 2005) apud Leung (2009:1341)), by asking questions, making comments and providing positive affective signals such as laughter (Coupland & Jaworski, 2003:88); (Goodwin, C. and Goodwin, M., 1990); (Jefferson, 1978); (Ochs et al., 1992). *Co-narration* has been found out to occur mostly in conversational interactions among friends or family members (Ochs et al. (1996)); (Polanyi (1985) apud Leung (2009:1341)), functioning as a means of reinforcing friendship or asserting family membership, shared values, feelings, and memories but also for comparing different points of view (Coates (2005); Norrick (1997); Ochs et al. (1996); Polanyi (1985); Coates (2005) apud Leung (2009:1342)). Collaborative narratives or joint productions strengthen social relationships and confer co-membership status by means of the storytellers' joint account and evaluation of past events, aligning the parties together (Norrick, 1997:205); (Ochs et al. (1996) apud Leung (2009:1342)). Gender studies examining the language use in women groups of friends have pinpointed the collaborative nature of women's talk and the storytelling's force of binding women friends together (Coates (1988; 1996; 2005) apud Leung (2009:1342)).

With respect to the most commonly used linguistic and interactional *features* in the co-tellers' construction of conversational narratives, studies in the literature have revealed 'the *repetition* of phrases, clauses, or sentences; the *rephrasing* of ideas; *latching*[88] between speakers; *overlapping speech*; the shared construction of utterances with one narrator completing another's utterance; and frequent use of *back channeling* (e.g., I see, that's right, OK)' (Coates (2005:91-92)); (Coates, 1988) apud Leung (2009:1342)). It has been pointed out that the presence of *humour* (mostly signalled by frequent laughter) in narratives of shared experiences reinforces friendship and *solidarity* and contributes to the intensification of *group rapport*, often functioning as a backchannel device, which is indicative of the recipient's attention and interest in the ongoing narrative (Tannen (1989) apud Lambrou (2003:170-171)).

The narratives in excerpts (48) and (49) are instances of collaborative accomplishments which prove that the tellability of a narrative may also reside in the speakers' involvement with the event they relate.

*(48) Chiul//*Cutting class
1B: mai ții minte Oana când plecam de la ultimele ore când aveam meditație la istorie
      Oana do you remember when I used to cut the last classes when I had private History classes
2   și veneam la tine să-nvă::ț ? ((râde))
      and I used to come to your place to study ((laughs))
3O: da::
      yeah
4   și-o prostea pe bunică-mea [((râde))]
      and she used to fool my grandma ((laughs))
5B: [((râde))]
                                  ((laughs))
6O: că cică io am mai stat știi?
      she said that I was still at school you know
7   io-am mai stat mai mult în plus la școală [((râde))]
      I stayed extra at school   ((laughs))
8 B: [((râde))]
                                  ((laughs))
9 O: nu zicea că ea chiulește știi? ((râde))
      she wouldn't say she was cutting class you know ((laughs))
10   cică „Oana mai stă (0.2) mai stă puțin ="
      she went 'Oana is staying extra'
11B: = da' io veneam la ea să-nvăț că eram disperată că aveam meditații la istorie (0.3)
      and I went to her place to study cause I was desperate cause I had private history classes
12   și dacă nu-nvățam îl suna pe taică-mio și-i zicea=
      and if I didn't study he would call my father and tell him about it
13O: = și când plecai cu Ioana Avram
      what about when you used to leave with Ioana Avram
14   o corupeai să plecați și dup-aia a zis că te zice mai știi ?

---

[88] The phenomenon of *latching* (symbolized in the transcript by =) indicates that the turns speakers take follow each other without any gap.

you used to talk her into leaving together and then she said she was going to tell the headteacher about it do you still remember
15B: *da*
yes

The narrative in the fragment above is co-told by two of the participants to the conversation. The narrated events are shaped through the contributions of the two speakers, who permanently interrupt and complete one another. The aim of the narrative is not to recount a new event, rather, it regards the solidarity between the co-narrators, the pleasure to relive a shared funny past experience, when the two attended secondary school and B used to skip the last classes and lie in order to manage to study in History. In this sense, humour, signalled by frequent laughter – lines 2, 4-5, 6-7 and 9–, plays an essential part.

With a view to the linguistic and interactional features that signal the co-tellers' building of the present narrative, the following features stand out: instances of latching (both speakers, O and B, follow one another in speeech without discernable silence) – lines 10-11, 12-13, overlapping talk – in fact joint laughter – lines 4-5 and 6-7, word repetition (the interlocutors sometimes make use of the same words used previously by their conversational partners – e.g., *a zice* (to tell) – lines 9, 12 *('(nu) zicea')* ('she wouldn't say') ('he (would) tell') and 14 *('zice')* ('she was going to tell'); *a pleca* ('to leave') – lines 1 *('plecam')* ('used to cut') and 14 *('plecați')* ('leaving'), rephrasal of the story opener/preface – lines 1 and 14 *('mai ții minte')*/*('mai știi')* ('do you remember?').

(49) *Râde ciob de oală spartă/* The pot calls the kettle black
1C: ua::i **mai ții mai ții minte** *faza cu profa de is- de geografia Angliei?* ((râde))
    oh do you recall the incident with the teacher of English geography ((laughs))
2 *și (0.1) ((râde)) Cristina Pop (0.1)* **nu mai știi** *[((râde))*
    and ((laughs)) Cristina Pop don't you recall it ((laughs))
3T: [*da*
                                                              yeah
4C: *ua:i ((râde)) deci aveam o profă de geografia Angliei (0.2)*
    oh ((laughs)) well we had a teacher of English geography
5 *slăbu::tă mai urâți::că așa săraca*
    really skinny and ugly poor thing
6 *și tot timpul era grăbi:tă tot timpul era în întârziere*
    and she was always in a hurry always late
7B: *făceați istoria Angliei geografia Angliei ?=*
    did you study English history English geography
8C: *=[da păi am fost la secție specială de] engleză am fost*
     well yes cause we were in an English specialty class
9T: *[da păi am fost la bilingv   ]*
     yes cause we were in a bilingual class
10C: *și făceam chestiile astea în engleză știi (0.2) ((își drege vocea))*
     and we did this stuff in English ((clears her throat))
11T: *da' ea ea preda practic (0.1) era profă de geografie la: (0.1) Pedagogic știi*
     but she was in fact teaching she was a geography teacher at the Pedagogical highschool you know

```
12    și normal că alerga pentru o singură [oră la noi] pe săptămână sau două ore aveam
         and it's only natural that she practically ran up to our highschool for a single class a week or did we have two
classes
    13C:                                   [da:      ]
                                            yeah
    14T: nu mai știu o oră sau două °aveam°?
         I can't remember we had a class or two
    15C: do:uă (0.1) nu mai știu
         two I really can't tell
    16T: nu știu în fi:ne DE-ASTA ERA TOT TIMPU' GRĂBI:TĂ știi (0.4)
         I don't know all in all this is why she was always in a hurry you know
    17   și-și trântea plasa aia=
         and she used to throw her bag
    18C: =pe bune așa urâțică era săraca abia mai avea păr pe cap=
         really so ugly was the poor thing she barely had any hair left
    19T: = [((râde))]
           ((laughs))
    20C:  [era] na mă rog
          she was well
    21T: ((râde))=
         ((laughs))
    22C: = și-aveam noi una în clasă pe nume Cristina Pop
         and we had one classmate Cristina Pop was her name
    23B: (        )?
    24T: [da]
         yes
    25C: [da] pe nume Cristina Pop și-aia săraca urâțică rău
         yes Cristina Pop was her name and really ugly too poor thing
    26T: [((râde))]
         ((laughs))
    27C: [((râde))] parcă era îmbătrânită devreme
         ((laughs)) as if she got old early
    28   parcă avea boala aia știi gena aia când îmbătrânești devreme
         as if she had that illness you know when one gets old early
    29T: hai să trecem peste asta
         let's skip this shall we
    30C: na mă rog și când intră asta odată în clasă [((RÂDE))         ]
         well and one day she enters the classroom ((laughs))
    31T:                                             [și-a făcut permanent]
                                                     she got a perm
    32   își făcuse permanent (0.1) la două fire cât avea ea
         she had got a perm to the two hairs she had
    33C: stai puțin și-nainte cu două săptămâni îi spusesem
         wait a minute and two weeks beforehand I had told (Teo)
    34   "tu Teo oare nu i-ar sta mai bine dacă și-ar face permanent păru'?"
         Teo I wonder wouldn't she look better if she got a perm
    35   io (mă gândeam) că permanent e mai bogat
         I reckoned that the perm might make it look thicker
    36T: horror
         horrid
    37C: și ((râde)) vine asta și-i stătea ori:bil
         and ((laughs)) in she comes looking horrid
    38T: parcă te-a auzit=
         as if she had heard you
    39C: =și toată clasa a început să râ:dă
         and all the class started laughing
    40   și cine râdea mai tare era Cristina Pop care era oribilă săraca ea însăși=
```

    and the one that laughed loudest was Cristina Pop who was horrid herself poor thing
41T: =*ea însăși* ((*râde*))
    herself ((laughs))
42C: *și-atunci îi zic io lu' Teo* "**râde ciob de oală spartă**" ((*râde*))
    and then I tell Teo the pot calls the kettle black ((laughs))
43T: *și și ea a zis „ce faci Cristina râ:zi"* ?
    and she herself said 'laughing Cristina are you'

The story in the fragment above (an amusing situation from the narrators' common past, namely the highschool years) is an instance of a collaborative narrative, which is clearly not told for its novelty in point of content but for social purposes, that is, for the reinforcement of the friendship holding between the two narrators, C and T. Thus, in spite of the fact that the two interlocutors know the story very well (as it is a first-hand experience), it is co-told anyway, first of all, for their own amusement, and secondly, for the entertainment of a third party, a friend of C's, who has no knowledge whatsoever of the recounted event. The technique used by the two co-tellers consists of establishing *common ground with the addressee* – a positive politeness technique, functioning as a social bound between the interactants (Brown & Levinson, 1987:103). Several strategies are employed by the two narrators. One such strategy is *intensifying interest to the hearer* (ibid.:106-107) through the use of 'the vivid present', which 'pulls the hearer right into the middle of the events being discussed', increasing the interest to him/her – lines 30 *('na mă rog și când intră asta odată în clasă [((RÂDE))')* ('well and one day she enters the classroom ((laughs))') and 37 *('și ((râde)) **vine** asta și-i stătea ori:bil')* ('and ((laughs)) in she comes looking horrid'). In fact, this instance of the conversational historical present is included in a larger switch, back and forth, between the past – lines 4 *('ua:i ((râde)) deci aveam o profă de geografia Angliei (0.2)')* ('oh ((laughs)) well we had a teacher of English geography'), 6 *('și tot timpul era grăbi:tă tot timpul era în întârziere')* ('and she was always in a hurry always late'), 12 *('alerga pentru o singură [oră la noi] pe săptămână sau două ore aveam')* ('she practically ran up to our highschool for a single class a week or did we have two classes'), 17 *('și-și trântea plasa aia=')* ('and she used to throw her bag'), 18 *(' =pe bune așa urâțică era săraca abia mai avea păr pe cap=')* ('really so ugly was the poor thing she barely had any hair left'), 22 *('= și-aveam noi una în clasă pe nume Cristina Pop')* ('and we had one classmate Cristina Pop was her name'), 28 *('parcă avea boala aia știi gena aia când îmbătrânești devreme')*, ('as if she had that illness you know when one gets old early') 31 *('[și-a făcut permanent]')* ('she got a perm'), 39 *('=și toată clasa a început să râ:dă')* ('and all the class started laughing'), 40 *('și cine râdea mai tare era Cristina Pop care era oribilă săraca ea însăși=')* ('and the one that laughed loudest was Cristina Pop who was horrid herself poor thing') and present tense – lines 30 and 37. The use of the directly quoted speech is another feature of the above-mentioned strategy, which is at work in this collaborative narrative – lines 34 (*"tu Teo oare nu i-ar sta mai bine dacă și-ar face permanent* *păru'?")* ("Teo I wonder wouldn't she look better if she got a perm"), 42 *('și-atunci îi zic io lu' Teo "râde ciob de oală spartă" ((râde))')* ('and then I tell Teo the pot calls the kettle black ((laughs))') and 43 *('și și ea a zis "ce faci Cristina râ:zi"?')* ('and she herself said 'laughing Cristina are you').

The second strategy is seeking agreement through repetition ((ibid.:112-113). By repeating C's utterance in the previous turn, T stresses emotional agreement with it, as in lines 13-14 *('ea însăși')* ('herself').

All in all, this narrative shows that relevance may also consist of social and emotional bonding between the interlocutors.

The next interactional feature of conversational narratives that we will discuss is the speakers' right of telling stories.

4.1.2 Tellability rights or speakers' right of telling stories

A potential narrator does not only have to persuade the hearers that the story he/she is about to tell deserves their attention, but also that he/she is the right person to tell it. Storytelling rights depend a great deal on the degree of *knowledge of,* or familiarity with the recounted *events*. That is why a narrator who actually took part in a certain event (through a first-hand experience) goes first in telling a story before another participant to the conversation who found out about that respective event from someone else's story, and who, obviously, knows less on the matter than his interlocutor. Or, in other words, 'personal experience grants ownership, and shared experience grants joint ownership' (Blum-Kulka, 1993:383).

Storytelling rights also depend on *contextual and social factors,* as, for example, *age* and *power relations*[89] holding between the interactants (Norrick, 2000). For instance, an older person goes before a younger person and an employee yields his/her right to tell a story to his/her employer/superior. Another social factor allocating the speaker's right of telling stories is, according to the data in our corpus, the recognition by the auditors of the *speaker's talent as* an exquisite *performer*.

---

[89] Power relations also influence the communicative contributions at the level of conversation, the more powerful speaker tending to take more elaborate turns and to interrupt his/her interlocutor (Vasilescu, 2007c:211).

Fragments (50) and (49) point out that storytelling rights are established socially and contextually.

(50) D-na Miki / Mrs. Miki
1 E: *Roxana cum făcea doamna aia (0.3) hai te rog spune?*
     Roxana how did the lady do that please tell us
2 R: *care doamnă?=*
     what lady
3 E:= *doamna aceea Miki*
      that lady the one they called Miki
 ((*R și E râd*))
 ((R and E laugh))
4 E: *hai te rog spune*
     please tell us
5 R: (   )
6 E: *da hai că tu spui mai b::ine*
     yes come on you tell it better

In the present fragment both speakers are would-be storytellers, as they are both equally familiar with the event to be recounted (they both have a first-hand experience of the respective event). The decisive factor in assigning the telling right is, in this case, the *social factor*: the right to tell a story is assigned to R, as E yields the latter her own right to narrate, by virtue of the principle that the best or the most talented must come first – line 6 (*'da hai că tu spui mai b::ine'*) ('yes come on you tell it better'). E's attempt to persuade her interlocutor into telling the story is strategically built. For a start, E uses an indirect speech act, a directive, her request being masked under the guise of a question (Searle, 1969) – line 1 (*'Roxana, cum făcea doamna aia' (0.3)*) ('Roxana how did the lady do that please tell us'), then, after a few seconds' break, in which there is no reply from her interlocutor, E reformulates her request by means of a direct speech act (*'hai te rog spune'*) ('please tell us'), a request which she reiterates in line 4, this time stressing the verb emphatically (*'spu::[ne]'*) ('tell us'). Taking into account R's hesitation in responding to her interlocutor's demand to narrate (it takes E four requests to get R started), one feels entitled to claim that the directive speech acts addressed by E to R are interpreted by the latter as a threat to her negative face, in the sense that R is being imposed to tell a story. Perceiving her mistake, E is trying to repair it by adopting a positive face-saving strategy (Brown & Levinson, 1987), by mitigating her request through the address of a compliment, a linguistic unit which she emphatically stresses in line 6 (*'da' hai că tu spui mai b::ine'*) ('yes come on you tell it better').

Coming back to fragment (49), we notice that the narrative is co-told, since both narrators have first-hand knowledge of the respective event. However, the main narrator is clearly C, who is also the initiator of the narrative. The variables of distance and power are irrelevant in this case, since the two interlocutors are of the same age and the relationship holding between them is one of friendship. T's role as a storyteller is to support C, by supplying further details concerning the recounted situation or by adding glosses, accounting for the main character's odd behaviour (always being late) – lines 16-17 or even by sanctioning her co-storyteller when one of her remarks – lines 27 *('[((râde))] parcă era îmbătrânită devreme')* ('((laughs)) as if she got old early') and 28 *('parcă avea boala aia știi gena aia când îmbătrânești devreme')* ('as if she had that illness you know when one gets old early') constitutes a real threat to one of the character's positive face – line 29 *('hai să trecem peste asta')* ('let's skip this'). Although T's latter action, which represents a threat to her interlocutor's negative face by imposing her what to do, may have some consequences on their friendship, T takes the risk relying on their solid relationship.

The next feature to be examined in the present section is the interactive nature of conversational narratives.

4.1.3 The interactive, often polyphonic nature of conversational narratives

As embedded in conversation, narratives may become *dialogic*[90] or *polyphonic*[91], since they involve several participants[92] in the process of narration (Blum-Kulka, 1993:385). This implies that conversational narratives are by-products of the negotiations between interlocutors, since, in most cases, auditors do not behave like passive recipients but play an active role in the co-construction of stories. The plurality of voices present in the act of co-narration entails the achievement of rapport or high-involvement between co-tellers, instantiated in showing interest and enthusiasm (Blum-Kulka, ibid.); (Tannen, 2005:100).

The fragment below is illustrative of the polyphonic character of ongoing narratives:

(51)D-na Miki/Mrs. Miki
1R: *da' ea era foarte satisfăcută că tu râzi =*
   she was very satisfied you were laughing
2 *= deci se uita la tine dar defapt ei îi plăcea și să fie în centrul atenției*
   I mean she looked at you but she actually liked being the centre of attention

---

[90] *Dialogic narratives* are constructed through a question-answer sequence.
[91] *Polyphonic narratives* are jointly constructed by several parties.
[92] In considering this classification, we started from Bakhtin's assertion that any discourse is dialogically oriented (Bakhtin, 1981:279); (Billig, 1996:17).

```
 3 E: [da]
       yes
 4R: [nu] nu-i așa adi::că exagera unele lucruri?
      didn't she I mean she used to exaggerate certain things
 5 E: mai povestea niște chestii de nu mă mai puteam
      she also told us some stuff that I couldn't
 6    știi cu râsul ăla al meu mă-necam
      you know that laughter of mine I was choking
((toți râd))
((all laugh))
 7E: zicea "ce-ai fata mea? te-neci ? ce-ai? ai probleme cu ca[::pu']?"
     she said  what's the matter girl are you choking what's the matter are you nuts
 8R:                                                        [apoi] ne-a povestit ea cum s-au cunoscut cu (0.2) soțu'
                                                            then she told us how she met her husband
 9    defapt ne-a povestit cum și-au petrecut luna de miere=
      in fact she told us how they spent their honeymoon
10E:= în deltă
       in the delta
11R: în deltă izolați și (0.2) în prima noapte (0.3) soțu (0.2)' a intrat în comă=
     in the delta isolated and during the first night her husband fell into a coma
12E:= alcoolică
       alcoholic (coma)
       ((toți râd))
       ((all laugh))
13R: de ce crezi?
     guess why
14I: că (0.2) nu știu
     cause I don't know
15R: erau doi ardeleni pe-acolo nu știu ce făceau [ei]
     there were two people from Ardeal over there I don't know what they did
16 E:                                             [ei]
                                                  they
17I: beau pălincă=
     they drank 'pălincă'
18R: =nu
      no they didn't
```

Fragment (51) contains, as shown above, a story which is co-told by two of the participants in the conversation. The style adopted by the two interactants is 'a high involvement style', which is alert and characterized by overlaps, being nevertheless non-competitive – meaning that it denotes the speakers' collaboration and not their competition for turn-taking (Schegloff, 2000:32-33). This kind of style is used by the speakers for building rapport and signalling involvement and solidarity (Tannen, 1984, 1989). In the present fragment, this style can be traced in the speakers' use of *discourse markers* for seeking agreement *('nu-i așa?')* ('didn't she') – line 4 and *('știi')* ('you know') – line 6. The two interactants' turns do not only overlap (lines 3-4, 7-8, 15-16), but they also complete one another (as, for example, in lines 7-8 or 9-10-11-12 (R: '*a intrat în comă*'/E: '*alcoolică*') (R:'fell into a coma/E:alcoholic (coma)'), (R: '*și-au petrecut luna de miere*''/E: '*în deltă*')) (R: 'they spent their honeymoon/E: in the delta') – and even invite the hearer, I, to take part actively in the process of storytelling: for instance, in line 13, through an apparent question *('de ce crezi?')* ('guess why'), R produces an indirect speech act (namely a directive (Searle, 1969)), through which she prompts I to anticipate the continuation of the story.

Returning to excerpt (49), we can claim that it is illustrative of the interactive and dialogic character of conversational narratives. The present story is told by two narrators, C and T, who permanently cut-in to complete each other's remarks with comments and personal impressions, thoughts or remembrances about the narrated event. Although each of the storytellers' voice is unique and brings different details into the audience's attention, nevertheless, C and T succeed in creating the impression of a unitary performance through the use of lexical or semantic repetition of the linguistic units used by one or the other speaker – lines 36 *('horror')* ('horrid') and 37 *('și ((râde)) vine asta și-i stătea ori:bil')* (and ((laughs)) in she comes looking horrid'), 40 *('care era oribilă săraca ea însăși=')* ('who was horrid herself poor thing') and 41 *('=ea însăși ((râde))')*('herself ((laughs))'), 42 *("râde ciob de oală spartă" ((râde)))* ('the pot calls the kettle black ((laughs))') and 43 *('și și ea a zis „ce faci Cristina râ:zi")* ('and she herself said "laughing Cristina are you"').

We will now consider another characteristic of stories in talk-in-interaction, namely their unfolding across several turns of talks.

4.1.4 The unfolding of stories across several turns of talks

Stories-in-interaction unfold across several turns of talks or utterances (Ionescu-Ruxăndoiu, 1991:38). According to Sacks (1992, vol.2:19), a story represents the speaker's attempt to control the discussion across an extended series of utterances. That is why, in terms of the sequential organization of conversation (which signals whose turn it is to speak), it is important that the would-be tellers indicate by means of special cues their intention of telling a story, so that the other interactants may comment or make remarks on the topic tackled by the narrator but in the end give the floor back to the speaker who has announced his/her intention of telling a story (Sacks, ibid.); (Norrick, 2000:107).

Fragments (52) and (46) prove that a story may extend across several turns of talk.

(52) Examene auto picate/Failed driving tests
1C: a: a doua oară=

```
         the the second time
2A:  = atunci începi să-ți dai seama că nu prea poți să-l iei ((râde))
         it is then you realise you can't really pass it ((laughs))
3C: nu:: a doua oară a fost așa
     no the second time it was like this
4    ă: (0.3) instructorul a plecat avea alte chestii
     the driving instructor left as he had other things to do
5    și a trimis pe altcineva iar persoana asta (0.5)
     and he sent someone else in his place and this person
6    cum a venit a vrut să ia banii să scape repede
     as soon as he came he wanted to take the money and to get the job over with quickly
7    și m-a pus să să (0.3) deci m-a pus a doua mașină
     and he had me drive second
8    deci n-am mers cu mașina să văd cum merge mașina
     I mean I hadn't driven that car beforehand to see how it works
9    n-am pornit mașina ca la [(    )
     I didn't start the car as in
10A:                          [(    )
11C: și era aceeași marcă era aceeași marcă dar alt tip (0.3)
     and it was the same brand it was the same brand but another type
12   are fiecare mașină are=
     each car has a
13A: =normal
     naturally
14C: are altfel setările știi?
     it has different settings you know
15A: îhî
     yeah
16C: și ce nu mi s-a-ntâmplat mie în luni de zile când conduceam pe mașina celuilalt
     and what hadn't happened to me for months while I had been driving the other person's car
17   mi s-a întâmplat acuma mi s-a oprit motoru'
     happened to me now the car engine stopped
18   o dată de două ori ceea ce nu e grav (0.2)
     once or twice which is not serious
19   deci se poate opri de trei ori și abia după trei ori se consideră greșeală
     I mean it can stop three times and only then it's considered to be a mistake
20   deci nu e o greșeală da' eram atât de emoționată
     so it's not a mistake but I was so nervous
21   și nu mă mai gândeam decât cum să meargă motoru'
     and the only thing I could think of was how to get the engine started
22   trebuia să o fac la dreapta ă: (0.2) aveam verde
     I had to turn right uhm the traffic light was green
23   da' trecerea era pe partea pietonilor și:: (0.5)
     but the crossing was on the pedestrians' side and
24   n-am călcat pe nimeni ((râde))
     I didn't hit anyone ((laughs))
     ((toți râd))
     ((all laugh))
25C: n-am acordat prioritate=
     I didn't yield the right-of-way
26   = și am picat foarte ușor cu douășiunu de puncte
     and I just failed with twenty-one points
```

In the excerpt above, one of the participants to the conversation, C, recounts how she failed her driving test for the second time. C's interlocutors recognize her intention of telling a story and, although they interrupt her several times, at *transition-relevance places*[93], either in order to make an ironic remark on the topic tackled in the story – line 2 (*'atunci începi să-ți dai seama că nu prea poți să-l iei'*) ('it is then you realise you can't really pass it ((laughs))') – or to express their alignment with C's utterances – lines 13 (*'normal'*) ('naturally') and 15 (*'îhî'*) ('yeah') –, they constantly give the floor back to C, so that she could finish her story. Therefore, under the plea of telling a story, the narrator obviously succeeds in dominating the conversation by producing much more utterances than her interlocutors.

Coming back to the story in excerpt (46), we may assert that it represents another instance of the narrator's manipulation of the conversational interaction across several turns of talk. The recipient, P, acknowledging Speaker's E intention of telling a story, has brief interventions, as for example, when making comments – line 16 (*'ce se întâmplă aici'*) ('what's happening in here'), guesses – lines 50 (*'=erau bărbați mă gândesc'*) ('they were men I reckon'), 59 (*'a și ăia or fi fost'*) ('oh and those folks must have been') or asking for explanations regarding the topic of the narrative – lines 22 (*'erau la rugăciune ce făceau?'*) ('were they praying or what') and 36 (*'tot acolo sau la'*) ('to the same place or'), but gives the floor back to E to continue and finish her story.

Last but not least, we will examine the fragmentary nature of stories across extended and interrupted discourse.

4.1.5 The fragmentary nature of stories across extended and interrupted discourse

Across an extended and interrupted discourse, ongoing stories are often fragmented (Ionescu-Ruxăndoiu, 1991:38). This fragmentation or discontinuity of the story reflects 'the exigencies of real-time verbalization for an active conversational audience' (Norrick, 2000:3). Besides the narrator's unavoidable false starts[94] and self-repairs[95] (Dascălu Jinga & Ştefănescu, 2009:193-194), we have identified two main factors which favour the discontinuity of a story, namely the narrator's frequent or

---

[93] For more information on *transition-relevance places* see chapter 1.
[94,8] we will not insist on these phenomena, since we have treated them in chapters 1 and 2.

extended digressions from the narrative proper and the recipients' cut-ins of the narrative thread, as for instance, in order to request various details connected to the events presented by the narrator.

Returning to the story in fragment (51), we may conclude that its fragmentary character is given by the co-tellers' preoccupation for building rapport and creating a joyous atmosphere. This is why the narrative line comes in second, the story becoming a sum of various sequences and impressions selected by each speaker, taking into account the factors that have marked their experience individually and have meant to shape an eccentric character. For instance, E does not relate what the character in the narrative said exactly, but the effect which the latter had on her – line 5 ('*mai povestea niște chestii de nu mă mai puteam*') ('she also told us some stuff that I couldn't'), whereas R selects and sketches briefly an unexpected incident, meant to attract the recipient's attention and even to shock her – lines 9-12–. Therefore, as long as narratives do not render the actual facts, but they rather reconstruct them (they are '*construals* of happening' in Ochs' terms (1997) and *selections*, rather than reflections of reality (cf. Burke, 1962)), it is to be expected that, in the process of co-telling in which two narrators present the events through their own individualities, the stories should be fragmented.

The next excerpt is also illustrative of the fragmentary character of narratives embedded in conversation:

<u>(53) *Tratament*/</u>Treatment
1C: *și eu nu mai puteam să vin și a doua zi că trebuia să stau cuminte acasă (0.2) în pat*
    but I could not come the next day cause I had to rest at home in bed
2   *și:: i-am încredințat mamei rețeta a doua zi*
    and the next day I entrusted Mum the prescription
3   *mama s-a dus la farmacie*
    Mum went to the pharmacy
4A: *la <u>pri</u>ma farmacie ((râde))*
    to the nearest pharmacy ((laughs))
5C: *mă rog (0.1) era printre primele far<u>macii</u> (0.1) de lângă <u>casă</u>=*
    well it was among the phamarcies nearest to our home
6A :=<u>*așa*</u>
    right
7C: *că noi avem Catena Dona ă: avem mai multe și Sensiblu*
    cause there are Catena Dona uhm there are several (pharmacies) even Sensiblu
8A: *((râde))*
    ((laughs))
9L: *e raiu' farmaciilor*
    it's the pharmacies' heaven
10A: *da: ((râde))*
    yeah ((laughs))
11C: *mă rog și din moment ce cei de la Helpnet ne promiseseră că ne ajută*
    well and since the people from Helpnet had promised to help us

12 și io lăsasem rețeta la ei (0.1)
    and I had left the prescription with them
13 A și L: a::::::
    A and L: oh
14C: că la ei lăsasem rețeta ă:: mama a apărut la ei
    cause I had left the prescription with them uhm Mum showed up there
15C: și (0.2) ei ăstia i-au spus "tanti noi nu avem medicamentu' ăsta (0.2)
    and they these guys told her 'we haven't got this medicine m'am'
16 dar vă putem da un înlocuitor"
    but we can give you a substitute
17A: a::: (0.4)
    oh
18C: și (0.2) mama de bună credință a luat înlocuitoru'
    and Mum in good faith took the substitute
19 a plătit banii că altfel [dacă l-ar fi luat] după rețetă ar fi fost gratis
    she paid the money cause otherwise if she had taken the one in the prescription it would have been for free
20A: [nu (   )]
                             no way
21L: a:::: și cât a plătit
    oh and how much was it?
22C: un milion jumate
    a million and a half
23L: fii atent (arătând spre un băiat din parc)
    watch this (pointing to a boy in the park)
24A: ăhă
    yeah
25C: după ce-am ajuns io acasă=
    when I came home
26L: fii atent fii atent
    watch this watch this
27C:a:::: și io am rămas cu undița agățată într-un copac odată
    oh I myself got my fishing line stuck in a tree once
28 asta când mergeam cu ea pe umăr fără să mă uit la nimic în jur
    this was while I was walking with it on my shoulder without looking around
29 ((L și A râd))=
    ((L and A laugh))
30C:=și eram cam așa:în mijlocul sălbăticiei (0.1)
    and I was almost in the middle of the wilderness
31 adică n-avea cine să m-ajute pe-acolo
    I mean there wasn't anybody to help me there
32L: și ce [(   )?]
    and what
33C: [făcusem rost] de un scăunel de pescuit parcă cum să zic=
            I managed to get a fishing chair or something
34A: =((râde))
    ((laughs))
35C: bine am tăiat firu' până la urmă [((râde))]
    well I eventually cut the thread ((laughs))
36A: [((râde))] și?
                                      ((laughs)) and what next?
37C: așa și (0.5) deci ă:: unde rămăsesem io cu povestea?=
    well so where was I ?
38A:= ((râde))
    ((laughs))
39C: că trebuia mama să se ducă la farmacie
    Mum had to go to the chemist's
40 i-au dat un înlocuitor=

       they gave her a substitute
41A := *a plătit un milion jumate (0.1) a plătit=*
       she paid a million and a half
42C:= *da a plătit un milion jumate și ă: (0.2)*
       yeah she paid a million and a half and uhm
43   *cât mi-a adus medicamentele io mi-am făcut injecția*
       by the time she got my medicine I had done my injection
44   *după la ceva vreme după aceea când mi-am făcut timp*
       after that in a while when I found time for it
45   *că mă uitam și la emisiuni la televizor (0.2) treburi importante deci*
       cause I was also watching TV important matters therefore
46   *ă: am citit prospectu' de la :: (0.3) injecție*
       uhm I read the injection prospectus
47   *pe pilulele pe care trebuia să le iau*
       on that of the pills I was supposed to take
48   *scria că sunt antiimflamatoare nesteroidiene (0.5)*
       it read they were non-steroid anti-imflammatory
49   *pe cel al injecțiilor spunea că nu sunt compatibile*
       on that of the injections it read they weren't compatible
50   *cu antiimflamatoarele nesteroidiene (0.2) [((râde))]*
       with the non-steroid anti-imflammatory pills ((laughs))
51A: *[((râde))] ai auzit Laura?=*
                                  ((laughs)) got it Laura?
52L:=*da*
       yes
53A: *ma::mă și?*
       oh my God and what next?
54C: *atunci io- am lăsat să treacă o zi și din ziua următoare*
       then I let a day pass by and from the next day onwards
55   *am continuat să iau antiimflamatoarele nesteroidiene adică pilulele (0.5)*
       I went on taking the non-steroid anti-imflammatory medicine I mean the pills
56   *injecțiile le-am lăsat (0.2) pe (0.1) pe mai târziu*
       I left the injections for some other time
57   *când o vrea cineva să (0.2) să (0.1) să-i consume să le ia le-oi da*
       when somebody wants to use them to take them I'm going to give them away
58A: *da' pentru ce erau injecțiile*
       what were the injections for anyway
59C: *erau niște chestii contra coagulării sângelui (0.1) să nu formezi cheaguri*
       they were some stuff against blood coagulation which impede clot formation

The conversational narrative in the fragment above is clearly discontinuous. This fragmentation or discontinuity of the story is due to two main sources. One such cause consists of the narrator's frequent or extended digressions from the narrative proper. Thus, the storyteller, C, deviates from the story line to inform his interlocutors on the multitude of pharmacies in his neighbourhood – lines 5 (*'mă rog (0.1) era printre primele farmacii (0.1) de lângă casă='*) ('well it was among the phamarcies nearest to our home') and 7 (*'că noi avem Catena Dona ă: avem mai multe și Sensiblu'*) ('cause there are Catena Dona uhm there are several (pharmacies) even Sensiblu') –, to make an ironic comment regarding his frivolous preoccupations and his lack of priority at a time when he was ill – line 45 (*'că mă uitam și la emisiuni la televizor (0.2) treburi importante deci'*) ('cause I was also watching TV important matters therefore') and to start a new report on a time when he had some trouble with his fishing line, when his attention is drawn by L on a similar situation – lines 27-35.

The other source of discontinuity is represented by the recipients' cut-ins of the narrative thread, as when L interrupts the story in order to draw the participants' attention on an incident in the immediate surroundings – lines 23 and 26, which eventually prompts C into engaging into another report and as when A asks for more details concerning the prescribed injections – line 58. A's and L's ironical comments on the recounted event – lines 4 *('la prima farmacie ((râde))')* ('to the nearest pharmacy ((laughs))') and 9 *('e raiu' farmaciilor')* ('it's the pharmacies' heaven'), the latter expression being a metaphor, as well, and their expression of disappointment at C's and his mother's reckless decisions – lines 13 and 17 *('a:::')* ('oh') are other instances of cut-ins from the narrative thread.

4.2 Conclusions

This chapter has shown that Romanian conversational narratives, just like the English ones in the literature, evince a series of *interactional features,* which we exemplified with relevant excerpts taken from our own corpus of Romanian ongoing narratives. For the analysis of these features, we have relied on the model of organization and structuring of conversation elaborated by Sacks, Schegloff and Jefferson (1974) and Sacks (1992) and on the sociological variables of age, gender and level of education of speakers, which influence the discursive strategies of positive and negative politeness (Brown and Levinson, 1987 [1978]) and positive and negative impoliteness (Culpeper, 1996); (Culpeper et al., 2003).

The *interactional features* of conversational narratives depend on the power/solidarity relations holding among the interlocutors. Therefore, we found that some of these properties vary with the age of the participants and with the setting in which the stories are told, whereas others do not.

One characteristic aspect deriving from the turn-taking rules (Sacks, Schegloff and Jefferson, 1974) is the *relevance or tellability* of a story, which has been pointed out to consist of two factors: the *novel content* of the story for the recipient and the *interactants' involvement* in the act of narration. The tellability of a *story*, both in point of the novelty of the story's content and in that of the interlocutors' involvement in the ongoing story has been found not to vary with age. In formal settings, unlike in the familiar ones, in cases of unequal power relations holding between conversationalists or in relations characterized by social distance, conversationalists do not normally engage in telling stories, unless they are new and relevant to the local context. In familiar settings, on the other hand, in the case of equal power relations and with no social distance holding between the interlocutors, a story does not necessarily have to be new to be relevant. Story relevance is often synonymous with the interactants' involvement with the narrated event and with each other.

Another interactional feature of conversational narratives is the speakers' *rights of telling stories*, which are secured by the stories being *relevant or newsworthy* in the interactional context in which they are embedded. It has been shown that storytelling rights depend on the degree of *familiarity with* the recounted *events*, as well as on c*ontextual and social factors*, as for example, the *age* and *power relations* holding between the interactants. Thus, a younger person and an employee yield their right to tell a story to an older person and to the employer/superior, respectively. A particular *speaker's talent as* an exquisite *performer* has also proved to be a decisive factor, providing the right of telling stories.

Conversational narratives have been shown to be *interactive*, more or less *polyphonic*, representing the result of negociations between the interlocutors. This interactive feature seems to be favoured by familiar settings and by the solidarity relation holding between the interlocutors.

A conversational narrative has been pointed out to unfold across more than one turn of talk or utterance by virtue of regarding the story as a speaker's attempt to control the discussion across an extended series of utterances. This property is invariant with the participants' age, formal/informal setting or the power and social distance variables.

Most stories have also been described to be *fragmented across extended and interrupted discourse*, due to either the teller's digressions from the storyline or to the hearers' cut-ins to ask for various details concerning the reported events. This property has been found to be influenced by the power and social distance variables and by the formal setting of the act of telling.

The present chapter has also examined other aspects related to the interaction between the two types of discourse, dialogue and narrative. It has been pointed out that the insertion of narratives in conversation gives rise to specific narrative forms, such as *rounds of narratives* or *story sequences*. In this particular case, the solidarity relation holding between conversationalists has been shown to be marked by the recurrence, in close proximity, of the same story pattern. Another issue characteristic of narratives embedded in conversation has been shown to be the occurrence of another special type of narratives, *collaborative stories*. These joint productions strengthen social relationships and confer co-membership status by means of the interactants' assertion of shared values, feelings, and memories.

All in all, the Romanian corpus we have examined and analysed proves that the interactional features of conversational stories recurring in the English corpus appear in Romanian conversational narratives, as well.

CHAPTER 5.
FINAL CONCLUSIONS

The present study has focussed on *conversational narratives,* a unique form with specific features arising from the fact that it combines two discursive modalities: *narrative* and *dialogue* (or conversation). The investigation of the double nature of narratives in talk-in-interaction has required an appropriate theoretical framework, an eclectic perspective based on two approaches to discourse: *conversation analysis* and *narrative analysis*. It has been pointed out that conversation analysis views *conversation* as a *characteristic mode of behaviour* and that, similarly, *narratives* represent *typical modes of organizing experience*. We have also shown that in the analysis of conversational turns we have relied on *pragmatic theories*: Speech Act Theory (Searle, 1969), including Grice's Cooperative Principle (CP) (1975) and its four related maxims, as well as Politeness Theory (Brown and Levinson, 1987 [1978]) and Impoliteness Theory (Culpeper, 1996); (Culpeper et al., 2003).

The general properties of the narrative, such as its *fixed structure,* consisting of *a beginning, a middle* and *an end,* and its focus on *temporally ordered events* have been pointed out to be preserved in conversational narratives, as well. In addition to these features which conversational narratives share with classical narratives, we have identified a set of *linguistic features*, bestowed upon narratives by their being embedded within the larger framework of conversation (**chapter 2**). In this sense, narratives have been shown to acquire an oral character, given by special *syntactic and lexical features, characteristic of spoken language*. Special attention was given to the linguistic traits marking the passage between the discourse genres of dialogue and narrative: *opening/closing formulas* and *the switch in tense* from the present tense of the conversation to the past tense of the narrative. The *future* tense, as well as the *narrative present* have also been proved to be an option. *Tense alternation* from the past to the present tense and back again has been shown to be a linguistic phenomenon characteristic of narratives in interaction, whose role is to separate episodes in the story or mark the climax of the narrative.

The various ways in which a story is triggered in conversation have also been considered. Thus, we have noticed that a particular detail in the conversational interaction may trigger the so-called *entailed* narrative, whereas a question asked by a conversationalist may engender an *elicited* narrative.

Alternatively, the presence of an object or person in the local environment may give rise to an *environmentally cued* narrative.

As to the *oral character* of conversational narratives, we have discussed it in point of the *syntactic structure* and *vocabulary* of conversational narratives, which are characteristic of spoken language. At the syntactic level, we have emphasized the fact that conversational narratives favour brief utterances and *co-ordination* by means of the conjunction 'and' or by juxtaposition. Other syntactic characteristics of conversational narratives as samples of spoken language are: *the simple structure of the noun phrase*, characterized by few proper names and few relative clauses, *fragmented verbal sequences* and/or *incomplete sentences, syntactic disorder,* illustrated by means of *ellipsis, anacoluthon, self-correction, false starts*, followed by *rephrases and repetitions*. The use of *interjections* and *exclamatives*, of *address terms* (such as *first names, endearment forms* and *diminutives*), *discourse markers, phatic elements (or fillers), back-channel signals* and *general extenders* has also been shown to contribute to the orality of interactional narratives.

Among the various ways of reporting the characters' speech in conversational narratives we have found that *direct reported speech* is by far preferred to indirect speech, having the role of marking the key elements of the story or of creating the impression of involvement in the narrated event. In fact, DRS has been reinterpreted as *constructed dialogue,* since the so-called reported utterances do not actually belong to the characters but represent the storyteller's contribution, a positive politeness strategy meant to create involvement between interlocutors.

As to the vocabulary used by storytellers in conversational narratives, we have identified a series of colloquial lexical items, characteristic of spoken language: *idioms, slang, taboo terms, words derived by diminutival or augmentative suffixes* with the purpose of expressing affect, *vague language or generic terms*. We have also pointed out that the amount of synonymic terms is rather low and that there is a particular preference for the *repetition* of certain lexical items, whose role is to emphasize the dramatic effect of the story or the storyteller's attitude with respect to an aspect presented in the story.

Chapter 3 has discussed the *pragmatic functions* of conversational narratives from the double perspective of conversational narratives as a form of narrative and as being enclosed within the larger frame of conversational interaction. It has been pointed out that the analysis *concentrates on* the *narrative passages*, rather than on the whole conversation, since any narrative, whether conversational or not, can be discussed from the point of view of its pragmatic functions.

Our research on this issue started from the communicative purposes listed in the literature. However, we observed that the perspective was incomplete, as we could not subsume part of our findings (the metalinguistic and the poetic functions) to the already inventoried functions. Therefore, we have set upon the task of enlarging the respective perspective by adopting Halliday & Hasan's (1989) model of language functions. This paradigm has proved closer to our pragmatic perspective, since it characterizes the language serving referential goals (*the ideational function*), the narrator and the interlocutor, as well as the relationship holding between them (*the interpersonal function*) and the text (*the textual function*). We then decided to opt for Jakobson's model of language functions, since it is less abstract than Halliday & Hasan's, permitting us, for instance, to treat the interpersonal function in relation to the speaker (the *emotive or expressive* function), the interlocutor (the *conative or persuasive* function) and the channel of communication (the *phatic* function).

The identification of the functions of conversational narratives has been a challenging aspect, since, according to the principle of the *multifunctionality of language*, the functions of language are co-present or overlap in any given message (Jakobson, 1960); (Halliday & Hassan, 1989). After listing all the possible functions of a particular conversational narrative, we arranged them hierarchically, from the dominant function to the secondary, minor, or peripheral ones. The dominant function was identified by relying on *the intention-based criterion*, which is synonymous with Grice's (1975) and Searle's (1979) idea of the purpose of a speech act. In other words, we identified the dominant function according to the main speech act structuring the conversational exchange.

Our findings have revealed that the ***ideational function,*** comprising language as a system of signs, is omnipresent in every conversational narrative. **The interpersonal function** has been found to be on top in an overall classification of the dominant functions of conversational narratives. By relating Halliday and Hassan's (1989) interpersonal function to Jakobson's (1960) emotive/expressive, conative/persuasive and phatic functions, we discovered that *the phatic function* is favoured. The most common situations in which it occurs are: entertaining the audience, gossiping, and establishing, maintaining or transforming social relationship, ratifying group/family membership and reinforcing group norms and values. The *emotive function* has been found to overrule the other minor functions when the storyteller constructs a certain identity for himself/herself and when he/she explores the moral implications of personal experience, whereas the *persuasive function* is dominant when the speaker uses a story to illustrate a point he/she is advocating in conversation and to justify or account for his/her actions.

The metalingual function has been found to be prominent when the storyteller engages upon telling a story in order to clarify a particular linguistic term. As to *the poetic function*, it only occurs as a secondary function in interactional narratives, when the storytellers seek to obtain a certain dramatic effect. This was shown to be achieved by means of various linguistic devices, such as the *selection of lexical items* providing the details of the story, the use of *repetition*, the use of *humour (punning, irony, banter)*, of *constructed dialogue and* of *tense alternation* (from the past tense to *the conversational historical present*).

Last but not least, *the referential function* was shown to be always a minor function, supporting all primary functions.

Aside from the strict examination of the functions of conversational narratives, other aspects have been tackled in relation to these functions. For instance, related to the interpersonal function is the use of *topics*, which is revealing for the storyteller's socio-cultural identity, for his/her relationship with the interlocutors and for the context/cotext of occurrence of a particular narrative. The sociological variables of *age, gender, and level of education* have been pointed out to be influential with respect to topic selection.

In connection with the textual function of narratives, which has an explanatory role regarding the narrative as a final text or product, we have discussed the *internal structure* of conversational narratives, discriminating between *canonical* and *non-canonical narratives*.

While in chapter 2 we have examined a series of linguistic properties characterizing narratives in talk-in-interaction, in **chapter 4** we have dealt with the *interactional features* of conversational narratives, pointing out that they are the result of the embedding of narratives in conversation, as well as the product of the sociological variables of age, gender and level of education of speakers, which bear on conversational behaviour.

The *relevance or tellability* of a story has been discussed starting from the turn-taking rules (Sacks, Schegloff and Jefferson, 1974). It has been shown that two factors secure the speakers' right of telling stories: the *novel content* of the story for the audience and the *interactants' involvement* in the act of narration. The tellability of a *story*, both in point of the novelty of its content and in that of the interlocutors' involvement in the ongoing story, has been found to be invariant with respect to the age variable. As to the setting in which the narrative is told, we have found that in formal settings, in cases of unequal power relations holding between conversationalists or in relations characterized by social distance, the speakers do not normally engage in telling stories unless they are new and relevant to the local context. In familiar settings, on the other hand, in the case of equal power relations and with no social distance holding between the interlocutors, a story does not necessarily have to be new to be relevant. Story relevance is often conferred by the conversationalists' involvement with the narrated event and with each other.

The speakers' *right of telling stories* has been shown to be granted if the upcoming story appears *relevant or newsworthy* in the interactional context in which it is introduced. It has been pointed out that storytelling rights depend on the degree of *familiarity with* the recounted *events*, as well as on c*ontextual and social factors*, as for example, the *age* and *power relations* holding between the interactants. Thus, a younger person and an employee yield their right to tell a story to an older person and to the employer/superior, respectively. Moreover, our corpus has provided evidence that the audience's acknowledgement of a particular *speaker's talent as* a *performer* can also secure the right of telling stories.

Another interactional property of ongoing stories has been shown to be their *polyphonic nature*, which implies that they are the result of negociations between the interactants. This trait has been found to be favoured by familiar settings, which foster relations of solidarity between conversationalists.

The *unfolding* of conversational narratives *across more than one turn of talk* or utterance by virtue of the fact that telling a story represents the speaker's attempt to control the discussion across an extended series of utterances has been found to be invariant with the participants' age, formal/informal setting or the power and social distance variables.

The fragmentariness of stories across extended and interrupted discourse, due to either the teller's digressions from the storyline or to the hearers' cut-ins to ask for various details concerning the reported events, has been described to be influenced by the power and social distance variables and by the formal setting of the act of telling.

Our research has revealed the existence of specific types of narratives, engendered by the intersection of the two modes of discourse – narrative and conversation: *rounds of stories (*or *story sequences)* (characterized by the recurrence, in close proximity, of the same story pattern) and *collaborative accomplishments* (defined as joint story productions). It has been shown that in both cases what comes first is the solidarity relation holding between conversationalists.

All in all, throughout this thesis, we have shown that *conversational narratives* may be approached in various ways: as *a type of text* (chapter 2), as *an act of communication* (chapter 3), and as *an interactional act,* as *part of the conversational behaviour* (chapter 4).

Finally, we propose that our research may represent the basis for the development of *a typology of conversational narratives,* starting from a series of **criteria** which we found pertinent for the present research. Thus, with respect to the internal structure of conversational narratives we may identify *canonical* and *non-canonical stories* (Georgakopoulou, 2006b; Ervin-Tripp and Küntay, 1997; Ochs and Capps, 2001; Labov and Waletzky, 1967). The examination of the ongoing narratives from the point of view of their source leads to the binary opposition: *firsthand* versus *secondhand* narratives (Schank (1990) apud Özyildirim (2009:1210)), whereas with a view to the degree of fictionality of the events presented in the conversational narratives, we may distinguish between *fictional* and *non-fictional* narratives (Preece,

1992). According to the contribution of one or several narrators to the enfolding narrative, we can discriminate between *narratives told by a single narrator* and *collaborative accomplishments* (Goodwin, C. & Goodwin, M., 1990; Jefferson, 1978; Ochs et al., 1992; Norrick, 2000; Sacks, 1992; Sacks, 1978), whereas according to the frequency of the succession of nearly identical narratives in conversation, we may identify *single narratives* and *rounds of narratives* or *story sequences* (Sacks, 1992; Kűntay and Șenay, 2003; Coates, 2003; Arminen, 2004). Finally, in point of the context/cotext of occurrence of conversational narratives, we encounter the following categories of narratives: *entailed narratives, elicited narratives* and *environmentally cued narratives* (Kűntay and Șenay, 2003). Several types of narratives may be added to the already existing typology by grouping them according to the following criteria of classification: the novelty of the narrative's informational content for the recipient and the topic selection in the conversational narratives. In point of the former criterion, we can distinguish between *narratives presenting new information* and *narratives based on old information*, whereas in point of the topic tackled by the narrators in their stories, we may draw a larger list.

As to the relevance of our study for the current research of narratives in talk-in-interaction, the present dissertation is meant to be a *comprehensive work* on Romanian conversational narratives. It is worth mentioning that, at the time we started our thesis, there was no research in Romanian concerning conversational narratives. However, in the meantime, a few aspects have been tackled by several studies, among which none is as extensive as ours. The various issues discussed in relation to conversational narratives have been illustrated with relevant fragments taken from our corpus of narratives engendered by conversation. This *corpus* amounts to about 30 hours of naturally-occurring, face-to-face conversational interactions, containing genuine conversational narratives, which were recorded in familiar settings, during casual chats among friends and/or family members, as well as in more formal settings, during professional meetings. Considering the amount of our recorded material, we may claim to contribute to the enrichment of the data of spoken Romanian with *conversations comprising ongoing narratives*.

BIBLIOGRAPHY

ABMA, T. A. (2004) 'Narrative Analysis'. *Encyclopedia of Evaluation.* SAGE Publications. Retrieved 3 May 2010 from <http://www.sage-ereference.com/evaluation/Article_n359.html>.

ARDINGTON, A. (2006) 'Playfully negotiated activity in girls' talk'. *Journal of Pragmatics,* vol. 38, pp. 73-95.

ARISTOTLE (2000) *The Poetics of Aristotle.* Butcher, S. H. (trans.). The Pennsylvania State University.

ARMINEN, I. (2004) 'Second stories: the salience of interpersonal communication for mutual help in Alcoholics Anonymous'. *Journal of Pragmatics,* vol. 36, pp. 319-347.

BAKHTIN, M. (1981) *The Dialogic Imagination.* Four essays by M. M. Bakhtin. The University of Texas Press.

BAMBERG, M. (1997) 'Positioning between structure and performance'. *Journal of Narrative and Life History,* vol. 7 (1-4), pp. 335-342. Lawrence Erlbaum Associates, Inc.

BAMBERG, M. (2004a) 'Considering counter narratives'. Bamberg, M. & Andrews, M. (eds.) *Considering Counter-Narratives. Narrating, resisting, making sense.* John Benjamins Publishing Company, Amsterdam/ Philadelphia, pp. 351-371.

BAMBERG, M. (2004b) 'Talk, Small Stories, and Adolescent Identities'. *Human Development,* vol. 47, pp. 366–369.

BAMBERG, M. and GEORGAKOPOULOU, A. (2008) 'Small stories as a new perspective in narrative and identity analysis'. *Text & Talk* 28-3, pp. 377-396.

BARBU, V. (2011) *Les actes de langage dans l'incipit de l'interaction didactique.* Thèse de doctorat. Universitatea din București.

BARTHES, R. & DUISIT, L. (1975) 'An Introduction to the Structural Analysis of Narrative'. *New Literary History,* vol. 6, no. 2 On Narrative and Narratives, pp. 237-272. The Johns Hopkins University Press.

BAUMAN, R. (1986) *Story, performance, and event. Contextual studies of oral narratives.* Cambridge University Press, Cambridge.

BĂLĂȘOIU, C. (2004) *Discursul raportat în textele dialectale românești.* Editura Universității din București.

BESNIER, N. (1989) 'Information Withholding as a Manipulative and Collusive Strategy in Nukulaelae Gossip'. *Language in Society*, vol. 18, no. 3, pp. 315-341. Cambridge University Press.

BILLIG, M. (1996) *Arguing and thinking. A rhetorical approach to social psychology.* Cambridge University Press.

BLUM-KULKA, S. (1993) '"You Gotta Know How to Tell a Story": Telling, Tales, and Tellers in American and Israeli Narrative Events at Dinner'. *Language in Society*, vol. 22, no. 3, pp. 361-402.

BLUM-KULKA, S. (1997) *Dinner-Talk: Cultural Patterns of Sociability and Socialization in Family Discourse.* Lawrence Erlbaum, Mahwah, New Jersey and London.

BLUM-KULKA, S. (2005a) 'I will tell you the whole true story now': Sequencing the past, present and future in children's conversational narratives'. Ravid, D. D. & Bat-Zeev Shyldkrot, H. (eds.) *Perspectives on Language and Language Development.* Essays in honor of Ruth A. Berman. Springer, pp. 275- 288.

BLUM-KULKA, S. (2005b) 'Rethinking Genre: Discursive Events as a Social Interactional Phenomenon'. Fitch, K. L. & Sanders, R. E. (eds.) *Handbook of Language and Social Interaction.* Lawrence Erlbaum Associates, Inc., Mahwah, New Jersey, London, pp. 275-300.

BOGAN, D. (1992) 'The Organization of Talk'. *Qualitative Sociology*, vol. 15, no. 3, pp. 273- 295. Human Sciences Press, Inc.

BREWER, W. F. & LICHTENSTEIN, E. H. (1982) 'Stories are to entertain: a structural-affect theory of stories'. *Journal of Pragmatics*, vol. 6, pp. 473-486. North-Holland Publishing Company.

BROWN, G. & YULE, G. (1983) *Discourse Analysis.* Cambridge University Press.

BROWN, P. & LEVINSON, S. (1987) (first edition, 1978). *Politeness. Some universals in language usage.* Studies in Interactional Sociolinguistics 4. Cambridge University Press, Cambridge.

BRUNER, J. (1990) *Acts of meaning.* Harvard University Press, Cambridge, London.

BUCHOLTZ, M. & HALL, K. (2005) 'Identity and interaction: a sociocultural linguistic approach'. *Discourse Studies*, vol. 7, no. 4–5, pp. 585–614. SAGE Publications.

BUJA, E. (2008) *Relating events in narrative. A case study of Romanian.* Editura Universității 'Transilvania' din Brașov.

BURIDANT, C. (2006) « L'interjection : jeux et enjeux ». *Langages*, vol. 1, no. 161, pp. 3-9. Armand Colin.

BUTLER, C. S. & TAVERNIERS, M. (2008) 'Layering in structural-functional grammars'. *Linguistics: an interdisciplinary journal of the language sciences.* Walter de Gruyter GmbH & Co. KG, available online at http://findarticles.com/p/articles/mi_hb195/is_4_46/ai_n32406385/

BÜHLER, K. (2011) *Theory of Language. The representational function of language.* John Benjamins Publishing Company. Amsterdam/Philadelphia.

THE CAMBRIDGE ENCYCLOPEDIA OF THE LANGUAGE SCIENCES (2011) Hogan, P.C. (ed.). Cambridge University Press.

CARTER, R. & McCARTHY, M. (2006) *The Cambridge Grammar of English.* Cambridge University Press.

CATON, S. C. (1987) 'Contributions of Roman Jakobson'. *Annual Review of Anthropology*, vol. 16, pp. 223-260. Annual Reviews.

CHAFE, W. (1994) *Discourse, consciousness, and time. The flow and displacement of conscious experience in speaking and writing.* The University of Chicago Press, Chicago & London.

CHAFE, W. (2001) 'The Analysis of Discourse Flow'. Schiffrin, D., Tannen, D., Hamilton, H. E. (ed.) *Handbook of Discourse Analysis.* Blackwell Publishers Ltd, UK, pp. 673-687.

CHAFE, W. & TANNEN, D. (1987) 'The Relation between Written and Spoken Language'. *Annual Review of Anthropology*, vol. 16, pp. 383-407. Annual Reviews.

CHATMAN, S. (1975) 'Towards a Theory of Narrative'. *New Literary History*, vol. 6, no. 2, On Narrative and Narratives, pp. 295-318. The Johns Hopkins University Press.

CHATMAN, S. (1978) *Story and Discourse. Narrative Structure in Fiction and Film.* Cornell University Press, Ithaca and London.

CIOLAC, M. (1999) *Sociolingvistică românească.* Editura Universității din București, București.

CLARK, H. H. & GERRIG, R. J. (1990) 'Quotations as Demonstrations'. *Language*, vol. 66, no. 4, pp. 764-805. Linguistic Society of America.

CLIFT, R. & HOLT, E. (2006) 'Introduction'. Holt, E. & Clift, R. (ed.) *Reporting Talk: Reported Speech in Interaction.* Cambridge University Press.

CHIRICU, I. (2007) 'Aspecte ale discursului raportat în 'Interacțiunea verbală în limba română actuală. Corpus (selectiv). Schiță de tipologie". Ionescu-Ruxăndoiu, L. (coord.) *Interacțiunea verbală (IV II). Aspecte teoretice și aplicative. Corpus.* Editura Universității din București, pp. 227-251.

COATES, J. (2000) 'Small talk and subversion: female speakers backstage'. Coupland, J. (ed.) *Small talk.* Pearson Education Limited, pp. 241-263.

COATES, J. (2003) *Men talk. Stories in the making of masculinities.* Blackwell Publishing.

COATES, J. (2005) 'Masculinity, collaborative narration and the heterosexual couple'. Thornborrow, J. & Coates, J. (ed.) *The sociolinguistics of narrative.* John Benjamins Publishing Company, Amsterdam, pp. 89-106.

COHAN, S. & SHIRES, L.M. (1988) *Telling stories. A theoretical analysis of narrative fiction.* Routledge, London and New York.

CONSTANTINESCU, M. (2007) "ce-aţi făcut în /uichend/ ↑ <@ aţi vorbit la mobil ↓ un cent pe minut.>'. Umorul în conversaţie'. Ionescu-Ruxăndoiu, L. (coord.) *Interacţiunea verbală (IV II). Aspecte teoretice şi aplicative. Corpus.* Editura Universităţii din Bucureşti, pp. 171-197.

CORNILESCU, A. & CHIŢORAN, D. (1994) *The Theory of Speech Acts.* Editura Fundaţiei "Chemarea", Iaşi.

COSORECI-MAZILU, S. (2010) *Dissociation and Persuasive Definitions as Argumentative Strategies in Ethical Argumentation on Abortion.* Unpublished doctoral dissertation. Universitatea din Bucureşti.

COUPLAND, J. (2000) 'Introduction: Sociolinguistic perspectives on small talk'. Coupland, J. (ed.) *Small talk.* Pearson Education Limited, pp. 1-25.

COUPLAND, J., COUPLAND, N. & ROBINSON, J. D. (1992) '"How Are You?": Negotiating Phatic Communion'. *Language in Society*, vol. 1, no. 2, pp. 207-230. Cambridge University Press.

COUPLAND, J. & JAWORSKI, A. (2003) 'Transgression and Intimacy in Recreational Talk Narratives'. *Research on Language and Social Interaction*, vol. 36, no.1, pp. 85–106. Lawrence Erlbaum Associates, Inc.

CULPEPER, J. (1996) 'Towards an Anatomy of Impoliteness'. *Journal of Pragmatics,* vol. 25, pp. 349-367.

CULPEPER, J., BOUSFIELD, D. and WICHMANN, A. (2003) 'Impoliteness revisited: with special reference to dynamic and prosodic aspects'. *Journal of Pragmatics,* vol. 35, pp. 1545–1579.

DASCĂLU JINGA, L. (2002) *Corpus de română vorbită (CORV). Eşantioane.* Oscar Print, Bucureşti.

DASCĂLU JINGA, L. (coord.) (2011) *Româna vorbită actuală (ROVA). Corpus şi studii.* Editura Academiei Române, Bucureşti.

DASCĂLU JINGA, L. & ŞTEFĂNESCU, A. (2009) 'Despre caracterul fragmentar al discursului oral'. *Limba română,* nr. 2, pp.192-201.

DAVIES, C. E. (2003) 'How English-learners joke with native speakers: an interactional sociolinguistic perspective on humor as collaborative discourse across cultures'. *Journal of Pragmatics*, vol. 35, pp. 1361–1385.

DEDAIĆ, M. N. (2005) 'Ironic denial: tobože in Croatian political discourse'. *Journal of Pragmatics*, vol. 37, pp. 667–683.

DE FINA, A. (2003) *Identity in Narrative. A study of Immigrant Discourse*. John Benjamins, Amsterdam and Philadephia.

DICŢIONAR GENERAL DE ŞTIINŢE. ŞTIINŢE ALE LIMBII (1997) Bidu-Vrănceanu, A., Călăraşu, C., Ionescu-Ruxăndoiu, L., Mancaş, M. & Pană-Dindelegan, G. (eds.) Editura Ştiinţifică, Bucureşti.

DINNEEN, F. P. (1995) *General Linguistics*. Georgetown University Press, Washington, D.C.

DOMINTE, C. (2003) *Introducere în teoria lingvistică. Antologie pentru seminarul de teorie a limbii*. Universitatea din Bucureşti.

DREW, P. (2005) 'Conversation analysis'. Fitch, K. L. & Sanders, R. E. (eds.) *Handbook of Language and Social Interaction*. Lawrence Erlbaum Associates, Inc., Mahwah, New Jersey, London, pp.71-102.

DRUMMOND, K. & HOPPER, R. (1993) 'Back channels revisited: Acknowledgement tokens and speakership incipiency'. *Research on Language and Social Interaction*, vol. 26, no. 2, pp. 157–177.

DUBOIS, B. L. (1989) 'Pseudoquotation in Current English Communication: "Hey, She Didn't Really Say It"'. *Language in Society*, vol. 18, no. 3, pp. 343-359. Cambridge University Press.

DUNBAR, R. (1996) *Grooming, gossip and the Evolution of Language*. Faber and Faber Limited, London.

DUNCAN, S. JR. (1974) 'On the Structure of Speaker-Auditor Interaction during Speaking Turns'. *Language in Society*, vol. 3, no. 2, pp. 161-180. Cambridge University Press.

DURANTI, A. (1997) *Linguistic Anthropology*. Cambridge University Press, Cambridge.

DYER, J. & KELLER-COHEN, D. (2000) 'The discursive construction of professional self through narratives of personal experience'. *Discourse Studies*, vol. 2, no. 3, pp. 283–304. SAGE Publications, London, Thousand Oaks, CA and New Delhi. www.sagepublications.com

EEMEREN, F. H. van (2002) 'Argumentation: an overview of theoretical approaches and research themes'. *Argumentation, Interpretation, Rhetoric*. Online Journal, issue 2. EEMEREN, F.

H. van & GROOTENDORST, R. (1992) *Argumentation, Communication, and Fallacies. A pragma-dialectical perspective.* Lawrence Erlbaum Associates, Inc., New Jersey.

THE ENCYCLOPEDIA OF COMMUNICATION AND INFORMATION (2002) Schement, J. R. (ed.), vol.2. Macmillan Reference USA, Gale Group.

ERVIN-TRIPP, S. & KÜNTAY, A. (1997) 'The occasioning and structure of conversational stories'. Givón, T. (ed.) *Conversation: cognitive, communicative and social perspectives.* Benjamins, Amsterdam & Philadelphia, pp. 133–166.

FISHER, W. R. (1987) *Human communication as narration: Toward a philosophy of reason, value and action.* University of South Carolina Press, South Carolina, USA.

FLEISCHMAN, S. (1993) 'Tense and narrativity. From medieval performance to modern fiction'. *Journal of Pragmatics,* vol. 19, pp. 83-98. Book review, reviewed by Bertinetto, P. M. .

FLUDERNIK, M. (2009) *An introduction to narratology.* Routledge, Abingdon.

FOX, B. A. (1987) *Discourse structure and anaphora. Written and conversational English.* Cambridge University Press.

FRANZOSI, R. (1998) 'Narrative Analysis-Or Why (And How) Sociologists Should be Interested in Narrative Author(s)'. *Annual Review of Sociology,* vol. 24, pp. 517-554. Annual Reviews. Stable URL: http://www.jstor.org/stable/223492.

GAFU, C. (2009) *Naraţiunile familiale în mediul urban actual.* Editura Etnologică, Bucureşti.

GARSON, G. D. (2008) "Narrative Analysis". *Statnotes: Topics in Multivariate Analysis.* Retrieved 03/03/2010 from http://faculty.chass.ncsu.edu/garson/pa765/statnote.htm

GELLNER, E. (1998) *Language and solitude. Wittgenstein, Malinowski and the Habsburg Dilemma.* Cambridge University Press.

GEORGAKOPOULOU, A. (1997) *Narrative Performances. A study of Modern Greek storytelling.* John Benjamins Publishing Company, Amsterdam.

GEORGAKOPOULOU, A. (2006a) 'The other side of the story: towards a narrative analysis of narratives-in-interaction'. *Discourse Studies,* vol. 8, no.2, pp. 235–257. SAGE Publications, London.

GEORGAKOPOULOU, A. (2006b) 'Thinking big with small stories in narrative and identity analysis'. Internet version at http://www.clarku.edu/~mbamberg/Papers/Alex%20Georgakopoulou.doc

GEORGAKOPOULOU, A. (2007) *Small Stories, Interaction and Identities.* John Benjamins Publishing Company, Amsterdam.

GEORGAKOPOULOU, A. (2008) 'Narrative Genre Analysis'. *The Sage Encyclopedia of Qualitative Research Methods.* SAGE Publications.

GHIGA, G. (1999) *Elemente fatice ale comunicării în româna vorbită.* Editura Alcris-M94, București.

GOFFMAN, E. (1986) ([1974]) *Frame Analysis: An essay on the organization of experience.* Northeastern University Press, Boston.

GOODWIN, C. (1981) *Conversational Organization: Interaction Between Speakers and Hearers.* Academic Press, New York.

GOODWIN, C. (1984) 'Notes on Story Structure and the Organization of Participation'. Atkinson, M. & Heritage, J. (ed.) *Structures of Social Action.* Cambridge University Press, Cambridge, pp. 225-46.

GOODWIN, C. & GOODWIN, M. H. (1990) 'Interstitial argument'. Grimshaw, A. (ed.) *Conflict talk.* Cambridge University Press, Cambridge.

GOODWIN, M. H. (1982) '"Instigating": Storytelling as Social Process'. *American Ethnologist*, vol. 9, no. 4 Symbolism and Cognition II, pp. 799-819. Blackwell Publishing.

GOODWIN, M. H. (1990) *He-Said-She-Said. Talk as Social Organization among Black Children.* Indiana University Press, Bloomington.

GRAMATICA LIMBII ROMÂNE (2005) Guțu Romalo, V. (coord.). Editura Academiei Române, vol. I & II, București.

GRUNDY, P. (1995) *Doing Pragmatics.* Edward Arnold, London.

GÜNTHER, U. K. (2003) *What's in a laugh? Humour, jokes and laughter in the conversational corpus of the BNC. Unpublished doctoral dissertation.* Philosophy Faculty, Albert-Ludwigs University, Freiburg i. Br. Available online at http://www.freidok.uni-freiburg.de/volltexte/735/pdf/thesis.pdf

HALLIDAY, M. A. K. & HASAN, R. (1983) [1976] *Cohesion in English.* Longman, Singapore.

HALLIDAY, M. A. K. & HASAN, R. (1989) *Language, context and text: aspects of language in a social-semiotic perspective.* Oxford University Press.

HANDBOOK OF LANGUAGE AND SOCIAL INTERACTION (2005) Fitch, K. L. & Sanders, R. E. (eds.). Lawrence Erlbaum Associates, Inc., Mahwah, New Jersey, London.

HARRIS, F. (2007) *(Re)-Constructing Māori children as Achieving Learners.* Unpublished doctoral dissertation, University of Canterbury.

HAYDEN, R. M. (1987) 'Turn-taking, overlap, and the task at hand: ordering speaking turns in legal settings'. *American Ethnologist,* vol. 14, no. 2, pp. 251-270. Blackwell Publishing.

HÉBERT, L. (2007) *Dispositifs pour l'analyse des textes et des images*. Presses de l'Université de Limoges, Limoges. Also available online at http://www.signosemio.com/jakobson/a_fonctions.asp

HERMAN, D. (2005) 'Histories of Narrative Theory (I): A Genealogy of Early Developments'. Phelan, J. & Rabinowitz, P. J. (ed.) *A companion to narrative theory*, Blackwell Publishing, UK, pp. 19-35.

HERMAN, D. (2009) *Basic elements of narrative*. Wiley-Blackwell, Singapore.

HILBERT, R. A. (1990) 'Ethnomethodology and the Micro-Macro Order'. *American Sociological Review*, vol. 55, no. 6, pp. 794-808. American Sociological Association.

HOLMES, J. & MARRA, M. (2005) 'Narrative and the construction of professional identity in the workplace'. Thornborrow, J. & Coates, J. (ed.) *The sociolinguistics of narrative*. John Benjamins Publishing Company, Amsterdam, pp. 193-213.

HORNOIU, D. (2008) *Language and Gender. An Analysis of Conversational Discourse in English and Romanian*. Ovidius University Press, Constanţa.

HUTCHEON, L. (2005) *Irony's Edge. The theory and politics of irony*. Routledge, London and New York.

IONESCU-RUXĂNDOIU, L. (1991) *Naraţiune şi dialog în proza românească – Elemente de pragmatică a textului literar*. Editura Academiei Române, Bucureşti.

IONESCU-RUXĂNDOIU, L. (1999) *Conversaţia. Structuri şi Strategii. Sugestii pentru o pragmatică a românei vorbite*. All Educational, Bucureşti.

IONESCU-RUXĂNDOIU, L. (coord.) (2007) *Interacţiunea verbală (IV II). Aspecte teoretice şi aplicative. Corpus*. Editura Universităţii din Bucureşti.

IONESCU-RUXĂNDOIU, L. (2010) 'Impoliteţea in absentia în discursul parlamentar românesc'. Ionescu-Ruxăndoiu, L. (coord.) *Dialog, discurs, enunţ. In memoriam Sorin Stati*. Editura Universităţii din Bucureşti, pp. 59-72.

IORDACHE, L. (2008) 'The Function of Story-telling in Conversation'. *Analele Universităţii Spiru Haret*, Seria: Filologie – Limbi şi Literaturi Străine – An X, nr. 10, pp. 239-244. Editura Fundaţiei România de Mâine, Bucureşti.

IORDACHE, L. (2009a) 'The Topics of Conversational Narratives'. *Limbă, Cultură, Civilizaţie – Noi Căi spre Succes*, vol.1, pp. 316-321. Editura Politehnica Press, Bucureşti.

IORDACHE, L. (2009b) 'The Typology of Conversational Narratives'. *Analele Universităţii Spiru Haret*, Seria: Filologie – Limbi şi Literaturi Străine – An XII, nr. 12, vol.1, pp. 213-230. Editura Fundaţiei România de Mâine, Bucureşti.

IORDACHE, L. (2010a) 'Time in Conversational Narratives'. *Regards croisés sur le Temps*, pp. 278-290. Editura Universității din București, București.

IORDACHE, L. (2010b) 'Interactional Features of Conversational Narratives'. *Analele Universității Spiru Haret*, Seria: Filologie – Limbi și Literaturi Străine – An XIII, nr. 13, vol.1, pp. 77-86. Editura Fundației România de Mâine, București.

IORDACHE, L. (2010c) 'Formulaicity and Repetition in Conversational Narratives'. *Limbă, Cultură, Civilizație: Idei în dialog*, pp. 227-233. Editura Politehnica Press, București.

JAKOBSON, R. (1960) 'Linguistics and Poetics'. Sebeok, T. (ed.) *Style in Language*. M.I.T. Press, Cambridge, MA, pp. 350-377.

JAKOBSON, R. (1980) *The framework of language*. Michigan Studies in the Humanities. Horace H. Rackham School of Graduate Studies, University of Michigan.

JAKOBSON, R. (1987) 'Linguistics and poetics'. Pomorska, K. & Rudy, S. (ed.) *Language in literature*. The Jakobson Trust, USA.

JAWORSKI, A. (2000) 'Silence and small talk'. Coupland, J. (ed.) *Small talk*. Pearson Education Limited, pp. 110-132.

JAWORSKI, A. & COUPLAND, J. (2005) 'Othering in Gossip: "You Go out You Have a Laugh and You Can Pull Yeah Okay but Like..."'. *Language in Society*, vol. 34, no. 5, pp. 667-694. Cambridge University Press.

JAWORSKI, A. & COUPLAND, N. (2006) 'Introduction: Perspectives on Discourse Analysis'. Jaworski, A. & Coupland, N. (eds.) *The Discourse Reader*, second edition. Routledge, pp.1-37.

JEFFERSON, G. (1972) 'Side Sequences'. Sudnow, D. (ed.) *Studies in Social Interaction*. The Free Press, New York, pp. 294-451.

JEFFERSON, G. (1973) 'A Case of Precision Timing in Ordinary Conversation: Overlapped Tag-Positioned Address Terms in Closing Sequences'. *Semiotica*, pp. 47-96. Mouton & Co. N.V. Publishers, The Hague.

JEFFERSON, G. (1974) 'Error Correction as an Interactional Resource'. *Language in Society*, vol. 3, no. 2, pp. 181-199. Cambridge University Press.

JEFFERSON, G. (1978) 'Sequential aspects of storytelling in conversation'. Schenkein, J. (ed.) *Studies in the organization of conversational interaction*. NY: Academic Press, New York, pp. 219-248.

JEFFERSON, G. (1984) 'A sketch of some orderly aspects of overlap in natural conversation'. Yucker, A.H. (ed.) *Conversation Analysis – Studies from the first generations by G.H. Lerner*. John Benjamins Publishing Company, Amsterdam/Philadelphia, pp. 43-59.

JEFFERSON, G. (1986) 'Notes on 'latency' in overlap onset'. *Human Studies*, vol. 9, pp. 153-183. Martinus Nijhoff Publishers, Dordrecht, the Netherlands.

JEFFERSON, G. (1987) 'On exposed and embedded correction in conversation'. Button, G. & Lee, J. R. E. (eds.) *Talk and social organization*. Clevedon, UK: Multilingual Matters, pp. 86-100. [Originally in *Studium Linquistik* (1983) vol. 14, pp. 58-68.]

JEFFERSON, G. (1989) 'Preliminary notes on a possible metric which provides for a 'standard maximum' silence of approximately one second in conversation'. Roger, D. & Bull, P. (eds.) *Conversation: An Interdisciplinary perspective*. Intercommunication 3, Multilingual Matters LTD, Clevedon, Philadelphia, pp. 166-196.

JEFFERSON, G. (2007) 'Preliminary notes on abdicated other-correction'. *Journal of Pragmatics*, vol. 39, pp. 445–461.

JEFFERSON, G., SACKS, H. & SCHEGLOFF, E. (1987) 'Notes on laughter in the pursuit of intimacy'. Button, G. & Lee, J. R. E. (eds.) *Talk and social organization*. Multilingual matters LTD, Clevedon, pp. 152-205.

JOHNSTONE, B. (2001) 'Discourse analysis and narrative'. Schiffrin, D., Tannen, D., & Hamilton, H. (eds.) *The Handbook of Discourse Analysis*. Blackwell Publishers, Oxford, pp. 635–650.

KENDALL & TANNEN (2001) 'Discourse and Gender'. Schiffrin, D., Tannen, D., & Hamilton, H. E. (eds.) *The Handbook of Discourse Analysis*. Blackwell Publishers, Oxford, UK, pp. 548-567.

KERBRAT-ORECCHIONI, C. (1997) *La enunciación. De la subjetividad én el lenguaje*. Edicial, Buenos Aires.

KINNEAVY, J. L. (1971) *A theory of discourse. The aims of discourse*. Prentice-Hall Inc., Englewood Cliffs, N. J., USA.

KOTTHOFF, H. (2003) 'Responding to irony in different contexts: on cognition in conversation'. *Journal of Pragmatics*, vol. 35, pp. 1387–1411.

KÜNTAY, A. & ERVIN-TRIPP, S. M. (1997) Conversational Narratives of Children: Occasions and Structures. *Journal of Narrative and Life History*, vol. 7, pp. 113-120.

KÜNTAY, A. C. & ŞENAY I. (2003) 'Narratives beget narratives : rounds of stories in Turkish preschool conversations'. *Journal of Pragmatics*, vol. 35, pp. 559-587.

LABOV, W. (1972) *Language in the Inner City: Studies in the Black English Vernacular*. University of Pennsylvania Press, Philadelphia.

LABOV, W. (1997) 'Some Further Steps in Narrative Analysis'. Special issue of *The Journal of Narrative and Life History*, vol.7, no. 1-4. Available online at http://www.ling.upenn.edu/~wlabov/sfs.html

LABOV, W. (2011) 'Narratives of Personal Experience'. Hogan, P. C. (ed.) *The Cambridge Encyclopedia of the Language Sciences*, Cambridge.

LABOV, W. & WALETZKY, J. (1967) 'Narrative analysis'. Helm, J. (ed.) *Essays on the Verbal and Visual Arts*. University of Washington Press, Seattle, pp. 12-44.

LAMBROU, M. (2003) 'Collaborative oral narratives of general experience: when an interview becomes a conversation'. *Language and Literature*, vol. 12, no. 2, pp. 153-174. SAGE Publications, London, Thousand Oaks, CA and New Delhi.

LEECH, G. (1991) [1983] *Principles of Pragmatics*. Longman, London.

LEECH, G. & SHORT, M. (1981) *Style in Fiction. A linguistic introduction to English fictional prose*. Longman Group Limited, London & New York.

LEUNG, C. B. (2009) 'Collaborative narration in preadolescent girl talk: A Saturday luncheon conversation among three friends'. *Journal of Pragmatics*, vol. 41, pp. 1341-1357.

LEVINSON, S. C. (1983) *Pragmatics*. Cambridge University Press, Cambridge.

LEVEY, S. (2006) 'Tense Variation in Preadolescent Narratives'. *Journal of English Linguistics*, vol. 34, no. 2, pp. 126-152. SAGE Publications.

LI, C. (1986) 'Direct speech and indirect speech: A functional study'. Coulmas, F. (ed.) *Direct and Indirect Speech*. Mouton de Gruyter, Berlin, pp. 29-45.

LIDDICOAT, A. J. (2004) 'The projectability of turn constructional units and the role of prediction in listening'. *Discourse Studies*, vol. 6, pp. 449-469.

LINDE, C. (2001) 'Narrative in Institutions'. Schiffrin, D., Tannen, D., & Hamilton, H. E. (eds.) *Handbook of Discourse Analysis*. Blackwell Publishers, Oxford, UK, pp. 518-535.

MANCAŞ, M. (1972) *Stilul indirect liber în româna literară*. Editura Didactică şi Pedagogică, Bucureşti.

MANDELBAUM, J. (1991) 'Conversational Non-Cooperation: An Exploration of Disattended Complaints'. *Research on Language and Social Interaction*, vol. 25, pp. 97-138.

MANDELBAUM, J. (2003) 'How to 'do things' with narrative: a communication perspective on narrative skill'. Greene, J. O. & Burleson, B. R. (eds.) *Handbook of Communication and*

Social Interaction Skills. Lawrence Erlbaum Associates Publishers, London, pp. 595-633.

MEY, J. L. (1993) *Pragmatics: An Introduction*. B. Blackwell, Oxford, UK & Cambridge, USA.

MOESCHLER, J. (2001) 'Speech act theory and the analysis of conversation. Sequencing and interpretation in pragmatic theory'. Vandervecken, D. & Kubo, S. (eds.) *Essays in Speech Act Theory*. John Benjamins, Amsterdam, pp. 239-261. PDF version (pp. 1-32) available online at http://www.unige.ch/lettres/linguistique/moeschler/publication_pdf/speech_acts_conv.pdf

MONDADA, L. (2007) 'Multimodal resources for turn-taking: pointing and the emergence of possible next speakers'. *Discourse Studies,* vol. 9, no. 2, pp. 194-225, SAGE Publications, Los Angeles, London, New Delhi and Singapore.

MULLIGAN, K. (1997) 'The Essence of Language: Wittgenstein's Builders and Bühler's Bricks'. *Revue de Métaphysique et de Morale*, vol. 2, pp. 193-216.

NEWMARK, P. (1988) *A Textbook of Translation*. Shanghai Foreign Language Education Press Prentice Hall, New York, London, Toronto, Sydney, Tokyo.

NICULA, I. (2011) 'Utilizări ale verbului A VEDEA în româna vorbită'. Dascălu Jinga, L. (coord.) *Româna vorbită actuală (ROVA). Corpus și studii*. Editura Academiei Române, București.

NIEMELÄ, M. (2005) 'Voiced Direct Reported Speech in Conversational Storytelling: Sequential Patterns of Stance Taking'. *SKY Journal of Linguistics,* vol. 18, pp. 197-221.

NORRICK, N. R. (1997) 'Twice-Told Tales: Collaborative Narration of Familiar Stories'. *Language in Society*, vol. 26, no. 2, pp. 199-220. Cambridge University Press.

NORRICK, N. R. (2000) *Conversational Narrative. Storytelling in Everyday Talk*, John Benjamins Publishing Company, Amsterdam & Philadelphia.

NORRICK, N. R. (2003) 'Issues in conversational joking'. *Journal of Pragmatics*, vol. 35, pp. 1333–1359.

NORRICK, N. R. (2005) 'The dark side of tellability'. *Narrative Inquiry,* vol. 15, pp. 323-343. John Benjamins Publishing Company.

NORRICK, N. R. (2007) 'Conversational Storytelling'. Herman, D. (ed.) *The Cambridge Companion to Narrative*. Cambridge University Press, UK, pp. 127-141.

NORRICK, N. R. & SPITZ, A. (2008) 'Humor as a resource for mitigating conflict in interaction'. *Journal of Pragmatics*, vol. 40, pp. 1661–1686.

NÖTH, W. (1990) *Handbook of Semiotics*. Indiana University Press, Bloomington and Indianapolis.

OCHS, E. (1997) 'Narrative'. Dijk, T. A. van (ed.) *Handbook of discourse: a multidisciplinary introduction*. SAGE, London, pp. 185-207.

OCHS, E. (2004) 'Narrative Lessons'. Duranti, A. (ed.) *A Companion to Linguistic Anthropology*. Blackwell, Oxford, pp. 269-289.

OCHS, E., SMITH, R. & TAYLOR, C. (1989) 'Detective Stories at Dinnertime: Problem-solving through co-narration'. *Cultural Dynamics*, vol. 2, no. 2, pp. 238-57.

OCHS, E. & TAYLOR, C. (1992) 'Family Narrative as Political Activity'. *Discourse & Society*, vol. 3, no. 3, pp. 301-340. SAGE Publications, London, Newbury Park and New Dehli. www.sagepublications.com.

OCHS, E. & CAPPS, L. (2001) *Living Narrative: Creating Lives in Everyday Storytelling*. Harvard University Press, Cambridge.

ÖZYILDIRIM, I. (2009) 'Narrative analysis: An analysis of oral and written strategies in personal experience narratives'. *Journal of Pragmatics*, vol. 41, pp. 1209–1222.

PADILLA CRUZ, M. (2005) 'On the Phatic Interpretation of Utterances: Complementary Relevance-Theoretic Proposal'. *Revista Alicantina de Estudios Ingleses*, no. 18, pp. 227-246.

PARSONS, T. (2002) 'Eventualities and Narrative Progression'. *Linguistics and Philosophy*, vol. 25, pp. 681-699. Kluwer Academic Publishers, The Netherlands.

POLANYI, L. (1979) 'So What's the Point?'. *Semiotica*, vol. 25, pp. 207-41.

POLANYI, L. (1982) 'Linguistic and Social Constraints on Storytelling'. *Journal of Pragmatics*, vol. 6, pp. 509-524. North-Holland Publishing Company.

POLANYI, L. (1989) *Telling the American Story: a Structural and Cultural Analysis of Conversational Storytelling*. MA: MIT Press, Cambridge.

POP, L. (2006) 'Peut-on parler de style communicatif interjectif ? Le cas du roumain'. *Langages*, vol. 1, no. 161, pp. 24-36.

PREECE, A. (1992) 'Critics and collaborators and critics: The nature and effect of peer interaction on children's conversational narratives'. *Journal of Narrative and Life History*, no. 2, pp. 277-292.

PRIDHAM, F. (2001) *The Language of Conversation*. Routledge, London.

REBOUL, A. & MOESCHLER, J. (2001) *Pragmatica, azi*. Ed. Echinox, Cluj Napoca.

RIESSMAN, C. K. (2008) 'Narrative Analysis'. *The SAGE Encyclopedia of Qualitative Research Methods*. SAGE Publications. Retrieved 4 May 2010 from <http://www.sage-ereference.com/ research/Article_n273.html>.

ROMAINE, S. & LANGE, D. (1991) 'The Use of like as a Marker of Reported Speech and Thought: A Case of Grammaticalization in Progress'. *American Speech*, vol. 66, no. 3, pp. 227-279. Duke University Press.

SACKS, H. (1992) *Lectures on Conversation*, vol. 1 & 2. Basil Blackwell, Oxford.

SACKS, H., SCHEGLOFF, E. A. & JEFFERSON, G. (1974) 'A Simplest Systematics for the Organization of Turn-Taking for Conversation'. *Language*, vol. 50, no. 4, part 1, pp. 696-735. Linguistic Society of America.

SAMS, J. (2010) 'Quoting the unspoken: An analysis of quotations in spoken discourse'. *Journal of Pragmatics*, vol. 42, pp. 3147–3160. Elsevier.

SĂFTOIU, R. (2007) *Limba și Literatura Română. Teoria și practica limbii*. Available online at http://www.scribd.com/doc/34044011/Teoria-Si-Practica-Limbii.

SĂFTOIU, R. (2009) *Discursul fatic: un ritual interacțional*. Editura Universității din București, București.

SĂLĂVĂSTRU, C. (2003) *Teoria și practica argumentării*. Polirom, Iași.

SCHEGLOFF, E. A., JEFFERSON, G., & SACKS, H. (1977) 'The preference for self-correction in the organization of repair in conversation'. *Language*, vol. 53, no. 2, pp. 361-382, Linguistic Society of America.

SCHEGLOFF, E. A. (1988a) 'On an actual virtual servo-mechanism for guessing bad news: A single case conjecture'. *Social Problems*, vol. 35, no. 4, pp. 442-457.

SCHEGLOFF, E. A. (1996b) 'Confirming allusions: Toward an empirical account of action'. *American Journal of Sociology*, no. 102, pp.161-216.

SCHEGLOFF, E. A. (2000) 'Overlapping talk and the organization of turn-taking for conversation'. *Language in Society*, vol. 29, pp. 1-63.

SCHIFFRIN, D. (1981) 'Tense variation in narrative'. *Language*, vol. 57, pp. 45-62.

SCHIFFRIN, D. (1994) *Approaches to Discourse*. Blackwell, Oxford, UK and Cambridge, USA.

SCHIFFRIN, D. (1996) 'Narrative as self-portrait: sociolinguistic construction of identity'. *Language in Society*, vol. 25, pp. 167-203.

SCHMID, W. (2010) *Narratology. An introduction*. De Gruyter, Berlin.

SCHOLES, R., PHELAN, J. & KELLOGG, R. (2006) *The Nature of Narrative*. Fortieth anniversary edition, revised and expanded. Oxford University Press.

SILVA-CORVALAN, C. (1983) 'Tense and Aspect in Oral Spanish Narrative: Context and Meaning'. *Language*, vol. 59, no. 4, pp. 760-780. Linguistic Society of America.

SMITH, C. (1999) 'Activities: states or events?'. *Linguistics and Philosophy,* no. 22, pp. 479-508. Kluwer Academic Publishers, The Netherlands.

SOKOLOVA, I. (2003) 'Realization of subjective modality in texts-announcements'. *The USSE Messenger*, vol. 2, pp. 123-126.

SOREA, D. (2007a) *Pragmatics: Some cognitive perspectives.* Editura Universității din București.

SOREA, D. (2007b) *Translation. Theory and Practice.* Editura Coresi, București.

STEIN, N. L. (1982) 'The definition of a story'. *Journal of Pragmatics*, vol. 6, pp. 487-507. North-Holland Publishing Company.

STENSTRÖM, A. B. et al. (2005) 'Trends in Teenage Talk: Corpus Compilation, Analysis and Findings'. *Journal of Pragmatics,* vol. 37, pp. 589–593. Book review by Androutsopoulos, J. K. .

ŚWIĄTKOWSKA, M. (2006) 'L'Interjection: entre Deixis et Anaphore'. *Langages,* vol. 1, no. 161, pp. 47-56. Armand Colin.

ȘERBĂNESCU, A. (2007) *Cum gândesc și cum vorbesc ceilalți. Prin labirintul culturilor.* Editura Polirom, Iași.

ȘTEFĂNESCU, A. (2007) *Aspecte pragmatice. Incursiuni în limba română actuală.* Editura Universității din București.

ȘTEFĂNESCU, A. (2011) 'Marcatorii discursivi în narațiunea conversațională: un studiu de caz. Dascălu Jinga, L. (coord.) *Româna vorbită actuală (ROVA). Corpus și studii*, pp. 275-306. Editura Academiei Române, București.

TANNEN, D. (1980) 'Spoken/Written Language and the Oral/Literate Continuum'. *Proceedings of the Sixth Annual Meeting of the Berkeley Linguistics Society*, pp. 207-218.

TANNEN, D. (1982) 'Oral and Literate Strategies in Spoken and Written Narratives'.
Language, vol. 58, no. 1, pp. 1-21. Linguistic Society of America.

TANNEN, D. (1983) 'I take out the rock --dok!": how Greek women tell about being molested (and create involvement)'. Anthropological Linguistics, vol. 25, no. 3, pp. 359-374.

TANNEN, D. (1986) 'Introducing constructed dialogue in Greek and American conversational and literary narrative'. Coulmas, F. (ed.) *Direct and Indirect Speech.* Mouton de Gruyter, Berlin – New York – Amsterdam.

TANNEN, D. (1987) 'Repetition in Conversation: Toward a Poetics of Talk'. *Language*, vol. 63, no. 3, pp. 574-605. Linguistic Society of America.

TANNEN, D. (1993) 'What's in a frame? Surface evidence for underlying expectations'. Tannen, D. (ed.) *Framing in discourse.* Oxford University Press, pp. 14-56.

TANNEN, D. (1995b) 'The Power of Talk: Who Gets Heard and Why'. *Harvard Business Review,* pp. 138-148.

TANNEN, D. (1995a) 'Waiting for the Mouse: Constructed Dialogue in Conversation'.

Tadlock, D. & Mannheim, B. (eds.) *The Dialogic Emergence of Culture.* University of Illinois Press, Urbana and Chicago.

TANNEN, D. (2005) [1984] *Conversational Style: Analyzing Talk Among Friends.* Oxford University Press.

TANNEN, D. (2007) [1989] *Talking Voices: Repetition, dialogue, and imagery in conversational discourse.* Cambridge University Press.

THOMAS, J (1996) *Meaning in interaction.* Longman, London and New York.

THORNBORROW, J. & COATES, J. (2005) 'The sociolinguistics of narrative identity, performance, culture'. Thornborrow, J. & Coates, J. (eds.) *The sociolinguistics of narrative.* John Benjamins Publishing Company, Amsterdam, pp. 1-16.

THREADGOLD, T. (2005) 'Performing theories of narrative: Theorising narrative performance'. Thornborrow, J. & Coates, J. (eds.) *The sociolinguistics of narrative.* John Benjamins Publishing Company, Amsterdam, pp. 261-278.

TOOLAN, M. (2008) *Narațiunea. Introducere Lingvistică.* Editura Universității 'Alexandru Ioan Cuza', Iași.

TRUDGILL, P. (1995) *Sociolinguistics: An introduction to language and society.* The Penguin Group, London.

TUȚESCU, M. (2006) 'L'interjection – modalisation, axiologisation et grammaticalisation. Le cas des interjections roumaines zău et vai'. *Langages,* vol. 1, no. 161, pp. 37-46. Armand Colin.

UCHIDA, S. (1997) Immediate contexts and reported speech. *UCL Working Papers in Linguistics,* no. 9, pp.1-29, available online at http://www.phon.ucl.ac.uk/home/PUB/WPL/97papers/ uchida.pdf.

VACHEK, J. (in collaboration with DUBSKÝ, J.) (2003) *Dictionary of the Prague School of Linguistics.* Dušková, L. (ed.) John Benjamins Publishing Company. Amsterdam/Philadelphia.

VANDERVEKEN, D. (2002) 'Searle on Meaning and Action'. Grewendorf, G. & Meggle, G. (eds.) *Speech Acts, Mind and Social Reality.* Discussions with Searle. Studies in Linguistics and Philosophy. Dordrecht, Kluwer, pp. 141-161. PDF version (pp. 1-30) available online at http://www.uqtr.ca/~vandervk/ SearleOnMeaning.pdf

VAN DIJK, T. A. (1975) 'Action, Action Description, and Narrative'. *New Literary History*, vol. 6, no. 2, On Narrative and Narratives, pp. 273-294. 294. The Johns Hopkins University Press.

VAN DIJK, T. A. (2008) *Discourse and Context. A sociocognitive approach*. Cambridge University Press.

VASILESCU, A. (2007a) *Cum vorbesc românii. Studii de comunicare (inter)culturală*. Editura Universității din București, București.

VASILESCU, A. (2007b) 'Negocierea rolurilor communicative prin intermediul semnalelor de recepție ('back-channels'). O perspectivă (inter)culturală'. Ionescu-Ruxăndoiu, L. (coord.) *Interacțiunea verbală (IV II). Aspecte teoretice și aplicative. Corpus*. Editura Universității din București, pp. 15-43.

VASILESCU, A. (2007c) 'Distribuția contribuțiilor conversaționale în cultura română'.

Ionescu-Ruxăndoiu, L. (coord.) *Dialog, discurs, enunț. In memoriam Sorin Stati*. Editura Universității din București, pp. 177-216.

VÁSQUEZ, C. (2007) 'Moral stance in the workplace narratives of novices'. *Discourse Studies*, vol. 9, no. 5, pp. 653-675, SAGE Publications, Los Angeles, London, New Dehli and Singapore. www.sagepublications.com

VERSTRAETE, J. C. (2001) 'Subjective and objective modality: interpersonal and ideational functions in the English modal auxiliary system'. *Journal of Pragmatics*, vol. 33, pp. 1505-1528.

VINTILESCU, V. (2005) *Evaluation et actes de langage évaluatifs*. Thèse de doctorat. Universitatea din București.

YULE, G. (1996) *Pragmatics*. Oxford University Press.

WOLFSON, N. (1978) 'A Feature of Performed Narrative: The Conversational Historical Present'. *Language in Society*, vol. 7, no. 2, pp. 215-237. Cambridge University Press.

WOLFSON, N. (1979) 'The Conversational Historical Present Alternation'. *Language*, vol. 55, no. 1, pp. 168-182, Linguistic Society of America.

ZAFIU, R. (2000) *Narațiune și poezie*. Bic All, București.

ZAFIU, R. (2001) *Diversitate stilistică în limba română actuală*. Editura Universității din București.

ZAFIU, R. (2010) *101 cuvinte argotice*. Humanitas, București.

www.ingramcontent.com/pod-product-compliance
Lightning Source LLC
Chambersburg PA
CBHW082059230426
43670CB00017B/2896